Contents

List of Tables

The National Foundation for Educational Research

The National Foundation for Educational Research in England and Wales was founded in 1946 and is Britain's leading educational research institution. It is an independent body undertaking research and development projects on issues of current interest in all sectors of the public educational system. Its membership includes all the local education authorities in England and Wales, the main teachers' associations, and a large number of other major organizations with educational interests.

Its approach is scientific, apolitical and non-partisan. By means of research projects and extensive field surveys it has provided objective evidence on important educational issues for the use of teachers, administrators, parents and the research community. The expert and experienced staff that has been built up over the years enables the Foundation to make use of a wide range of modern research techniques, and, in addition to its own work, it undertakes a large number of specially sponsored projects at the request of government departments and other agencies.

The major part of the research programme relates to the maintained educaitonal sector – primary, secondary and further education. A further significant element has to do speciafically with local education authorities and training institutions. The current programme includes work on the education of pupils with special needs, monitoring of pupil performance, staff development, and information technology in schools. The Foundation is also the national agency for a number of international research and information exchange networks.

The NFER-NELSON Publishing Company are the main publishers of the Foundation's research reports. These reports are now available in the *NFER Research Library*, a collection which provides the educational community with up-to-date research into a wide variety of subject areas. In addition, the Foundation and NFER-NELSON work closely together to provide a wide range of open and closed educational tests and a test advisory service. NFER-NELSON also publish *Educational Research*, the termly journal of the Foundation.

Acknowledgements

The project team would like to express their gratitude to all those whose ready cooperation and assistance have enabled this research to be undertaken. We are particularly grateful to all those advisers, officers, heads and teachers in the case study LEAs who willingly gave of their time to guide us round the issues.

We are indebted to our Steering Committee, the members of which are listed on page 218, for their advice and sustained interest in this project, as well as for their comments on the draft of this report.

Within the National Foundation for Educational Research we would wish to thank Margaret I. Reid, who was the project director for most of the project's life, and Dick Weindling, who took over when she left. We would also like to thank Derek Foxman, Lesley Kendall and Neil Rubra for all their assistance, and last but not least, Hazel Menenzes, our secretary.

AS
MG

I *Introduction*

Historical background to the research

Some 45 years ago section 77(3) of the Education Act 1944 gave the then 154 local education authorities the right to inspect their schools, and by implication, the right to set up and fund the necessary services. A small number of inspection and advisory services had existed before then and this legislation paved the way for all LEAs to provide the service:

Any local education authority may cause an inspection to be made of any educational establishment maintained by the authority, and such inspections shall be made by officers appointed by the local education authority.(Education Act 1944)

Between 1944 and 1974 there were more local education authorities (LEAs) than we see today. The majority were smaller than at present, and indeed, with a number further devolving their responsibilities to the even smaller units of divisional executives and 'excepted districts', some were very small indeed. It is no surprise therefore that there was enormous variation in how this part of the legislation was interpreted; it was reported that, in 1974, the size of the services ranged from four to 94 advisers (DES, 1977). Some LEAs had built on past practice and continued to employ inspectors, whereas others, if they really employed any central staff other than officers, employed small numbers of organizers who concentrated mainly on the practical subjects of PE, domestic science, music and rural studies (see e.g. Pearce, 1986). The organizer's role was typically one of providing equipment, running orchestras, organizing county teams and seeing to health and safety, such as it was then.

---

1. Unless stated otherwise, the term 'adviser' is used throughout to refer to LEA advisers and inspectors equally.
2. The term 'chief adviser' (without capital letters) is used to refer to all those people in charge of advisory services – i.e. those who are the chief advisers. The term 'Chief Adviser' (with capital letters) is used to refer to those whose title is Chief Adviser or Chief Inspector; not all chief advisers will be Chief Advisers.

During the 1960s and early 1970s there was a growing emphasis on curriculum development, and pressure was exerted on LEAs to employ expertise in the more academic areas. In such a climate, the limitations of the organizer's role soon became apparent and most of these posts were phased out and replaced by those for advisers. The new role was still designed to concentrate on the single subject and to be self-motivating and independent, but there was now a greater focus on the curriculum and its development – the role had changed to suit the times. It should be noted, however, that to a large extent, the organizers' duties were never really taken away and that much of the change was effectively achieved by adding the new roles on top of the old – concerts and orchestras still had to be organized and county teams needed running.

With the local government reorganizations of 1968 (metropolitan) and 1974 (county), the minimum size of the local authorities and of their advisory services became significant issues (see Fiske, 1977). Most of the smaller LEAs disappeared and many authorities now gained their first reasonable establishment of advisers. Many new advisers were taken on and numbers rose nationally much above the 1,260 figure of 1968 (House of Commons, 1968). Quite how high they rose is not certain as conflicting figures have been offered for this theoretically rising figure; thus, for 1974, the DES offered 1,849 and Kogan offered about 3,000 and, for 1975, Pearce offered 1,650 (DES, 1977; Kogan, 1974; Pearce, 1986). It is from this time that we really see the beginnings of the services as we now know them.

In rationalizing the size of LEAs the local government reorganization allowed the first real opportunity for the new authorities to influence the organization of their new advisory services. In his presidential address to the National Association of Inspectors of Schools and Education Organizers, Mr Matthew Bagot was reported as saying: 'make no mistake about it, local government reorganisation presents us with the greatest chance we have had for a decade of getting establishments, conditions and salaries nearer to the point of justice.' (*Education*, 6.10.72).

The new authorities also had the opportunity to redesignate some or all of the posts, and because there were now sufficient posts, to consider how their advisers should be deployed to cover the broad range of activities. The desire for some form of balance and rationalization in the advisers' tasks – a theme that will arise many times throughout this book – had been talked of for some time, and basically centred around three polarizations, though they could be seen in several ways. Kogan commented that:

Their [advisers'] tasks can be broadly defined as advisory,
inspectorial and administrative. Many have to perform all three
tasks and find that the triple role produces conflict and
difficulty. (Kogan, 1974)

The same conflict was also expressed in terms of the 'the Janus role',
the problem of advisers having to 'face' towards both teachers and
administrators (see e.g. Bolam, 1978). The issue was raised implicitly, in
1976, in a paper presented to the ILEA Schools Sub-committee. A brief
statement about the paper commented that:

The report explains that the inspectorate's tasks might be
divided into two broad but inter-related categories: advice and
information to members and officers of the Authority; and
service to the staff of the Authority's schools and colleges by
advising them and helping them in their professional
development.

The integrated nature of these activities is stressed in the
report. For example, a full inspection of a school or college
serves to inform the sub-committee but also benefits the staff
by the preparation for the inspection, the clarification of their
own objectives, the discussions with inspectors during the
inspection and the suggestions for improvement which are
usually made in the report. The fundamental feature to emerge
from this is the balance between the formal inspection process
and the role of support and development of teaching staff.
(Birchenough, 1976)

The 1974 reorganization obviously achieved some of the benefits that
had been sought of it. An 'Education Digest', in February 1976,
entitled, The Advisory Service, commented both on the balance of
work and on the management structure of the services:

Local Government reorganisation has resulted in a good deal of
rethinking about advisory staff structures. Many authorities have
moved to a much stronger emphasis on the pastoral role of the
adviser and now expect all or most of their advisers to have
some general pastoral responsibility for a group of schools.
Very often these advisers also have a subject specialism and
divide their time between the two activities.

Local government reorganisation has also encouraged a team
approach and although corporate management is not always
viewed favourably by those involved in it, advisory services
have almost certainly benefited from the development of
structures designed to foster teamwork. Many more authorities
than formerly now have a chief adviser responsible for
coordinating the work of the advisory team. Another result of

> the rethinking brought about by local government
> reorganisation is a clarifying of the place of the chief adviser
> within the overall structure of the education office. He is now
> most likely to be regarded as a member of the CEO's
> management team. (*Education*, 1976)

Despite the positive nature of this last report, it is still difficult to determine from what has been reported just where the balance lay between subject and general work and equally just how much emphasis was actually given to managing the services. The picture we gained, like that given by Bolam, Smith and Canter (1978), was certainly not as positive about the pastoral role being taken on by so many advisers. Many of those we interviewed described the position they remembered in the mid-1970s when, in many LEAs, the subject role predominated with an adviser being appointed for each of the main secondary (grammar school?) subjects. Little time was spent on cross-curriculum or general issues. Furthermore, although LEAs typically had more children in primary than secondary school, the majority of advisers were appointed for secondary work, and however much the subject specialists may have had a 'responsibility' for their subjects in the primary phase, their involvement was often very uncertain. Overall, the services had a strong secondary bias and adviser involvement in the further and higher education (FHE) and the special educational needs (SEN) fields showed the same reluctance to depart from the mainstream secondary school model – in both cases the achievement of regular involvement seemed to require external pressure.

During the 1970s the education system became embroiled in a further series of major changes. Immediately after the local government reorganization and the raising of the school leaving age, while many teachers were still trying to come to grips with the implications of comprehensive schooling, a financial crisis arose and was followed by falling rolls and a serious political questioning of the state education system, as recorded in the *Black Papers*, in James Callaghan's Ruskin speech and in the DES' *Four Subjects for Debate* (Cox, 1975; DES, 1977). These changes spelt uncertainty for all those in education, but for advisers there were three further issues which added to the discomfort:

> Firstly there was the protracted battle to secure for advisers the
> comparable benefit of the main Houghton award for teachers.
> Eventually advisers won but not before some of the points
> made against their case sowed uncertainties about the way their
> employers saw their work.
>
> Secondly, as the economic pressures of 1975 and 1976 grew
> steadily more fierce, individual authorities in pursuit of savings

on administrative costs left unfilled posts for advisers that came vacant through retirement or normal staff movements. It sometimes seemed that those posts which in 1973 and 1974 were often hard won in establishment debates could very lightly be left unfilled in the search for economies.

Then, in May of this year the president of the Headteachers' Association told his colleagues at their annual conference that there should be drastic and permanent reductions in the number of advisers employed by LEAs. (Fiske, 1977)

But while the doubts were being cast, there was also a series of reports which sought more from the advisory services, though as ever, their recommendations failed to reduce the conflict of tasks. Thus the Auld Report (1976) promoted stronger evaluative systems, and the 1977 Green Paper (GB. DES, 1977) promoted curriculum support. In looking at the role of governors the Taylor Report (1977) acknowledges these two emphases before going on to prescribe its own solution:

6.38: The purpose of the advisory service is to promote high standards of performance by teachers and of attainment by pupils both in basic skills and studies and in education in its wider sense. This purpose is principally achieved through the provision of advice, based on wide experience and knowledge, to head and other teachers and by reference to example to show where and how high standards are achieved and maintained. Whilst the relationship of advisers with teaching staff will normally be one of mutual support, the advisory team exercises a leadership role in the area of curriculum innovation, in-service training and staff development programmes. In those circumstances where the efficiency of a particular school or teachers is giving cause for concern, the advisory team may assume an inspectorial role and report as required to the governing body and to the local education authority.

6.39: . . . Although the opportunity presented by local government reorganisation was taken to achieve a better balance (of subject cover) and improved structure, there nevertheless remains a preponderance of advisers who are primarily subject specialists rather than general advisers who, in addition to having a specialist role, are able to take an overview, to assess and to give advice upon the school as a whole, its organisation, overall development and progress, following the tradition and practice of HM Inspectorate . . . We therefore regard it as a matter of urgency that more general advisers should be made available . . . if the role we have envisaged for the new governing bodies is to be filled.

With the decade of the 1980s came even more innovations: Technical and Vocational Educational Initiative (TVEI), Certificate of Pre-vocational Education (CPVE), General Certificate of Secondary Education (GCSE), SEN, Equal Opportunities and many more. But the intended role of the advisory services in their implementation still varied from the marginal to the essential – there certainly was no generally accepted view of the necessity to involve the advisory services when attempting to implement change in schools. Furthermore, when they have been involved, their introduction to the implementation was often a rushed affair. The reasons for this varying involvement are important and can be argued to reflect both a central uncertainty about the advisers' (and implicitly the LEAs') willingness to implement the innovation as writ, and also a continuing uncertainty about the advisers' role in general – little was actually known by central government about advisers and their advisory services. For instance, in the early 1980s the numbers of advisers employed by the LEAs was not known with any certainty; there were terminological problems of knowing who was, and who was not, an adviser; and when questions about subject coverage arose, even if it was known how much subject time was needed, there was little evidence to say how many advisers could devote how much of their time to any particular subject in any one authority. Cross-curricular emphases posed even more difficult questions. It was apparent that although the advisory services were being increasingly leant upon to support the implementation of various innovations in schools, and indeed to support the schools through this period of enormous change, there was very little knowledge about this whole field.

In 1985 the Secretary of State's Draft Statement on the Role of the Local Education Authority's Advisory Services (DES, 1985b) attempted to settle matters – and in a most welcome fashion – virtually for the first time in a recent government document, drew attention to the importance of the advisory services. The report went on to suggest, and to promote the view, that LEA advisory services had four interrelated groups of functions:

(1) monitoring and evaluating the work of the authority's services:
(2) supporting schools and other educational establishments;
(3) supporting and developing teachers and advising on their management;
(4) working on local initiatives.

One major difficulty with this suggestion was that it effectively ignored current practice and assumed that all LEAs were both willing and able to take on all four roles. But not all LEAs either wanted or were able to do this. Furthermore, the document supported a rather subject-oriented approach which, in many LEAs, had been long superseded by a strong generalist approach reached following both pragmatic and philosophical considerations. With the information to hand at the time, it assumed (falsely) a single model for the mainland advisory services, and on the basis of that one position, recommended a series of developments which with the benefit of hindsight, one could see would be unlikely to occur.

But the ideas in the Draft Statement, which was later withdrawn just prior to the general election of 1987, were fully endorsed by the House of Commons Education, Science and Arts Committee in its 1986 report, *Achievement in Primary Schools* (House of Commons, 1986). The committee felt that the first of the groups of functions listed above, the monitoring and evaluation role, should be enhanced. They commented:

> 10.12 Some LEA advisory services do not at present conduct formal inspections of schools. The draft statement to which we have referred suggests that all should consider the possibility of including such inspections. We recommend that all LEA advisory services should do so. We also recommend that consideration should be given to making such formal reports public as do the HMI.

The arguments about balance thus progressed from the 1970s into the 1980s and while the roles were well enough identified, there were still pressures being applied upon each of the elements – the conflict had not been resolved. But during this time schools and the curriculum had changed and there was a growing emphasis on management: the demands made upon the services followed suit and changed, too. As a result, there was an increasing call during the early 1980s for the advisory services to reshape themselves to be able to meet them more effectively – the 'fire fighting', single-subject, lone-worker role was being shunned and the words 'proactive' and 'team' were becoming more widespread. Once again, there was pressure for change in the way the services divided up their roles and in the way they managed their work and staff. But identifying the essential features of change can be difficult when there is little information available beyond that of one's own service, especially when no two LEAs have adopted the same system.

Given this need, and the fact that very little objective national information then existed, the National Foundation for Educational Research (NFER) sponsored and set up this research project to study the roles, management and practices of LEA advisory services throughout England and Wales. It was designed to work in close collaboration with LEA advisers and officers, and its aims included:

(1) describing the various roles and responsibilities of advisers;
(2) studying their working practices and identifying the skills, knowledge and strategies used in their jobs;
(3) describing various LEA policies on the role of the advisory service and on the recruitment of advisers;
(4) exploring the views of those they work and come into contact with; and,
(5) identifying their in-service training needs.

The LEA Advisers Project: research method

The research was undertaken in two main stages. In the first, the project team undertook detailed case-study work in 12 authorities in England and Wales, with the authorities being chosen to represent a variety of practice, demography and geography. For two months prior to the case studies the researchers visited a number of authorities around the country and conducted open-ended interviews with chief advisers, officers and advisers. These conversations were used to build up a picture of the current salient issues and to help phrase the questions for the more detailed interview schedules to be used in the actual case studies.

In each of the case-study LEAs, the project asked the chief adviser to arrange a two-week programme for one researcher, with the programme including interviews with the Chief Education Officer (CEO), the chief adviser, several of the advisers and one or two other officers. Over and above this, we asked to spend a day in each of two secondary schools where we might interview the head, a deputy, two heads of department and one or two teachers who were just out of their probation year. Half-day visits to two primary schools, one special school and, where possible, one FE college, were also requested, and again, a range of staff were interviewed. The case studies also offered observation of advisers 'at work', for instance, when running in-service education and training (INSET), attending governors' meetings, shortlisting or interview panels, and when coming together for team meetings both with and without their officer colleagues. The case studies provided a detailed and rich source of information for the research.

The information from them was used in three ways. First, all the interviews were noted by hand on to the schedules themselves, and a proportion were also tape recorded and transcribed. The written record was then entered into a computerized text handling system which allowed very thorough and fast access to all parts of all the interviews. The information contained in the interviews has been drawn upon consistently throughout this report. Secondly, the case studies developed the issues initially identified in the open-ended interviews, as well as providing a few more of their own. This was necessary material, not only for the research report, but also as it enabled us to write and structure the two questionnaires that were designed to provide the quantitative data to complement the case-studies' more qualitative approach. The interview data was also used in helping to phrase the questionnaire items in an appropriate manner with the right language and minimum ambiguity.

The second main research stage involved the use of two national postal surveys. The first questionnaire was sent to all those in charge of advisory services in England and Wales and sought information about them (as chief advisers) and about the policy and practice of how their LEA organized and deployed its advisory services. Accompanying this questionnaire was a large pro forma which sought detailed information on all the advisory posts supported by the authority at that time. The second questionnaire was sent to all advisers in England and Wales. This sought detailed information on their backgrounds, careers, in-service training and experience of appraisal, as well as information about the nature of the work they carried out and their reactions to it. Further details about both surveys are available in Chapters 2 and 3.

A final note on the research method should comment on the close contact the research team maintained with many advisers and officers throughout the research. Given the nature of this work, it would have been very difficult to operate successfully without being able to lean on a good number of (chief) advisers, (chief) officers, HMIs and trainers around the country who could offer guidance, suggest avenues of study, and act as sounding-boards for our ideas.

Layout of the report

The presentation of the research findings starts in Chapter 2, with a broad, nationally based description of the LEA advisory services and their adviser and advisory teacher posts. This is the predominantly quantitative picture which was provided, in the main, by the 68 chief advisers who responded to the questionnaire. The chapter starts by describing how the statistics were collected in the two surveys and how the populations were chosen to complete the questionnaires. We then look at the basic numbers, titles, subjects, salaries and funding agencies before considering the ratios of advisers and advisory teachers to the pupil, teacher, school and adult populations within the LEA. Finally, we turn to the issue of subject coverage and adviser deployment patterns, and in so doing, highlight the recent growth in advisory teacher numbers.

Where Chapter 2 concentrates on details about the posts, Chapter 3 provides the survey information about the advisers and chief advisers themselves – this chapter, then, is about the people. It starts by describing a number of their professional features, for instance, initial subject training and professional backgrounds, before going on to look at the actual work they undertake – and here a large number of tasks are looked at in respect of the 'hat' that is being worn when advisers undertake them. This analysis allowed us to group advisers according to the types of work they reported undertaking and then to compare the various characteristics of those advisers in each of these groups.

This analysis leads to a consideration in Chapter 4 of the various organizational differences that seem to be influential at the LEA level. It starts with a detailed consideration of the factors which have affected advisory services over the last few years and goes on to consider the various possible roles for advisers with respect to LEA thinking. The theme is developed with the presentation of a ten-part organizational model to provide a framework for understanding some features of the different managerial and hierarchical structures used in the management of the advisory services. This model allows us to relate the different reactions from advisers, officers and teachers to the organizational systems and contexts they work within.

One important aspect of management must concern the channels of communication that are built into the system. Thus a part of this research was directed towards looking at the nature of advisers' working relationships with schools and colleges, with advisory colleagues and with other LEA personnel. The project was also keen to explore the opportunities for advisers to meet and work together, to broaden their horizons and to contribute towards LEA decision-making. In Chapter 5 we thus describe the advisers' working relationships with their colleagues, the formal communication channels within the LEA and their opportunities for teamwork. The evidence was taken both from the case studies, which offer detailed evidence from a broad range of personnel in a small number of LEAs, and from the Advisers and Chief Advisers questionnaires which offer a more national picture.

But having looked at the national picture and the roles and the management structures, we were also interested in how individual advisers were helped with these developments. In Chapter 6 we look at adviser recruitment, why people joined, the induction and in-service training they need and have been offered, their career paths and the issues of appraisal.

In offering a conclusion to this report it was felt that however much a summary might be useful in bringing together all these threads, the real strength of the report must lie in considering change – this has been, after all, the most consistent theme of the work. Thus in Chapter 7 we offer a summary of the previous chapters as a context to three sections on change. The first considers the changes that the advisers reported seeking and the problems they perceived with these developments. The second repeats this exercise but from the chief advisers' point of view – the changes they wanted and the reasons for them. However, this section then draws upon their experiences of trying to plan and implement change over the last few years and reports on the problems they encountered. We then look forward to contemplate the new legislation and attempt to assess what the future will bring and its effects on the advisory services. In attempting to predict the future it is perforce contemplative and tentative, events may well turn in other directions; however, the issues we consider in the concluding chapter will remain whatever the outcome. As such it should provide some useful pointers for those setting out to review their services.

Finally, it is important to add that virtually all those we met liked their jobs and worked extremely conscientiously over long hours. But, they also emphasized the changing nature of what we were looking at and the difficulties they had experienced, or were still experiencing, with the process of change. Given the current rates of change, and the difficulties of processing it effectively, this study is as much a look at how change is handled as a description of LEAs' advisory services.

2 The Advisory Services – a Quantitative Description of Adviser and Advisory Teacher Posts

Introduction

One of the main aims of this research was to consider the management of LEA advisory services – an aim which has included the study of adviser recruitment, careers and training. To meet this aim a major part of the research has involved case-study work to provide the necessary detailed and intimate pictures of the issues and factors at play. But such close involvement in just 12 authorities can deny the perspective that allows observers to differentiate between the local and, perhaps, personal idiosyncrasies and the more widespread structural problems. Officers and advisers in other authorities may also not recognize where their LEA fits into the pattern. Therefore, the project used two techniques for collecting the information: the case study, which offered the detailed but localized and context-bound material, and the questionnaire survey, which offered the quantitative but far less personalized information. The two processes were designed to be complementary.

   This chapter sets out to provide the quantitative context for the later discussions on the more detailed aspects of advisers' work and management. It describes the surveys carried out by the project, and then presents a picture of the range and type of posts maintained by the advisory services in England and Wales. Here, in presenting this picture, the project team felt it necessary to include a considerable amount of information about advisory teachers, for while they are significantly different from advisers, their increasing employment in recent years has had a serious impact upon the role and deployment of advisers. With this in mind, this chapter considers the numbers of advisers and advisory teachers, their salaries and funding agencies, their ratios with the LEAs' adult, pupil, teacher and school populations, and finally, their subject coverage. In the main, the chapter draws upon the quantitative information provided by those in charge of the advisory services, although where appropriate, case-study and adviser survey information has also been brought in. Chapter 3, completes this overall survey by presenting the advisers' own survey account of themselves and their work. (As elsewhere in this report, the term 'adviser' includes advisers and inspectors.)

The Chief Advisers and Advisers surveys

The NFER LEA Advisers Project collected national data using two surveys in the autumn and winter of 1986/87. The subject-matter was directed towards those thought most appropriate. Thus issues concerning policy and deployment matters, and questions about the background and work of chief advisers or their equivalents, were addressed to those in charge of the advisory services; and questions about advisers and their individual working practices went to the advisers themselves. Both surveys set out to cover all 104 mainland LEAs in England and Wales.

The Chief Advisers survey

The Chief Advisers questionnaire was dispatched in September 1986 and included questions on the respondents' post and career backgrounds, the current organization of their advisory services, issues affecting change, adviser appraisal and training, systems of monitoring educational establishments and detailed sections on the deployment of advisers across a range of both old and new tasks. The questionnaire also contained a pro forma for collecting information about all the various advisory posts maintained within the authority. Details were sought about whether each post was filled or vacant; permanent, temporary or seconded; full time, part time or shared; whether it carried responsibilities for an area, division and/or a phase; whether it carried pastoral duties; whether it carried the right to inspect; what its main subject or curriculum responsibilities were (if any); and what pay structure and point of the pay scale applied, what agency funded the post and how long the post had been established.

This pro forma was also designed to provide the project with a list of post holders for the later Advisers questionnaire which, in November 1986, was sent out pre-addressed to all adviser posts in England and Wales. Apart from seeking details about individual advisers' working practices, career and training, it also sought their reactions to various LEA processes and procedures which had already been described for us in the first survey.

Unfortunately, statistics about local authority advisers are difficult both to collect and to understand. The main problem stems from the difficulty of knowing precisely what an adviser is. At the fringes of virtually any pre-defined definition the categorization tends to break down and it becomes difficult to know whether a person is, or is not, an 'adviser'. Title alone is insufficient, for there are advisers fully employed in officer jobs and officers who spend most of their time advising. Task-oriented definitions fare little better. When they are used at a distance, as in postal survey work, it is difficult to determine the minimum proportion of a person's working time that needs to be spent on advisory work in order for that person to qualify, and similarly, it is difficult to determine which of the considerable range of tasks, roles and statuses associated with advising might be deemed uniquely essential to the role, and here accept that a mere imbalance in the range can deny membership. For example, neither TVEI coordinators nor advisory teachers would normally be considered advisers, although they both have many functions in common with advisers, including in some cases the right to inspect. However, this problem of being able to identify advisers at a distance is not new, and in 1973 when seeking to draw up a research sample of advisers, Bolam commented:

> it was in any case impossible to select a country-wide sample of
> advisers on the basis of, say, job-specification or status. Accurate
> and detailed information about the number and type of
> advisory staff in each LEA is not widely available.
>
> (Bolam, Smith and Canter, 1978)

Bolam and his colleagues resolved the problem by asking the chief education officer in each LEA in their sample to pass the questionnaire to all their staff 'with advisory type responsibilities'. Having done this, the team then encountered considerable variation in how authorities interpreted this instruction:

> Some CEOs included Deputy or Assistant Education Officers,
> some included Educational Psychologists, or the wardens of
> Teachers' Centres and in a few cases individuals such as the
> Education Librarians were also included . . . Amongst the
> sample respondents there were, in fact, 22 different titles given
> to advisory staff.   (ibid.)

The NFER LEA Advisers Project was faced with the same kind of problems and, like Bolam, the Project's solution was to have the identification decisions made at local level. In our case, this required two decisions. First, although the person in charge of most advisory services could be readily identified through the published title of chief adviser or its equivalent in the *Education Year Book*, in some 30 or more LEAs neither the post nor its identifiable equivalent was listed. In these authorities the chief education officer was asked to identify the person who was either in charge of the advisory services, or, where no such specific post existed, the person who was in the best position to answer our questions. With this information to hand, the Chief Advisers questionnaire was sent to all 104 mainland LEAs, and the 68 returns show it to have been completed by a wide range of different LEA postholders (the distribution is shown in Appendix Table A2.1, page 209).

In the majority of cases (77 per cent) the questionnaires were completed by the Chief or Principal Adviser or Inspector, or altern-atively, by someone with an equivalent post but who had other aspects of their job listed in front of, or instead of, the chief adviser element, for example, a Deputy Director/Chief Adviser. However, approximately 10 per cent of the replies were from respondents who were occupying positions one might not have expected, for example, senior adviser or senior education officer posts. Through later conversations with a number of these respondents we learnt that some were filling in for absent chief advisers, for example, during an interregnum or period of illness, while in other cases there simply was no chief adviser or equivalent post in the authority. Although these respondents may have been the best people to answer the project's questions, a number of them described their positions as not offering particularly good or effective oversights of their advisory services, and this will bear upon the quality of the information returned in the questionnaires. Unfortu-nately, there seems no immediate solution to this research problem since it would appear to reflect reality. In a number of LEAs there is no one individual with an overall view of what is happening and with specific and effective responsibility for the management and planning of the advisory service (see Chapter 4 for more detailed discussion of chief advisers' roles and the structures of their services).

Reasons for non-responses to the Chief Advisers questionnaire

Analysis has shown that the 68 LEAs returning the Chief Adviser questionnaire and the pro forma were not significantly different from the 38 non-responding LEAs in terms of their pupil, teacher and school numbers, nor was their geographic spread significantly different from the regional (using the ten DES regions) and the metropolitan/county spread of the non-responding LEAs. In other words, in terms of educational numbers and geographic position, the responding LEAs did not appear to be unrepresentative of the whole population of LEAs.

By telephoning most of the non-responding authorities we learnt of three main causes for the questionnaires not being completed. First, as has been suggested, some authorities did not have anybody in a position to answer the questionnaire. Apart from the problems already described, difficulties were also created in the few cases where two or more advisers had been given equal responsibility and where neither individual felt they could answer for the other. In these cases our questionnaire was seemingly caught up in a structural impasse. The second reason was that some LEAs were in the throes of a major reorganization at the time of the survey and felt that they could not then give any reliable answers to our questions. Later, however, personal visits were made to a number of these LEAs to talk about why the reorganization had been instigated and what its outcomes had been. The third group of LEAs which were unable to respond reported being too busy to be able to spend time on questionnaires.

The Advisers survey

The second identification decision that had to be made locally concerned the listing of advisory posts. This was done when the chief advisers completed the survey pro forma and described the composition of their advisory service by listing the official titles of 'all those posts primarily concerned with advising on educational matters within this authority'. A note on the pro forma suggested that the list was not expected to include many people beyond advisers, inspectors and the various types of advisory teachers who were LEA or area based, but that if there were other posts which made a significant contribution to the work of the advisory service in that LEA, then their listing was at the respondent's discretion. As with Bolam, Smith and Canter (1978), the choice of who was, and who was not, to be included in our survey and thus which posts were to be defined as being advisory was made locally.

The Chief Advisers pro forma identified 2,474 posts in 64 LEAs, of which 1,258 were adviser or inspector posts (including 'general' adviser and inspector posts), 1,182 were advisory teachers and curriculum officers/consultants with the rest (34) being officers and advisory officers (see Table 2.1). However, the advisers and inspectors in the other 40 LEAs still needed to be identified if they were to receive addressed questionnaires. Using information provided over the telephone and further lists from the *Education Year Book*, the project team managed to identify most, if not all, of the remaining adviser and inspector posts. In the end, 2,210 adviser posts were identified for the survey. (It should be noted that the Advisers questionnaire was only sent to advisory teachers if the local identification had suggested that they carried the equivalent of a full adviser role, for instance, if they had full responsibility for a major subject within the authority, if they had the right to inspect or if they were paid on Soulbury scales.)

Table 2.1: *Advisory populations in 64 LEAs as described by the chief advisers – September 1986*

Post title*	No.	Percentage of total	Extrapolated nos for 104 LEAs†
Advisers	642	25.9	1,043
Inspectors	159	6.4	258
Adviser/Inspectors Inspector/Advisers	34	1.4	55
General Advisers	286	11.6	465
General Inspectors	137	5.5	223
Advisory Officers	18	0.7	29
Officers	15	0.6	24
Advisory Teachers	881	35.6	1,432
Curriculum Consultants/ Coordinators, etc.	301	12.2	489
(unspecified)	1	0.0	2
Total:	2,474	99.9	4,020

* The post titles are those supplied on the Chief Advisers pro forma.
† The 64 responding authorities did not significantly differ in size from the non-responding authorities, nor was there any significant regional or metropolitan/county imbalance. The extrapolation of figures in column 3 was achieved by multiplying the reported totals by 104/64. The result is an estimate of the population reported upon.

Of the 104 LEAs approached for permission to carry out this survey, only five declined to participate or to distribute the questionnaires. The actual distribution of the Advisers questionnaire was handled in all but one case by individually addressed questionnaires being sent *en masse* to one person in the LEA. They were then distributed, either through whatever system the authority used for its internal post or by hand at the next advisers meeting. (In the one LEA where this was not done, by prior agreement the questionnaires were sent individually to the advisers' home addresses.) A pre-paid envelope for return, was enclosed with each questionnaire for its individual posting to the NFER.

In all, 2,025 addressed questionnaires together with a small number of spare copies were actually sent out to advisers and inspectors in 99 LEAs. Of these, 1,116 were returned giving an estimated 55.1 per cent response and representing just over 50 per cent of the known advisers and inspectors at that time in late autumn 1986. It should be noted that these figures include the responses from the three pilot LEAs and from one LEA where the structure and procedures were sufficiently different to warrant a slightly different presentation of the same questions. Timing, layout and question differences between the pilot, individualized and main versions of the questionnaire were sufficiently small for most of the data to be combined with the main survey returns.

The project's survey data, therefore, offers three perspectives on the advisory services. The first is drawn from the data in the pro forma and gives the numbers of posts and subjects covered within each LEA, as well as providing a few details about the posts themselves. It is limited information, but since it covers nearly 2,500 posts in 64 LEAs, it offers some most useful analyses (four of the 68 chief adviser respondents did not complete the pro forma). This data was also amenable to being merged with the DES 'Form 7' school and pupil information collected in the same year (1986). When the LEAs' adult population figures were also included, it enabled analysis of adviser 'density' ratios in respect of the LEAs' adult, school, teacher and pupil populations.

The second perspective comes from the Chief Advisers questionnaire itself, which provided detailed policy and management information from the 68 responding LEAs. This information is, on the whole, more useful for the depth of information it provides when considering specific topics, than for quantitative exercises. The third perspective is given by the Advisers questionnaire which contains detailed information from over 1,100 advisers and inspectors in 99 LEAs.

Advisers and advisory teachers – basic numbers and titles

The Chief Advisers pro forma was completed for 64 LEAs. Table 2.1 gives the numbers of each type of post described. Although analysing questionnaire data can reduce the numbers of variants within any group, there were still nine different post titles here, all of which were involved with giving educational advice (see n.2 in the table). From the data on these posts it appears that the title 'adviser' was at least three times as frequent as that of 'inspector', and that the combined number of advisory teachers, curriculum consultants and coordinators in these LEAs was much the same as the total number of advisers and inspectors (1,183 and 1,258 respectively).

Understanding the meaning behind the various adviser and inspector titles is difficult. The full titles given to these posts often include terms like 'area', 'county', 'general' or 'senior', but as will be shown later many of these qualifications cannot be related to any specific activities, responsibilities or duties. The issue of whether an adviser's subject is listed with the title also appears ambivalent. For the majority of advisers and inspectors with subject responsibility, if the subject was mentioned in their titles at all, it tended to come after the term 'inspector' or 'adviser'. In the analysis, shown in Table 2.2, these posts would be listed as 'unspecified' since the subject did not particularly appear to be being used to qualify the post. However, in some cases, the subject preceded the post title and might have been thought to qualify and to differentiate it from other posts in the authority. These have been described as 'subject posts'. Throughout this work, this distinction should be seen as an attempt to record a nuance rather than to describe any exact differentiation, though there is an apparent difference in status when salary differentials are also considered in this light.

Table 2.2 confirms a number of facets that one might have expected. One, however, stands out. The first three rows in the table show that while 77 per cent of advisers occupied positions without any particular seniority within the advisory service, the parallel figure for advisory teachers was over 99 per cent. Given that there were estimated to be approximately 2,000 people engaged in advisory teacher work in LEAs in 1986, and that this figure is growing so rapidly that by the end of the academic year 1987/88 it could involve nearly 3,000 people, it is surprising that there was virtually no career structure within this arm of the profession. It is accepted, of course, that a few will take up adviser posts, but as is evident in Chapter 3, the numbers to date have been fairly small, with only 21 per cent of existing advisers having held advisory teacher posts.

In looking at advisory work we might also consider how permanent it is. Of the 1,162 advisory teacher *posts* described, 54 per cent were permanent, with only 13 per cent being temporary and a further 33 per cent being seconded from teaching positions. (In comparison, the

Table 2.2: Within-service hierarchical and organizational positions (information from the Chief Advisers pro forma describing 64 LEAs)

Title	Advisers* total	General Advisers total	Inspectors* total	General Inspectors total	All Advisers and Inspectors total	%
Unspecified	246	238	43	94	621	49.4
Subject†	129	0	25	8	162	12.9
County	108	21	19	34	182	14.5
Area	9	11	6	0	26	2.1
Phase	32	0	8	0	40	3.2
Senior	111	16	52	1	180	14.3
Staff	3	0	5	0	8	0.6
Principal	9	0	4	0	13	1.0
Chief‡	16	0	10	0	26	2.1
Missing	0	0	0	0	0	0.0
Total	663	286	172	137	1258	100.0

Title	Advisory teachers total	Advisory officers and officers total	Advisory teachers and advisory officers total	%
Unspecified	1,089	20	1,109	91.2
Subject†	81	2	83	6.8
County	1	0	1	0.1
Area	1	5	6	0.5
Phase	0	0	0	0.0
Senior	9	4	13	1.1
Staff	0	0	0	0.0
Principal	1	1	2	0.2
Chief‡	0	1	1	0.1
Missing	0	1	1	0.1
Total:	1,182	34	1,216	100.1

* The joint titles of 'Adviser/Inspector' and 'Inspector/Adviser' have been listed according to the first part of the title.

† Where a subject precedes the post title these have been called 'subject' posts.

‡ Not all respondents to the Chief Advisers questionnaire listed themselves on this pro forma.

advisers' figures for the same categories were as follows: 99 per cent permanent, 0.5 per cent temporary and 0.6 per cent seconded.)

From the data it would also appear that the majority of advisory teacher posts are more recent creations than those of advisers. Only 7.5 per cent of the current advisory teacher posts existed prior to 1974, the year of the major local government reorganization, and although this figure was more than doubled in 1974 alone, this still represents the creation of only a further 10.3 per cent of the current posts. Thus 82 per cent of advisory teacher posts were created after 1974, with some 37 per cent of the total current advisory teacher posts being brought in between 1984 and the summer of 1986. In comparison, 43 per cent of the 1986 adviser posts were already in existence by 1974 and a fairly startling 19 per cent (nearly one-fifth of the current total) were then created in that year alone. Only eight of current adviser posts have been introduced between 1984 and 1986. Thus, while the majority of adviser posts can be seen to have been introduced over a fair number of years and to have grown in number at a fairly constant rate since 1974, the majority of advisory teacher posts appear to be a more recent phenomenon. (The emphasis on 'current', or 1986 posts, is important since the method of collecting data ignored posts which had been taken out of service. The apparently smooth growth in the creation of current posts does not necessarily indicate a smooth growth in the number of people employed in the advisory services over the same time.)

Advisers and advisory teachers – salaries and funding agencies

The funding situation within advisory services is fairly confused since not all funding is derived wholly from just one or another body and patterns differ between advisers and advisory teachers; However, Table 2.3. shows the major differences. It appears that the vast majority of advisers are funded by their LEAs, whereas this is only the case for some 62 per cent of advisory teachers, the rest being funded by some five or six other bodies. This raises a problem for the LEAs in having to keep track of the various different contracts and in upholding the prime purpose of each differently funded post, especially when it is recalled that a large number of new posts have been created recently and that there is overlap between adviser and advisory teacher work.

The advisers and advisory teachers pay structures are given in Table 2.4 and are basically distributed across three scales: Soulbury, Burnham Head Teacher and Burnham Teaching Scales. (Since this research was carried out, the Soulbury pay scales have been adjusted and their direct link with headteacher salaries has been broken. Appendix Table A2.2, page 210, shows the new salary structures as of November 1987. All of the following analyses apply to the old system; however, it is thought that many of the trends revealed will still apply to the new system.) The

Table 2.3: *Comparisons of adviser and advisory teacher funding*

	LEA	DES	ESG/DES	MSC	HO	MP/DTI	Totals
			Funding agencies*				
Advisers	98.2%	0.5%	0.5%	0.3%	0.5%	0.0%	100%
N =	1274	6	7	4	6	0	1272

(Information not provided for 2 advisers: analysis includes 18 advisory officers)

	LEA	DES	ESG/DES	MSC	HO	MP/DTI	Totals
Advisory Teachers	62.5%	14.1%	15.7%	6.3%	1.2%	0.2%	100%
N =	703	159	176	71	13	2	1124

(Information not provided for 58 advisory teachers)

* The exact proportion of funding provided by each of these separate agencies is not known. All that this table suggests is that these agencies provide 50 per cent or more of the funding. The differences between ESG and DES/ESG funding appear more to do with inexact responses than specific differences in the allocation of funds.

majority of adviser posts (96 per cent) were described by their chief advisers as being paid on the Soulbury scales, while the majority of advisory teachers (86 per cent) were paid according to the Burnham Teaching Scales. But the distribution of the two populations across the three scales was not totally clear-cut since a small proportion of both advisers and advisory teachers were paid on the Burnham Head Teacher (HT) scales, and surprisingly, a number of advisers were on the Burnham Teaching Scales, while some advisory teachers were on Soulbury.

If the Burnham HT and Soulbury scales are treated as the same and combined, the average scale point for adviser posts in 1986 was 8.9. If posts created before and after the beginning of 1980 are considered separately, it appears that there has been a small but significant decrease in recent years – i.e. the average scale point in 1986 for adviser *posts* created before 1980 was 9.0, compared with 8.7 for those created since then. Adviser pay can also be seen to differ significantly when the LEAs are split by their north/south position and by whether they are metropolitan or county: average scale points for adviser posts in the north and south are 8.85 and 9.05 respectively; and for metropolitan and county, 8.9 and 8.95 respectively. (All differences are significant at 0.01 level or better.)

Until the summer of 1987 the Soulbury scales were tied to the Burnham Head Teacher scales – the salary and status relationships between advisers and headteachers was seen as a matter of considerable concern to many of those we interviewed. This linking also had important ramifications within LEAs because of the differentials it

Table 2.4: Percentages of advisers and advisory teachers on the different salary scales

(Percentages given out of populations for which information was provided – i.e. 1,191 advisers and 1,094 advisory teachers)

(a) Soulbury scale points

	4	5	6	7	8	9	10	11	12	13	14	Total
Advisers	0.0	0.1	0.9	5.7	35.2	22.7	23.6	5.8	1.3	0.3		95.6
N =	0	1	11	68	422	272	283	70	15	4		1146
Advisory Teachers	0.1	0.1	0.1	0.2	1.0	0.5	0.2	0.0	0.0	0.0		2.2
N =	1	1	1	2	11	6	2	0	0	0		24

(b) Burnham Head Teacher scale points:

up to	4	5	6	7	8	9	10	11	12	13	14	Total
Advisers	0.1	0.0	0.1	0.0	1.2	0.2	1.8	0.3	0.1	0.0	0.0	3.8
N =	1	0	1	0	14	3	21	4	1	0	0	45
Advisory Teachers	6.9	0.3	1.2	0.9	1.0	0.9	0.2	0.1	0.0	0.1	0.1	11.5
N =	75	3	13	10	11	9	2	1	0	1	1	126

(c) Burnham Teaching Scales (1986):

	1	2	3	4	Senior teacher	Deputy head	Total
Advisers	0.0	0.2	0.2	0.3	0.0	0.0	0.7
N =	0	2	2	4	0	0	8
Advisory Teachers	4.5	10.1	34.8	27.7	8.9	0.4	86.3
N =	49	110	381	303	97	4	944

Note: Information not provided for 77 advisers and 88 advisory teachers

created between officers' and advisers' pay. Furthermore, within advisory services the issue of advisers' salaries was seen to affect their career structures and to influence considerations when attempting to establish new posts and when looking at various ways to reorganize the service. Another result of this linking was that the main difference between the two scales used for advisers (Soulbury and Burnham HT) was not money, but conditions of service, length of holidays, and so on. Notionally, advisers on Burnham HT scales could follow the normal teaching arrangements in these matters, while advisers on Soulbury scales had more office-related conditions. In practice, however, as will be described later, the distinction was blurred as many Burnham HT advisers reported being unable to take their full leave and their school holiday 'entitlement' might often better be described as being less of a holiday and more of a time when they could catch up with office work and reading.

One unfortunate consequence of linking one scale with another was that whilst the chief advisers might know the difference and provide accurate information, many advisers seemed unsure of how to describe their pay scales. Within some authorities advisers would offer different explanations when in fact they were all on the same scales and working to the same conditions. The national position is similarly blurred and unhelpful with parallel adviser posts for different authorities often being advertised on different rates of pay. For example, on one double page in the *Times Educational Supplement* (17 July 1987) there were three different posts advertised on three different rates – i.e. Burnham HT, Soulbury, and Soulbury Burnham HT scales! It is not surprising that confusion exists.

Perhaps surprisingly, the highest-paid post described in the Chief Advisers pro forma was for an advisory teacher on Burnham HT 14. Table 2.4 shows that there were several advisory teacher posts with high scale points. This is due to these posts being occupied by seconded headteachers from large comprehensive schools with protected salaries.

Advisers and advisory teachers – ratios with adult populations

Over the years there have been a number of attempts to offer LEAs guidelines for the number of advisers they should employ. For the most part, these relate to the adult population within the LEA and are expressed as ratios. For instance, the National Association of Inspectors and Educational Organizers (NAIEO) recommended to the Redcliffe-Maude Committee on local government reorganisation that within each LEA there should be: a chief inspector; a general inspector for every 60,000 of the total population or for every 10,000 of the school population; and sufficient specialists to cover English, mathematics, social sciences, art, drama, home economics, handicraft, music, physical education (boys and girls), science and languages. (NAIEO, 1968).

Patently, any recommendation based on population ratios can only be an approximate measure since geographic and demographic factors will influence the effectiveness of any team as well as presenting localized demands and problems which could not be addressed by a single national formula. More recently, any recommendation would also have to take account of the numbers of other personnel working within the advisory service as a whole (advisory teachers, teachers' centre wardens, etc.) as the presence of these posts affects the advisers' workload.

The 64 LEAs responding to the Chief Advisers questionnaire had an average adult population of 452,000 people – a figure which was not statistically significantly different from that of the non-responding LEAs (see p. 15). The LEAs also had, on average, 19.9 advisers (s.d. 9.6), which is marginally below the 1968 NAIEO recommendation of 20.5 advisers for an LEA of this size. The figure of 19.9 advisers per 452,000 population represents 44.1 advisers per million adults in the LEA. When this ratio is calculated for individual responding LEAs, the minimum ratio was 23.8 advisers per million, and the maximum was, 109.2 per million. These figures show a considerable range of adviser 'density' with the most 'generous' LEA proportionately employing just over four and half times as many advisers as the least generous.

There were, on average, 18.5 advisory teachers per LEA and thus 40.9 advisory teachers per million adults. Included in this calculation, however, are the zero values from the seven chief advisers who reported having no advisory teachers with an LEA-wide brief working in their LEAs, a position endorsed by the chief advisers' comments recording the difficulties of convincing Education Committees of the need to appoint advisory teachers. The maximum LEA advisory teacher 'density' was 274.2 per million adults, some two and a half times more numerous than the greatest adviser 'density'.

This much larger range between the maximum and minimum values of the advisory teacher ratios compared with that for advisers would seem to reflect the relative newness and unsettled nature of the advisory teachers' employment and role in contrast to the relatively 'institutionalized' employment of the advisers, where the ratios are more constant. This can be seen in another way. The correlations produced between the number of advisers and the number of adults in each LEA and the number of advisory teachers and the number of adults in each LEA are $+0.9$ and $+0.3$ respectively. (Both figures are significantly different from zero.) Plainly, the size of the adult population in the LEA is much less of a guide to the number of advisory teachers than it is to the numbers of advisers.

When the numbers of advisers and advisory teachers in each LEA are combined to represent a single service, the average ratio becomes 86.3 advisory personnel per million adults, with a minimum value in one LEA of only 28.7 per million in contrast to a maximum in another of 335.2 per million. The small size of this minimum value suggests that the advisory teachers might not be being used in any great numbers to supplement or compensate for low ratios of advisers. Looking at individual LEA ratios for advisers and advisory teachers (not given here) reinforces this point. The correlation between the numbers of advisers and advisory teachers employed in individual LEAs is only +0.2 and non-significant, implying little consistent relationship between the numbers of advisers and advisory teachers employed.

Advisers and advisory teachers – ratios with pupils, teachers and schools

An alternative and, perhaps, more appropriate way to consider adviser 'density' is to compare their numbers with those of the people and institutions with which they work, that is to compare them with the numbers of schools, teachers and pupils in the LEA. For the sake of comparability between the various systems used in the different LEAs, the pupil, teacher and school numbers in these analyses all relate to the compulsory years of schooling, 5–16, and ignore nursery and sixth-form pupils and colleges.

The adviser densities with respect to pupils, teachers and schools for the 64 responding LEAs presented average values of 0.35 advisers per 1,000 pupils, 6.1 per 1,000 teachers and 101 per 1,000 schools. (For advisory teachers the parallel averages were 0.34(5) advisory teachers per 1,000 pupils, 6.1 per 1,000 teachers and 97 per 1,000 schools, see Appendix Table A2.3 (p. 211) for more detailed results.) The school figures are perhaps easier to appreciate as being about one adviser and one advisory teacher to ten schools. There is, as has already been suggested with the adult populations, a considerable variation between individual LEAs, with the maximum and minimum ratios for advisers per 1,000 pupils being 0.72 and 0.17 respectively, per 1,000 teachers being 12.0 and 3.2 respectively, and 1,000 schools 244 and 36 respectively. (If the LEA ratios for numbers of advisers in the service per 1,000 primary and 1,000 secondary schools are considered separately, then the average of the LEA ratios of advisers per 1,000 primary schools is 124, with a maximum of 306 and minimum of 41, and the average of advisers per 1,000 secondary schools is 579, with a maximum of 1,357 and a minimum of 212 – these figures refer to all advisers in the service and do not differentiate between those with different phase responsibilities.)

All the ratios have shown large variations between LEAs. The question arises as to whether these variations are idiosyncratic or influenced by some other feature or features. When the results are broken down into the DES' ten geographic regions, although care must be taken with the small numbers of LEAs concerned, a fair degree of regional variation does seem apparent, and it would be fair to suggest that there is a regional influence. It is difficult, however, to determine how it works – see Appendix Table A2.3.

Arising from this analysis is the question of whether these differences are at all influenced by the urban or rural nature of the LEAs or whether their sizes play any role. Table 2.5 takes the same information as used in Appendix Table A2.3 but divides the LEAs by whether they are 'metropolitan' or 'non-metropolitan'. From this table we can see that the adviser–pupil and adviser–school ratios are both significantly larger in metropolitan boroughs than in counties, and adviser to teacher ratios follow the same trend. Differences in adviser–school ratios can, of course, be partly explained by schools tending to be larger in urban areas, but this effect could not account for differences in pupil ratios. Differences in advisory teacher ratios are not so marked, and indeed, because of the smaller differences and larger standard deviations, not statistically significant.

Table 2.5: *Demographic variation in adviser 'density'*

LEA Type		Advisory staff/1,000 pupils (all pupils 5–16)			Advisory staff/1000 schools (all primary and secondary schools)		
		Advisers	Advisory teachers	All team	Advisers	Advisory teachers	All team
Metropolitan	mean	0.40	0.37	0.77	127.1	117.1	244.2
	SD	0.13	0.30	0.34	45.2	92.7	109.8
No. of LEAs		33	33	33	33	33	33
Non-metropolitan	mean	0.29	0.32	0.61	73.3	76.2	149.5
	SD	0.08	0.40	0.43	20.2	97.4	103.2
No. of LEAs		31	31	31	31	31	31
All LEAs	mean	0.35	0.34	0.69	101.0	97.3	198.3
	SD	0.12	0.35	0.39	44.3	96.5	116.0
No. of LEAs		64	64	64	64	64	64
		sig.*	non-sig.	sig.	sig.	non-sig.	sig.

Note: * Significance is stated where $p < 0.05$ or better

(Mean school size (pupils):
Metropolitan: 318 Non-met. 253 All LEAs 289)
(Mean pupil–teacher ratios:
Metropolitan: 17.1 Non-met. 18.6 All LEAs 17.7)

Although there is a strong relationship between LEA size and the number of advisers, a third perspective is still available if we look more closely at the influence of the size of the LEA's population. The NAIEO formula of 1968, with both its constant factor (12 subject advisers and one chief) and proportional factor (one general adviser to every 60,000 population) would have tended to enhance the ratios in small LEAs, and indeed this is just what we find. Thirty-one LEAs had adult populations in 1986 of less than a quarter of a million – of these, 14 were London boroughs and only three were counties. In contrast, 24 LEAs had in excess of 600,000 adults, and all but two of these, Birmingham and the ILEA, were counties. Information about the advisory services was available for 18 of the 31 small, and 14 of the 24 large, LEAs. The average adviser and advisory teacher ratios per 1,000 adult population in the small LEAs were 59.2 (s.d. 17.3) and 64.4 (s.d. 63.2) respectively, while for the large LEAs the average adviser and advisory teacher ratios were 34.8 (s.d. 6.4) and 21.9 (s.d. 21.5) respectively. Clearly, the smaller the LEA population, the larger the ratio. But size may not be the only factor since the small LEAs tend to be concentrated in the metropolitan and London boroughs, while the large LEAs are virtually all counties – a facet which stems from the different criteria used in the reorganization of the London boroughs some ten years before the reorganization of the rest of the country. In all, it would seem difficult to separate out the political, demographic and size influences in these ratios.

Advisers and advisory teachers – tackling the issue of subject coverage

One of the main reasons put forward for increasing the size of an LEA's advisory service often relates to the argued necessity for maintaining or increasing that service's subject coverage, that is the number or range of subjects or curriculum areas that it can advise upon. However, the issue of advisers' subject coverage is complex and difficult. One reason for this is that the advisers' subjects and responsibilities can be expressed in different ways, for instance, as subjects named in their official titles (and hence referred to as their 'title' subjects), as subjects in the lists of 'other' subjects which they have been formally given over the years or, finally, as subjects for which they unofficially and informally, or even only temporarily, hold a watching brief. While it is easy to understand why individual advisers have more than one responsibility, and why they may be described differently, it is often difficult for the outsider to pick up the relative importance of specific subjects when they are offered in these different ways and, one suspects, it creates problems for the advisory team too, though perhaps not to the same extent.

Advisers' subject responsibilities – the case-study experience

The case-study interviews showed that advisers acquired considerable numbers of 'other' subjects over time, and that these may be fundamentally very different from their original 'title' subject(s) for which they were primarily employed. Furthermore, these 'other' subjects may well eventually occupy more of their time than their original responsibilities. One adviser suggested that accretion took place, but that rarely was anything taken off. The idea of accretion is well demonstrated in the humanities area, where one adviser talked of being originally appointed as a tutor for environmental studies working with pupils as well as teachers. The advisory work grew and after five years he became the adviser for environmental and geographical studies and then he took on history. He added that he also tended to pick up social studies and economics.

One might expect that the majority of later additions to the advisers' responsibilities would reflect their existing subject expertise, but to some extent this is circumvented by the related subjects often already being subsumed into the adviser's title role, for instance, science tends to include biology, chemistry and physics. The experience of the case studies, however, suggested that in practice there can still be considerable divergence between the added subject and the adviser's original main subject. One PE adviser, having described her job description as requiring her to promote physical education in the county, commented that while it was simple and brief, it had never been revised and now bore little resemblance to what she actually did. A mathematics adviser described how careers and schools–industry links had been added on, and an arts adviser described her job as having been 'widened' to include home economics. (We noted that when there was no specialist home economics provision available, it was seen on more than one occasion to be 'given' to an adviser on the basis of sex rather than any known academic competence in the area.)

Some indication of how and why the tasks were handed out is perhaps appropriate, since although the end-product of this process may not always appear totally logical, it can be seen as the LEAs' attempt to meet changing needs during a period of economic recession. Thus we can understand why, as certain subjects and curriculum emphases come to the fore, they were added to advisers' responsibilities. Although many advisers reported finding difficulty with the number and range of subjects they now had to cover, it was not uncommon for them in interview to talk of accepting the changes fairly willingly as they said they appreciated the difficulties faced by those in charge. One adviser pointed out, though, that when the request was phrased as 'Will you do it or will you do it?', he had felt he had but little choice in the affair!

Collecting subject information in surveys

In developing the questionnaires a difficulty arose with the use of the term 'subject'. Not only does the concept of a subject beg questions as to how precise an area is being considered, but also it was occasionally interpreted both as shunning primary work where the idea of the 'curriculum area' might be more appropriate, as well as seeming to ignore the new areas of cross-curriculum and other non-traditional types of work. To help alleviate difficulties we asked on the Chief Advisers pro forma for the advisers' 'Main subject(s) or curriculum areas'. On the Advisers questionnaire, apart from asking for the title of the individual adviser's current post, we also asked advisers to list any other curriculum areas or aspects they officially covered.

We then encountered difficulties with classifying and analysing the enormous range of subjects offered in the open-ended survey questions. Not only did the respondents most reasonably record their pastoral, phase and other areas of non-curriculum work, thus giving a far broader interpretation than we had intended, but they also went into considerable detail in the more conventional areas and clearly differentiated between variations on various subject themes. In the end, for practical reasons, small differences between variants of single subjects could not be coded. For instance, algebra, arithmetic, trigonometry and geometry may all have been offered as individual responsibilities but they had all to be given the same code as mathematics, and in English no distinction could be made between English, English literature and English language. One result of this was that it became possible for an adviser to be recorded as being responsible for the same subject several times, a none-too-sensible outcome. To correct this anomaly second and subsequent same-subject entries were deleted in the analyses such that no subject would be counted more than once for any one adviser.

A second difficulty in describing and interpreting adviser subject coverage was caused by the surveys' representational problems across LEAs. Neither survey was fully representative of all LEAs. As such the data cannot be used to present any definitive statements about subject coverage around the country. However, for all these difficulties, there was still a wealth of information provided in the subject returns, and a number of points can be made.

Advisers and advisory teachers – subject coverage results

The main results from the subject coverage questions in both the Chief Advisers and the Advisers questionnaires are shown in Table 2.6. Columns 1 and 3 give the distributions of advisory teacher and adviser title subjects as provided in the Chief Advisers pro forma. Although 6.3 per cent of advisory teachers had no title subject listed, the majority had one subject, and a few had more such that the overall average was 1.01 subjects per advisory teacher. Compared with the advisory teachers, proportionately twice as many advisers had no title subjects (13.1 per cent). The average number of title subjects given to advisers in the pro formas was 1.1.

Columns 2 and 4 in the table give the percentage distribution for each title subject and demonstrate the differences in the internal balance of subject work between advisers and advisory teachers. The most notable differences are where the percentage for advisory teachers (column 2) is greater than that for the advisers (column 4) – i.e. where proportionately more advisory teachers than advisers are occupied in a particular subject area. In many cases these emphases show the government's recent and direct influences as enacted through the DES, the Manpower Services Commission (MSC), Welsh Office and Home Office funding, though LEA influence is also visible. This analysis highlights the following subject areas as having such emphases: Welsh, primary science, personal and social education (PSE) and health education, computing and microelectronics, mathematics and primary mathematics, multicultural work, special educational needs, Certificate of Pre-vocational Education (CPVE) and the pre-vocational areas, TVEI and TRIST.

In absolute terms, advisory-teacher numbers are also high in English, PE, music and primary phase work, but in all these instances the advisers are well represented too. In contrast, apart from in the primary phase field, advisory teachers are basically absent from phase work and from pastoral work in schools as a whole.

'Title', 'core' and 'other' subjects

As has already been suggested, the advisers' title subjects do not necessarily give a full indication of the subject areas in which they work: to gain a more comprehensive picture it is necessary to include the other subjects for which they also formally carry some responsibility. In Table 2.6 column 7 ('All subjects') takes the information

Table 2.6: *Advisers and advisory teachers – subject distribution listed by adviser frequency as given by chief advisers (subjects with less than 10 entries in all columns have been deleted)*

Column:	1	2	3	4	5	6	7	8	9	10
Population:	Advisory teachers		Advisers		Advisers		Advisers		Advisers	
Type of subject:	title subjects		title subjects		title subjects		all subjects		all subjects	
Source of data:*	Chief Advisers		Chief Advisers		Advisers		Chief Advisers		Advisers	
	N	%	N	%	N	%	N	%	N	%
Subject and cross-curricular responsibilities										
PE	30	2.5	92	7.2	74	6.6	105	8.2	87	7.8
English/drama	33	2.8	91	7.1	66	5.9	135	10.6	116	10.4
Music	48	4.1	70	5.5	58	5.2	78	6.1	62	5.6
CDT, design, tech.	23	1.9	64	5.0	60	5.4	82	6.4	104	9.3
Mathematics	135	11.4	61	4.8	64	5.7	81	6.3	89	8.0
Sciences	35	3.0	58	4.5	57	5.1	89	7.0	80	7.2
Modern languages	13	1.1	46	3.6	49	4.4	76	6.0	64	5.7
Computer, IT micro	65	5.5	42	3.3	38	3.4	76	6.0	88	7.9
Other humanities	12	1.0	42	3.3	41	3.7	74	5.8	108	9.7
Art	10	0.8	40	3.1	35	3.1	59	4.6	58	5.2
Home economics	10	0.8	30	2.4	33	3.0	42	3.3	52	4.7
RE	10	0.8	22	1.7	21	1.9	40	3.1	44	3.9
Multicultural	33	2.8	16	1.3	13	1.2	30	2.4	44	3.9
Environmental studies	15	1.3	13	1.0	12	1.1	22	1.7	27	2.4
PSE, health, drugs	14	1.2	12	0.9	24	2.2	34	2.7	119	10.7
Business studies	10	0.8	7	0.6	6	0.5	34	2.7	39	3.5
Careers	1	0.1	7	0.6	10	0.9	12	0.9	21	1.9
History	1	0.1	7	0.6	5	0.4	29	2.3	29	2.6
Geography and/or geology	0	0.0	6	0.5	8	0.7	32	2.5	35	3.1
Environmental science	1	0.1	5	0.4	4	0.4	9	0.7	23	2.1
Leisure pursuits	14	1.2	5	0.4	11	1.0	23	1.8	40	3.6
Welsh	46	3.9	4	0.3	5	0.4	6	0.5	7	0.6
TVEI	26	2.2	3	0.3	6	0.5	5	0.4	25	2.2
Primary maths	34	2.9	3	0.2	4	0.4	6	0.5	8	0.7
Primary science	69	5.8	2	0.2	1	0.1	6	0.5	15	1.3
Economics	1	0.1	2	0.2	4	0.4	10	0.8	28	2.5
Dance/drama	6	0.5	1	0.1	11	1.0	9	0.7	29	2.6
Classics	0	0.0	1	0.1	3	0.3	7	0.5	27	2.4
Textiles	0	0.0	1	0.1	0	0.0	5	0.4	10	0.9
E2L TEFL	1	0.1	1	0.1	2	0.2	4	0.3	10	0.9
Community languages	0	0.0	0	0.0	1	0.1	0	0.0	11	1.0
CPVE pre-vocational	6	0.5	0	0.0	2	0.2	6	0.5	39	3.5
Phase and other non-subject-type work:										
Primary phase	44	3.7	150	11.8	146	13.1	178	13.9	187	16.8
Special educational needs	209	17.7	80	6.3	60	5.4	92	7.0	97	8.7
Secondary phase	0	0.0	51	4.0	51	4.6	58	4.5	85	7.6
Nursery, early years	8	0.7	24	1.9	27	2.4	30	2.4	41	3.7
FE and FE + Adult	0	0.0	24	1.9	25	2.3	32	2.5	37	3.3
Youth and comm.	0	0.0	24	1.9	15	1.3	28	2.2	30	2.7
INSET/Staff development	5	0.4	19	1.5	23	2.1	29	2.3	73	6.5
Cross curricular development	13	1.1	16	1.3	8	0.7	21	1.6	39	3.5
Adult + prison education	4	0.3	14	1.1	10	0.9	15	1.2	17	1.5
Materials, resources buildings, design + ed. tech.	1	0.1	11	0.9	6	0.5	17	1.3	26	2.3
16–19 phase	0	0.0	8	0.6	11	1.0	11	0.9	24	2.2
Middle phase	0	0.0	5	0.4	13	1.2	10	0.8	19	1.7
TRIST	30	2.5	3	0.3	3	0.3	5	0.4	16	1.4
Assessment	0	0.0	2	0.2	1	0.1	7	0.5	22	2.0
Learning resources/ media, libraries	1	0.1	3	0.2	4	0.4	8	0.6	54	4.8
Schools/industry	7	0.6	2	0.2	1	0.1	6	0.5	25	2.2
Equal opportunities	13	1.1	1	0.1	3	0.3	5	0.4	27	2.4

Table 2.6: Continued

Column:	1	2	3	4	5	6	7	8	9	10
Population:	Advisory teachers		Advisers		Advisers		Advisers		Advisers	
Type of subject:	title subjects		title subjects		title subjects		all subjects		all subjects	
Source of data:*	Chief Advisers		Chief Advisers		Advisers		Chief Advisers		Advisers	
	N	%	N	%	N	%	N	%	N	%
Subject and cross-curricular responsibilities										
Pastoral work	0	0.0	0	0.0	10	0.9	0	0.0	193	17.3
Other	86	7.3	21	1.6	1	0.1	51	4.0	53	4.7
No subject given†	74	6.3	178	13.1	149	13.4	175*	13.7	28*	2.5
Total	1199	101.4%	1400	110.2%	1307	117.7%	2022	158.6%	2667	238.8%
Total entries	1182	1182	1276	1276	1116	1116	1276	1276	1116	1116
Total respondents	64	64	64	64	1116	1116	64	64	1116	1116

* The data was taken from either the Chief Advisers' responses on the pro forma or from the Advisers questionnaire.

† 'No subject given' was a specific coding category which was only used in the 'title' subjects. Where no subject was given in the title, subjects were still often given in the 'other' subjects spaces, 'No subject given' has been recorded only in the combined subject groupings where no subject was given in the title and then none other added in the other subjects column.

provided on the Chief Advisers pro forma and then lists the advisers 'title' and 'other' subjects combined with repeats removed. It is quite noticeable that the number of subjects covered has increased from that given as title subjects only in column 3· the advisers now have an average of 1.6 subjects each.

The comparison of the title and 'All subjects' columns (columns 4 and 8) shows whether the other subjects are a numerically representative extension of the 'title' subjects, or whether there are certain subjects which feature more strongly in this 'other' category. Since the 'All subjects' column records 1.44 times as many subjects as are in the title subjects column, one would expect the average entry for each subject in the 'All subjects' column to be 1.44 times larger than its title subject only equivalent. In practice, however, we see many subjects falling below this expected value, that is subjects where there are not as many entries in the 'other' category as we would expect, for instance, English, modern languages, science, PE, home economics, art, craft design and technology (CDT), mathematics, special needs and most of the phase work. In contrast, primary science, geography and geology, history, environmental studies, economics, leisure, dance and drama, personal and social education (PSE), business studies, computing, RE, and one or two more all have enhanced values in the 'All subjects' column – they appear to have greater coverage in the 'other' subjects category than in title subjects.

One tentative explanation for this pattern of distribution groups the subjects into three areas. First, there are the conventional, specialist, mainstream and basically secondary school type of subjects, which LEAs, the public and politicians would think important enough to warrant a full adviser post and which would need specialists to occupy them – i.e. subjects like English, mathematics and science, the core subjects. As such these subjects are more likely to appear as title rather than other subjects, and the specialisms are such that one would not expect someone from a different academic field to be able to offer to cover them in any real sense.

The second group of subjects might be described from this analysis as still being conventional, but this time, as having less political clout and also – rightly or wrongly – as being easier to accept as second subjects – i.e. geography, history, environmental science, etc. This group thus appears to be over-represented in the other subjects category.

The third group of subjects also appears over-represented in the other subjects category, but possibly for a different reason. These are the new emphasis subjects whose presence here reflects the advisory services' response to pressure for change – as seen, for example, in primary science, computing, multicultural, special education needs, etc. These are subjects which, as they come into the limelight, are added to the advisers' official list of responsibilities. With their new emphases, they attract political and financial attention, though not necessarily enough initial funding to warrant a full new adviser post. Quite often, the new initiative will also carry responsibility for the management and support of the advisory teachers associated with it.

These three groups have appeared as a result of data provided in the Chief Advisers pro forma. Where advisers have provided their own 'title' and 'all subjects' information, as seen in columns 3 and 9 of Table 2.6, these same three groups of subjects are again visible.

It is interesting to note that in terms of numbers of subjects, where the chief advisers only ascribed 1.6 different subjects to each adviser, the advisers described themselves as each having responsibility for some 2.4 subjects. The advisers' perception of their subject responsibilities involved half as many subjects again as their chief advisers credited them with. However, the larger figure perhaps corresponds more closely with the position seen in the case studies. To be fair, though, this is always a difficult area to be exact about, since when is an extra subject responsibility officially part of one's job and when is it not? This question must pose many difficulties for advisers when trying to prioritize their time.

It seemed a useful check to consider the correspondence between the advisers' and the chief advisers' descriptions of the advisers' roles. If the survey was accurate, and if communications were working well within the services, we would expect the advisers' descriptions of their own official title subject(s) to reflect how the people in charge of their service described them, and for the most part, this appears to be the case. The chief advisers' and the advisers' responses (see columns 4 and 6 in Table 2.6) contain very similar figures, especially when we consider that they have been filled in by different populations, and that although they both represent over 50 per cent of the country's advisers, they do not necessarily cover the same advisers. However, in the totals shown in the table, it is evident that advisers ascribe somewhat more official subjects to their titles than do their chiefs (1.18 subjects per adviser according to the advisers, compared with 1.10 as described by the chief advisers), but the difference is small and care must be taken over the possibility of different criteria being used; for instance, some advisers listed pastoral work under a subject heading, while no chief advisers did.

Deployment models for advisory teachers

The distribution of advisory teachers' 'title' subjects in Table 2.6 suggested that there might be some underlying patterns in their deployment. If both the distribution of subjects between advisers and advisory teachers and the sources of advisory teacher funding were considered, it would seem that the majority of advisory teachers had probably been deployed in one of just three ways. Table 2.7 shows advisory teacher subject distribution listed according to whether it is LEA or mainly non-LEA funded.

The first of the three ways of deploying advisory teachers related to the high concentration of LEA-funded advisory teachers found in just two curriculum areas: special education needs, and computing/information technology. This work involved 30 and 11 per cent of all LEA-funded advisory teachers respectively. These are both areas in which LEAs have recently had to respond and for which money has not, perhaps, been initially sufficient to allow for the creation of new adviser posts. A second LEA-funded deployment pattern occurred where the LEA seemed to be enhancing the support it already offered schools and teachers in the basically traditional fields. Relatively high numbers of LEA-funded advisory teachers were found in English/drama, Welsh, PE and sports, music and primary phase work.

The last and perhaps most significant deployment pattern appeared to be initiative led, and to have been brought into being by central government offering to pay for part or all of a large number of advisory teachers in certain selected areas. Thus we saw the vast majority of

Table 2.7: *Advisory teachers – subject responsibilities by funding agent*

Funding agent:	LEA		Non-LEA		Both		(Title subject)*	
	N	%	N	%	N	%	N	%
Subject and cross-curricular responsibilities:								
Special educational needs	202	29.5	5	1.2	207	18.7	209	17.7
Computer, IT micro	74	10.8	13	3.1	87	7.9	65	5.5
Music	46	6.7	1	0.2	47	4.2	48	4.1
PE and sports	37	5.4	0	0.0	37	3.3	30	2.5
English/drama	36	5.3	3	0.7	39	3.5	33	2.8
Welsh	24	3.5	16	3.8	40	3.6	46	3.9
Mathematics	18	2.6	125	29.7	143	12.9	135	11.4
Leisure pursuits	17	2.5	1	0.2	18	1.6	14	1.2
CDT, design, technology	16	2.3	16	3.8	32	2.9	23	1.9
Environmental studies	16	2.3	1	0.2	17	1.5	15	1.3
Dance/drama	12	1.8	0	0.0	12	1.1	6	0.5
Art	11	1.6	1	0.2	12	1.1	10	0.8
Business studies (comm.)	11	1.6	3	0.7	14	1.3	10	0.8
Other humanities	11	1.6	3	0.7	14	1.3	12	1.0
Home economics	10	1.5	2	0.5	12	1.1	10	0.8
Modern languages	10	1.5	2	0.5	12	1.1	13	1.1
Multicultural	9	1.3	19	4.5	28	2.5	33	2.8
RE	9	1.3	3	0.7	12	1.1	10	0.8
Sciences	9	1.3	32	7.6	41	3.7	35	3.0
Crafts	6	0.9	0	0.0	6	0.5	1	0.1
PSE, health, drugs	5	0.7	11	2.6	16	1.4	14	1.2
Primary science	5	0.7	70	16.6	75	6.8	69	5.8
E2L TEFL	4	0.6	0	0.0	4	0.4	1	0.1
History	3	0.4	0	0.0	3	0.3	1	0.1
CPVE pre-vocational	3	0.4	3	0.7	6	0.5	6	0.5
TVEI	3	0.4	23	5.5	26	2.4	26	2.2
Primary maths	2	0.3	48	11.4	50	4.5	34	2.9
Phase and other non-subject-type work:								
Primary phase	31	4.5	15	3.6	46	4.2	44	3.7
Equal opportunities	13	1.9	0	0.0	13	1.1	13	1.1
INSET/staff development	12	1.8	2	0.5	14	1.3	5	0.4
Nursery, early years	9	1.3	0	0.0	9	0.8	8	0.7
Schools/industry	8	1.7	1	0.2	9	0.8	7	0.6
(Cross) curricular development	4	0.6	13	3.1	17	1.5	13	1.1
Assessment	3	0.4	3	0.7	6	0.5	0	0.0
TRIST	1	0.1	30	7.1	31	2.8	30	2.6
Other	62	9.1	31	7.4	93	8.4	86	7.3
No subject given‡	50	7.3	9	2.1	59	5.3	74	6.3
No. of subjects	815	119.1%	506	120.0%	1321	119.3%	1199	101.4%
No. of respondents	685	100%	421	100.0%	1106†	100.0%	1182	100.0%

* The subjects refered to here are taken from the Chief Advisers pro forma and include 'title' and 'other' subjects. All repeats for indvidual advisers have been deleted.
† Full analysis based upon 1,182 records; information about funding missing in 76 cases.
‡ 'No subject given' was a specific coding category which was only used in the 'title' subjects. Where no subject was given in the title, subjects were still often given in the 'other' subjects spaces. 'No subject given' has been recorded only in the combined subject groupings where no subject was given in the title and then none other added in the other subjects column.

non-LEA funded advisory teachers were employed in just 11 subjects: science and/or primary science; mathematics and/or primary mathematics; and then Welsh, PSE and Health Education, CDT, computing, multicultural, TVEI, TRIST and the primary phase, and finally, in curriculum development.

The question has already been raised as to whether advisory teachers were being used in place of advisers. Although this did not appear to be the case when we considered all subjects together, it was thought that it might be happening for individual subjects. It thus became of interest to ask what happened in an LEA when a major subject was *not* covered by an adviser and what, if anything, the LEA did to compensate. Table 2.8 shows the number of LEAs without listed adviser coverage (either in the advisers' titles or 'other' subjects) for each of 16 main subject areas. Of these, only English, the sciences, CDT, mathematics, music and physical education appeared to be covered in over 90 per cent of authorities, and 'coverage' in this sense did not necessarily imply being an adviser's main or title responsibility.

Where an LEA had no adviser coverage in a certain subject, one might have expected advisory teachers to have been employed in a compensatory fashion – and to some small extent this was found to be the case. With the exception of music, where a lack of adviser cover was totally reflected by a lack of advisory teacher cover, in all the other subject areas we have considered some of the LEAs' adviser subject deficit was 'compensated' for, by the presence of advisory teachers, but the picture was not uniform across the subjects. In each of the small number of LEAs with no maths or PE advisers (three and four respectively) there was advisory teacher coverage, whereas in many other subjects only about a third of the LEAs made up for cover in this way. It would appear, then, that only a minority of LEAs were using advisory teachers to cover deficits of the traditional adviser 'school' subjects in a thorough way.

This, then, raises the question of how LEAs meet their own, and their schools' and colleges', subject 'needs' when in some subjects they have no specific adviser or advisory teacher expertise available, and when they have not passed the subject responsibilities on to advisers as second-string responsibilities. The case studies demonstrated that LEAs still had a fair degree of flexibility left and that, in some cases, they managed without necessarily appointing extra staff. For example, degrees of compensation were achieved in some instances through the use of national curriculum development initiatives, pilot management studies and research projects. LEAs also reported 'leaning' on local HMI, education officers, teachers' centre wardens, self-help groups, and so on. However, there is often a hidden

Table 2.8: *Deficit subject coverage and advisory teacher compensation*

Subject area	No. of LEAs without listed adviser cover in each subject area (N = 64) N	Percentage of LEAs without adviser cover %	No. of these LEAs with advisory teacher cover in each subject area* N	Degree of† compensation as percentage of number of LEAs %
Mathematics	3	4.7	3	100
PE	4	6.2	4	100
Craft, design, technology, etc.	6	9.4	3	50
Sciences	2	3.1	1	50
English language	5	7.8	2	40
Primary science‡	58	90.6	22	38
Home economics	25	39.1	9	36
Computing, IT, etc.	9	14.1	3	33
Multicultural, etc.	35	54.7	7	33
Primary maths‡	58	90.6	19	33
Health education/PSD, etc.	26	40.6	8	31
Modern languages	10	15.6	2	20
Humanities	8	12.5	1	12
Arts	11	17.2	1	9
Classics	56	87.5	1	2
Music	4	6.2	0	0

* This excludes advisory teachers with school-based remits.

† Caution should be exercised with these percentages. Their main purpose is to act as gross rather than fine indicators.

‡ Part of the reason for these low values may have arisen from some primary maths and science being *implicitly* subsumed in some maths and science advisers' roles.

cost in this practice in terms of the loss of time or emphasis on the main commitments of those people whose attention is now diverted to these other areas. It should also be recognized that the alternative practices may not be as effective, especially with the subject/personnel kind of work (appointments, setting up INSET, curriculum continuity and redeployment), as they might have been with an adviser with specialist knowledge taking the role. The case-study work would suggest that this is most apparent in the difficult and amorphous areas of adviser support for school management and organization, where experience, personnel and management skills, and objectivity, may be most necessary, even though we tend to lump these attributes together and describe them as 'generalist' work.

Conclusion

This chapter has set out to provide a national picture of the numbers, salaries and subject coverage of LEA advisers and advisory teachers. As with previous survey work in this field, most notably that of Bolam *et al.* in 1978, the terminology was found to present problems. Adviser nomenclature was far from uniform in its usage, and although problems for research are hardly grounds for change, the difficulties we encountered were also likely to face other advisers, officers, teachers and, possibly, parents and governors too. The range of activities that might or might not be included in an advisers' brief was such that task definitions also suffered problems, as we will see in Chapter 3; and even the old chestnut of whether a post is held by an 'adviser' or 'inspector' is a predominantly meaningless distinction in terms of the actual activity of inspecting.

The surveys also encountered difficulties in recording and categorizing advisers' subject, cross-curriculum and pastoral responsibilities since the range was enormous; and again, the terminology was often inexact. These difficulties were, however, far less marked for advisory teachers. Even though there were nearly as many of them as advisers, their range of subject responsibilities was both individually and collectively much reduced, and it tended to concentrate in relatively definable areas. By inference it would seem that advisory teachers were freer than advisers to concentrate on the main parts of their task, but there is of course no guarantee that if they stayed in their posts for a long time, they too would not start to accrue extra responsibilities.

The number of advisory teachers is expected to reach 3,000 by mid-1988, and as such it will by then have overtaken the number of advisers. In the main, compared with the relatively steady generation of adviser posts over the years with its one peak in 1974 and its long trough in the late 1970s, the existence of so many advisory teachers may be regarded as a relatively recent phenomenon, with less than one in ten of current posts going back before the local government reorganization in 1974 and more than one in three being brought in between 1984 and 1986.

Advisory teacher posts were found, as expected, to be mainly in the areas of the recent educational initiatives. What was, perhaps, surprising was that over half of these posts were permanent, and over 60 per cent were LEA funded. That a post is permanent, however, does not imply that the postholder has tenure or any career in that field. Looking at the hierarchical structures available to advisory teachers, it is apparent that this is an arm of the profession with virtually no career structure, since not even one per cent of advisory teachers occupied senior or elevated posts within this job.

In terms of salaries, the general pattern was clear. The majority of advisers were paid on Soulbury scales, while the majority of advisory teachers were on Burnham Teaching Scales. However, there was sufficient crossover between the two groups to confuse the situation. The presence of a third scale, the Burnham Head Teacher Scale, which applied both to a number of advisers and advisory teachers, muddied the water still further. In many ways the non-pecuniary differences between the parallel Soulbury and Burnham HT scales may be regarded as unimportant since practice seems to eliminate them, but even so it seems an unnecessary additional confusion in a profession where job descriptions and conditions of service documents, if they exist at all, often fail to reflect reality.

In part of this chapter we have looked at the ratios reached in different LEAs between the numbers of advisers and adult, pupil, teacher and school numbers within those LEAs – indicators of what might loosely be termed 'adviser density'. Across the country there appears to be a startling range of ratios, with some LEAs employing up to four and half times as many advisers per million adults as other LEAs. Patently, LEAs have varying financial constraints. Furthermore, they obviously operate different systems as they cater for what they perceive are their schools' and colleges' needs. Surely, there must also be some truth in the idea that an institution's external needs are partly determined (conditioned) by the authority's willingness or ability to meet them; but for all these circumstances, we must also be looking at the outcome of policy decisions.

The position is, of course, more complicated than that of deciding merely how much provision should be made available. The case-study experience clearly demonstrated the powerful influence within LEAs of the status quo – it often seemed difficult, for both political and practical reasons, for chief advisers to implement change, and even then they needed to be able to work with the existing personnel. As such the variation between LEAs is unlikely to diminish in the near future due to internal initiatives alone and even if external pressures are brought to bear to bring uniformity to the services, the combination of inertia and regional and demographic influences may well be seen as effectively trapping LEAs in their own status quo model, and that again will tend to maintain the status quo. (We return to the theme of managing change in the advisory service in Chapter 7.)

The employment of advisory teachers is seemingly not so prone to inertia as that of advisers, so it is perhaps not surprising that the individual LEA's ratios of advisory teacher to adult populations should have varied more than those of advisers. Given too that there appeared to be no relationship between the number of advisers in an LEA and the number of advisory teachers it employed, even though the numbers of advisers were fairly constant in relation to the adult population, then we can see that the whole advisory teacher employment pattern seemed far more unsettled than the relatively institutionalized pattern for advisers. When we conducted the survey, there were, for instance, LEAs with no advisory teachers, while others in contrast, employed hundreds.

In turning to the final part of this chapter, the information from the surveys gave a clear indication of the range of adviser subject coverage and allowed us to see where current emphases lie. The analyses also provided a glimpse of the relative importance afforded the different subjects and three subject groups were recognizable.

In the first group the subjects appear as high-profile, high-status and secondary-orientated subjects; they tended to be listed as advisers 'title' subjects and might nowadays be likened to the 'core' subjects. The subjects are politically important and deserve full adviser attention. Subjects in the second group, although present in the 'title' subjects, were also very noticeable in the advisers' 'other' subjects. In other words, they were more often to be found as second or 'watching-brief' subjects, and as such we may take them as having less status, though that is hardly any indication of their educational value or of their supportive needs in schools. There was also a third group of subjects, and these mainly appeared under the 'other' subject heading, but they certainly did not deserve any low-status position – these were the 'new' subjects arising out of the educational initiatives. At a time of financial shortage many advisory services have responded to these new subjects by giving them to advisers as extra responsibilities, and hence they appear as advisers' 'other' subjects, and sometimes then only in the advisers' lists and not in those of their chief advisers. The other method open to advisory services in demonstrating flexibility to changing educational needs is to appoint advisory teachers, and it is perhaps appropriate to end this chapter by considering the recent impact of the advisory teacher.

In looking at how advisory teachers were distributed across subjects we have seen that advisory teachers appear well 'used' where the government has wished to emphasize and fund new initiatives, as in primary science and mathematics, and equally, where the new initiatives attracted little funding, as in computing prior to the summer of 1987 and special education needs work. In contrast, except in English, Welsh, PE, music and primary phase work, we see them very thinly spread across the now not so emphasized traditional subjects. All this would suggest features about the employment of the advisory teacher which differ from those of the adviser.

The advisory teacher was less expensive to employ, almost half were in temporary posts and the vast majority were given no hierarchical or management matters to occupy their time or to attract them to stay on. The majority were not involved with responsibilities beyond their main role. Given too that most were taken directly from the teaching-pool with apparently little training being offered, and that there was the belief that they could be returned to that pool when their task was done or the funding ran out, then one can see why they were an attractive proposition to LEAs looking for a quick response to new 'needs'. Through using different people over the years, they offer a subject flexibility that the current arrangements for advisers would have difficulty in matching while still firmly locked into subject structures. Furthermore, in times of centralist leadership, they seem an attractive proposition since they can promote change relatively speedily and economically. While this is all very mechanistic and ignores experience and all the other important roles carried out by advisers, it does seem to pose something of a problem to the advisers since a most important part of what they used to offer is now undertaken by a different workforce. But then, as we have already suggested and will see again in the following chapters, the advisers' job has itself already changed considerably over the last few years. As one maths advisory teacher recently commented, 'Many schools now receive more mathematics advice then ever before, but they see much less of their mathematics adviser'.

3   The People and the Job

Introduction

Chapter 2 offered survey information about advisory posts in England and Wales. Apart from being able to detect national trends that cannot be seen at the local level, its aim was to present the beginnings of a context against which many of the more detailed and often localized considerations could be set. This chapter continues with this theme, but provides the survey information about the advisers and chief advisers themselves; that is, where Chapter 2 described the posts, this chapter describes the postholders. In so doing, this chapter starts by looking at a number of the professional features of chief advisers and advisers before going on to consider the actual work they undertake.

Chief advisers

Numbers

Assessing the exact number of Chief Adviser posts around the country is not easily done. This arises partly because of the nomenclature which often makes it difficult to know who actually is in charge, and partly because (as Chapter 4 shows) the existence of a Chief Adviser post is no indication of how much time the holder will be allowed to spend on that job. Apart from stating the obvious that, at least nominally, there is someone in charge of each of the 104 advisory services, we cannot give any precise and meaningful numbers to this post. However, despite these difficulties, our experience would suggest that there were moves at the time of the research in 1986–7 to create chief adviser posts in a number of LEAs which did not have them before, or to create 'full-time' Chief Adviser posts in authorities which had previously had only 'part-time' ones. As such the number of Chief Adviser posts should be increasing. This view is reinforced by figures compiled by the National Association of Inspectors and Educational Advisers (NAIEA). Between October 1986 and May 1987 they reported that ten authorities advertised for a Chief or Principal Adviser, two of which were newly established positions. What is not known, however, is how many such posts have lapsed and remained vacant upon the retirement or departure of the previous incumbent. Overall, it would appear that some LEAs are newly signalling the need for a specifically designated leader of the advisory service.

Time in-post

Sixty-six of the 68 respondents reported how long they had held their current posts. The longest was 14 years, with the average being just 6.2 years. Four people had been appointed before 1974 and 12 were appointed that year, that is virtually a quarter had been in post 12 or more years when we conducted the survey. However, just over a third of the respondents (25) had been appointed during the two years up to the survey, and this represents a fair degree of movement around the country.

Background

The Chief Advisers' backgrounds highlight a number of important themes. First, Appendix Table A2.1 shows that responsibility for advisory services varied from the adviser or inspector type of post to the education officer type appointment. The previous careers of the 68 respondents had a similar division, with 44 of them (65 per cent) having come from adviser posts and 16 (24 per cent) having come from officer posts. Of the remaining eight respondents, four came from headship posts, and one each from lecturing, from a head of department, from TVEI directorship and from curriculum officer posts at the Schools Council. It is noticeable that only four of the 68 had held both officer and adviser posts before taking charge of the service, though there are limitations to this type of analysis when the information is drawn from post titles rather than job descriptions.

The titular division between those with adviser and those with officer type titles is reinforced by the way the respondents' previous posts reflected the current split. Of the 13 respondents listed in Appendix Table A2.1 with 'officer-type' titles, ten came from officer backgrounds. By the same token, the majority of the postholders with 'adviser-type' posts had adviser backgrounds (i.e. 39 out of 55, with only six in this group having officer backgrounds).

A second theme comes from the six respondents who came to their current Chief Adviser posts directly from school or college (four headteachers, one school head of department and one from college), – i.e. just under nine per cent of the population. This must be one of the few senior professional managerial grades where appointments are made from outside the system. It would appear to have serious status and career implications for advisers.

Another theme concerns staff mobility between LEAs. Of the 68 respondents, 28 were promoted, or at least moved, to their current position from a position already within their current 'county hall' (20 from within the advisory service and eight from the administrative/executive side); four respondents were promoted from schools within their current authority. In total, half of those in charge of advisory services reached this position from within their current LEA. In some respects there will be the strengths of continuity – in contrast, only half the postholders bring in ideas from other authorities when they are appointed.

A fourth theme is derived from the respondents' university or college subject backgrounds. Of the 62 respondents who provided information in this area, the most frequently stated subject was English, (12), followed by history (11), other humanities subjects (9), languages (9), sciences (9), mathematics (3), technology (3) and other subjects (6). In all, 66 per cent of the respondents had arts and humanities backgrounds, and only 24 per cent came from the sciences and technology.

The final theme concerns the postholders' previous sector experience. The great majority of respondents reported having worked in the secondary schools, and only seven reported having worked in the primary sector. In addition, only one respondent stated that his main subject at college/university included primary education. However, FHE lecturing experience was relatively well represented among the respondents, with just under a third (20) having held lecturing posts at some time in the past. The preponderance of secondary sector experience was clearly inbalanced, as was the proportion of male to female postholders, with there being very few women Chief Advisers.

The Chief Advisers' job description

A recurring theme in the case studies was that advisory work was simply too nebulous to be categorized and written down. On the other hand, the expansion of the range of functions undertaken, the reported increased workloads and the greater emphasis on managing education have led to a greater, or at least more overt, interest in clarifying, rationalizing and defining what should be done and by whom.

The respondents to the Chief Advisers questionnaire were asked if they had a specific job description and if so whether they had been involved in its formulation. Of the 66 respondents, two-thirds (45) had been issued with job descriptions and one-third (21) had not. Of the 45 with job descriptions, only 18 reported that they had been involved in their formulation. There was no statistical evidence to suggest that job descriptions were more likely to be issued with any one of the three different chief adviser types than any other. Equally, there was no significant difference in the proportions of respondents having job descriptions when they were grouped into those appointed more than five years ago and those appointed since then. The incidence of job descriptions among those in charge of advisory services did not appear to be increasing.

Copies of a number of job descriptions were returned with the questionnaires and others were collected from the case-study LEAs. Even in their fullest and most detailed form, there was likely to be an enormous difference between the job description and the actual job that is done, though this was not always regarded negatively. A number of people we talked with reported preferring broadly phrased job descriptions, allowing them the freedom to concentrate on what they thought important.

Analysis of these documents can only be inexact, but on the whole, they revealed more similarities in the main functions than dissimilarities. The main functions they offered are listed as follows (though no order of priority is suggested):

(1) to advise the chief education officer;
(2) to develop and maintain standards of excellence/promote curriculum development;
(3) to monitor and review the delivery of the curriculum;
(4) to monitor and review teaching etc;
(5) to ensure the proper provision of professional development for teaching staff;
(6) to be responsible for the induction of new teachers;
(7) to lead the team of advisers.

In all the job descriptions, the postholder's responsibilities towards educational institutions were clearly stated. However, the postholder's contribution towards policy and decision-making was phrased rather more ambiguously. One specifically stated that a function of the postholder was to: 'Contribute as a member of the Education Management Team to the determination of policies and management practices in the department their development and co-ordination with those of the Authority as a whole'. This, however, was the only reference we saw to involvement in policy making – perhaps,

significantly, the document had been drawn up by external management consultants! Although one or two authorities' job descriptions
recommended chief advisers should be members of the senior
management team or recommended their presence at Education
Committee, their roles in these cases seemed that of information
providers – reporters, perhaps, more than advisers? One of these
postholders was required to 'Prepare policy reports and agenda items
for the Director of Education to submit to Council Committees and to
Governing Bodies as required', while another was simply required to
'Attend and report to meetings of the Authority's committees and the
governing bodies of schools and colleges'.

A number of chief advisers were required to work in conjunction
with education officers, and at least one was required to deputize for the
director as required. Others had specific liaison and coordinating
functions where they were required to 'Develop, promote and monitor
policies for the Educational Psychology service, in collaboration with
the Principal Educational Psychologist', or 'To convene and chair
regular meetings of the principal officers in the Youth Careers,
Psychological and Education Social Work Services in order that there
might be co-ordination of thinking and practice among all the
professional support services within the Directorate'. Only in one of
them was there a specific requirement that the postholder should be
concerned with the professional development of advisers themselves.
However, in this one at least, the issue appeared to have been
thoroughly addressed. The postholder was required to:

Give leadership and direction to the inspectorate by means of
induction, training, determination of objectives and strategy
and by regular review in order that, in the context of the
authority's policies, there exists within the team a unity of
understanding and purpose and a corporate awareness of
essential issues.

Perhaps it should be added that along with this job description, a copy of
the authority's adviser induction programme and a draft document on
appraisal were also enclosed.

The chief adviser's work

The chief adviser's work appears to fall into four areas: (1) work which is
nothing to do with being a chief adviser; (2) advisory work that is given
to the most senior adviser; (3) ordinary advisory work as in that being a
pastoral adviser or covering a subject for which there is no
other adviser; and (4) management work concerned with running the
advisory team. Looking at the second area, only eight of the 68

respondents stated that they had no special or 'hierarchical' advisory duties which specifically arose out of their position as the most senior adviser; with the 60 who listed 138 such duties between them, while the range was fairly extensive, it can be grouped into ten appropriate areas, as shown in Table 3.1.

Table 3.1:   *Advisory duties undertaken by those in charge of advisory services in the light of their senior position*

Area of duty	No.	Percentage of those with the duty
Interviewing for senior staff in schools/colleges	54	90.0
Member of LEA senior management team	23	38.3
Attendance at Education (Sub) Committee meetings	15	25.0
Representing CEO at various meetings	10	16.7
Member of working parties	9	15.0
Involvement in INSET provision	6	10.0
Giving management advice to schools & colleges	3	5.0
involvement in LEA non-teaching appointments	3	5.0
Attendance at governing body meetings	3	5.0
Shortlisting for headships	3	5.0
Other	9	15.0
Total tasks listed	138	230%
No. of respondents	60	60

The relative proportions of the numbers of respondents undertaking work in each of the ten areas is quite informative. For instance, 90 per cent of those in charge of advisory services reported interviewing senior staff for school and college posts. Obviously this is a major part of the role of most chief advisers but it begs the question as to why this should be so, and what and whose expectations are being met. The second most frequently reported task, that of membership of the senior management team, affected just under 40 per cent of respondents, but a trouble with open-ended questions is that it cannot automatically be inferred that those who did not list this activity were not doing it. For instance, chief advisers with officer roles may well have attended the senior management team because of their officer role and, therefore, not listed it in their chief adviser role. These were the two most frequently cited tasks, involving over half of all the responses. However, a considerable range of the other tasks was revealed and demonstrated a good deal of variation in practice.

The respondents were also asked if their job included aspects of the third area, namely work in schools or colleges as a subject, phase or pastoral adviser, and if so, they were asked to describe it. Thirty of the 68 respondents said that they undertook this kind of advisory work, while 37 said they did not. Table 3.2 offers examples of the types of work involved.

Table 3.2: *Standard advisory duties undertaken in schools and colleges by those in charge of advisory services*

Area of duty	No.	Percentage of tasks per respondent
Phase work	13	44.8
Subject work	11	37.9
Management and pastoral work	7	24.1
Involvement in inspections	2	6.9
INSET and GRIST	2	6.9
Other	5	17.2
Total tasks listed	40	137.8%
No. of respondents	29	29

(One respondent undertook this type of work but did not describe it in detail)

The range and number of duties in Tables 3.1 and 3.2 underlines the extent and diversity of the responsibilities given to, or adopted by, those appointed to manage the advisory services. In turn, this poses the important question of how much time is left to them to perform the appropriate management functions, a question that is taken up again in Chapter 4, when the organization of the service is considered.

Although the data have given only a brief look at the chief advisers themselves, a number of clear points have begun to emerge, perhaps the most important of which reflects difficulties with the role. If an LEA has a chief adviser at all, the post can be either officer or adviser orientated and the postholder need have no prior experience of working in an advisory service. In other words, there is yet to be a single accepted role for the chief adviser, and indeed, when we see the range of their titles, many of which encompass other roles, we see that there is yet to be a universally accepted need for a full-time role.

Another striking theme must surely be the CEOs' ambivalence about the chief adviser's role in policy making – we rarely saw any clear statement that an adviser-type chief adviser was to be fully involved in the authority's decision-making. But why not? In many authorities we might question just how much the chief adviser is a manager who plays an important role near the top of the LEAs, and just how much he is the senior adviser who does the senior adviser job and little more. Presumably it follows that the model set for the chief adviser also filters down to the advisers.

Advisers

The Advisers questionnaire was returned by 1,116 advisers. Table 3.3 shows the range of post titles for 1,109 of these respondents. As mentioned in Chapter 2, the decision as to who was to be included in the population of advisers was made locally. Of this population, 96 per cent of respondents had an adviser or inspector title, with the other four per cent comprising advisory teachers, advisory officers, (education) officers, and curriculum coordinators and consultants – i.e. 44 professionals in education who were regarded by those in charge of them to be carrying an adviser's role. Unless otherwise stated, these 44 will not be separated from their adviser colleagues in the following analyses and discussions.

The inclusion of some chief advisers' responses in the Advisers questionnaire data is problematic, but intentional. Chief advisers were invited to complete the Chief Advisers questionnaire, but not particularly invited to complete the Advisers questionnaire. As this latter questionnaire was intended to be completed by those with a significant LEA advisory role, where chief advisers have included themselves, we have kept their information in. More specific detail about chief advisers is given on pages 43 *et seq.* and 95.

The first four columns in Table 3.3 give the absolute numbers for the advisers and inspectors responding to the survey; 288 (27 per cent) of this group were inspectors, a figure that corresponds closely to the 25 per cent reported in the Chief Advisers pro forma (see Table 2.2, p.20), and 300 (28 per cent) gave themselves a 'General' title (compared with 34 per cent on the pro forma). Overall, the correspondence between Tables 2.2 and 3.3 is good – the two separate populations reported very similar proportions for the various title groups, and this suggests that the respondents to the Advisers questionnaire were basically representative of the population of advisers as described by those who completed the Chief Advisers questionnaire. Table 3.3 can also be used to look at the distribution of hierarchical positions within the advisory services; column 5, showing the percentages of advisers and inspectors in each of the different title positions, indicates that just over one in five of all advisers and inspectors had some form of senior position or designation.

The table also shows the distribution of posts by whether the postholder was in his/her first or subsequent advisory appointment. Just over three-quarters of the 'unspecified' adviser posts were occupied by first-time appointments. First-time advisers also occupied 90 of the 233 'senior' posts, denoted by asterisks – i.e. they held over a third of the services' senior positions, whereas nearly two-thirds were

Table 3.3: *The range and distribution of advisers' post titles*

Post	Ads	Gen Ads	Ins	Gen Ins	Ad+ Ins	Others Total	All Total	1st time appts		Subsequent appts	
Title	N	N	N	N	%+	N†	N	N	%‡	N	%‡
Unspecified§	167	201	71	82	48.9	25	546	424	77.7	122	22.3
Subject	102		7	1	10.3	5	115	91	79.1	24	20.9
County	113	3	12	5	12.5	1	134	90	67.2	44	32.8
Area	7		16		2.2	7	30	13	(43)	17	(57)
Phase	44	2	5		4.8		51	39	(76)	12	(24)
*Senior//	118	6	72		18.4	5	201	84	41.8	117	58.2
*Staff			10		0.9		10	2	(20)	8	(80)
*Principal	9		4		1.2	1	14	3	(21)	11	(79)
*Chief	5		3		0.8		8	1	(12)	7	(87)
Totals N	565	212	200	88	1,065	44	1,109	747		362	

+ The percentage in this column is based on the sum of the responding advisers and inspectors as known by these titles, 1,065.

† The term 'Others' included 'advisory teachers' (8), 'advisory officers' (13), 'officers' (7), and various types of 'coordinator' (16). These four groups have been included in the analyses on the grounds that their contributions to the advisory work of the LEA were deemed by the LEA to be similar to those of the advisers.

‡ These are row percentages. Thus of the 546 'unspecified' advisers, 77.7 per cent were first-time appointments and 22.3 were second or subsequent appointments.

§ 'Unspecified' includes advisers and inspectors with no other qualifying adjectives, those with a subject listed after the term adviser or inspector, 'Education', 'General' advisers and inspectors. This is the category for all those without one of the 'specified' titles.

// In line with the practice of categorizing advisers according to the highest hierarchical title given, 'senior' includes 'senior area'.

(Post title information was missing for seven of the 1,116 responding advisers, 4 of whom were first-time appointments and 3 were subsequent appointments.)

occupied by those who had held advisory posts beforehand. With the 'staff', 'principal' and 'chief' adviser posts (although the numbers are too small for detailed analysis), it is apparent that while the proportions of first-time advisers are lower than in other positions, these positions are not restricted to experienced applicants only. People are appointed to management positions within advisory services who have not worked in such services beforehand.

Another point of correspondence between the two sets of questionnaire data comes with the advisers' and the chief advisers' reports of the advisers' salaries. When the numerical values of the reported Burnham Head Teacher (HT) and Soulbury scales for advisers were combined for analysis, advisers reported that they were paid on an average salary point of 8.93, while the chief advisers put that figure at

8.92 – two very similar values which are not statistically significantly different. However, the chief advisers reported that only 3.8 per cent of advisers were paid directly on Burnham HT Scales (see Table 2.4, p.23.), while a much larger number, i.e. some 8.8 per cent of advisers, considered themselves on these scales – a confusion which was probably centred on the advisers' understanding of these matters. The question of salary scale raised a good deal of uncertainty in interviews in the case studies, but as has already been suggested in Chapter 2, there has in recent years been much confusion in advertising and the system has changed since the survey. The distribution of advisers' pay scales, as reported by the advisers, is given in Appendix Table A3.1.

Sex and age

Table 3.3 portrays a wide range of different advisory posts. In looking at the members of such a group the possibility arises of a pattern existing in their background, ages and sex which might be linked to the different roles or types of work undertaken. For example, while overall 75.5 per cent of the respondents were men and 24.5 per cent women, when we consider advisers' sex by their phase work there is a different pattern. Women occupy nearly 40 per cent of primary phase roles, but only 17.5 per cent of secondary and 15.3 per cent of youth and FHE phase work (see Table 3.4).

The same sort of variation can be seen in the ages at which the advisers were appointed to their *current* posts, that is, their 'appointment ages'. The average appointment age for the whole sample of advisers is 41.04 years. The average first-time adviser, of which there were some 751 representing 67 per cent of the service, was appointed to the advisory service when just over 40 years old (40.15 years), and for those 365 (33 per cent) who had held adviser posts beforehand, they last changed their adviser job when they were on average nearly 43 years old (42.9).

In looking at appointment ages by how long the adviser has been in post, it is possible to see if the average age at which advisers are appointed has changed over the years (see Table 3.5), but in so doing there is a spurious trend that first must be laid to rest. The table shows a marked decrease in appointment ages before 1974, but this decrease is most likely to be an artefact of the way the data were collected. Questionnaires were only sent to those in post. Given that retirement tends to be a characteristic of older age groups, and that retired (i.e. older) advisers were no longer in-post, retired advisers

Table 3:4:   *Sex distribution in advisers' phase work*

Sex	Primary phase		Secondary phase		Youth/FHE phase		No specific phase		All advisers	
	N	%	N	%	N	%	N	%	N	%
Male	116	(60.1)	66	(82.5)	61	(84.7)	598	(78.0)	841	(75.5)
Female	79	(39.9)	14	(17.5)	11	(15.3)	169	(22.0)	273	(24.5)
Total	195	(17.5%)	80	(7.2%)	72	(6.5%)	767	(68.9%)	1114	(100)

Note: Some advisers reported working in more than one phase and/or in more than one aspect within a phase – e.g. some worked in secondary and FE, and some in nursery and infant. For the purpose of this analysis each entry has been included as there was no way of separately apportioning these advisers' work (information missing from two of the 1,116 responding advisers).

would not have received questionnaires. Thus, in essence, the survey selectively ignored the 'older' of those advisers appointed some years ago while including their younger colleagues appointed at the same time. In only recording the appointment ages of the younger of the longer-serving advisers the analysis would progressively and artificially reduce the average appointment age the further back in time we look. However, this problem should not have been too influential over the more recent years and therefore, Table 3.5 offers some useful information.

The most noticeable aspect of advisers' appointment ages over recent years is that they appear to have remained very stable; furthermore, with the standard deviations hovering fairly constantly at approximately 5.8, the spread of appointment ages each year also appears to have remained basically constant. Table 3.5 also shows the number of advisers in the survey population who were appointed each year. Allowing for the fact that the survey method we used will have tended progressively to reduce the appointment numbers as we go back in time, recent-entry numbers still seem to be considerably enhanced. In fact, if the figures are extrapolated to the estimated full adviser population of nearly twice the survey population considered here, then the new intake number in 1986 should have exceeded the 200-mark for the first time since 1974. It is also apparent that the period from 1976 to 1979 seemed to have few entrants – in absolute terms probably no more than 50 in total in each of at least three of these years. Finally, Table 3.5 shows that despite the apparent reduction in numbers over time due to the survey method, the year 1974 (i.e. that of LEA reorganization) still stands out as the year when a relatively large number of advisers were appointed.

Table 3.5: Advisers' appointment ages by time in post, as recorded in autumn 1986

Years in post	Approx. date	All advisers Appt age years	N	1st time advisers Appt age years	N	Non-1st time advisers Appt age years	N	appointments %
<1	1986	42.0	144	40.7	105	45.7	39	27
1	1985	41.9	114	40.9	77	44.0	37	32
2	1984	42.7	103	41.7	69	44.8	34	33
3	1983	42.1	101	40.6	72	45.6	29	29
4	1982	41.4	63	40.6	38	42.7	25	40
5	1981	41.6	64	41.0	48	43.7	16	25
6	1980	41.7	41	40.6	23	43.2	18	44
7	1979	41.8	56	40.9	38	43.8	18	32
8	1978	40.4	42	39.6	26	41.7	16	38
9	1977	41.6	18	40.4	14	45.8	4	22
10	1976	42.8	34	41.9	22	44.4	12	35
11	1975	40.7	47	39.9	38	44.3	9	19
12	1974	39.0	149	38.24	93	40.2	56	38
13	1973	40.9	28	41.3	15	40.4	13	46
14	1972	37.8	19	35.7	10	40.2	9	47
15	1971	38.0	28	38.2	21	37.3	7	25
16	1970	38.1	13	38.0	10	38.6	3	23
17	1969	37.8	9	36.5	4	38.8	5	55
18	1968	36.1	10	34.0	3	37.0	7	70
>18	before '68	35.1	22	35.9	17	32.4	5	23
Totals:			1,105		743		363	32.9

Note: analysis based on 1,105 adviser with 11 missing.

One problem with these figures is that counting entrants into a profession cannot determine changes in its overall size simply because it ignores any comparable record for the numbers leaving. General consent would suggest however, that the LEA advisory services are increasing in size (see also pages 150-53) where estimated leaving rates are given).

While appointment ages may have remained constant over time, they can be shown to vary across subjects, with the more technical subjects recruiting at a significantly lower age than some of the other subjects, for instance, at a lower age than primary phase advisers' average appointment ages (see Table 3.6). Appointment ages also appear to vary between LEAs, with some authorities seemingly appointing their advisers around about the age of $36\frac{1}{2}$ years while others appoint, on average sometimes as much as seven years older – i.e. at 43 to $43\frac{1}{2}$ years. But two factors should also be considered here. First, among first-time advisers women tend to be appointed at a slightly but significantly, higher age than men (41.1 to 39.8 years respectively) and thus roles with high(er) proportions of women, for example, primary phase work, have enhanced appointment ages. (It may be, of course, that the process works in the other direction and that a sex effect at appointment influences the primary phase appointment age.) Secondly, and almost inevitably, money also plays a role. By looking at the average appointment ages for each of the main Soulbury scales we can see that as the posts' pay scales increase, so does the average age of first-time advisers appointed to those posts (see Table 3.7).

Table 3.6: Advisers' appointment ages by subject areas covered

Advisers' Subject Area	All advisers Appointment age		1st-time advisers Appointment age	
	years	N	years	N
(All areas)	41.04	1110	40.15	745
Technical subjects	40.20	92	39.48	66
Micro elect./IT/computing	39.90	73	39.04	55
Primary phase	43.28	199	42.30	140
Secondary phase	42.30	84	41.04	49
Youth/FE/Adult ed phase	40.77	81	39.27	55

Note: '1st-time advisers' had only held the one, their current, advisory post – thus their age of appointment was their age upon entry into the advisory profession. (Information missing from six respondents.)

Table 3.7: Advisers' appointment age by Soulbury scale for first-time advisers

Soulbury Scale	Mean appointment age	
	years	N
7	39.3	38
8	39.6	229
9	39.8	169
10	40.5	132
11	44.6	10
Total advisers		578

Note: Information based on (a) middle part of salary range, (b) first-time advisers only and (c) where appointment age has been given. This reduces adviser number.

Finally, at the time of the survey the average adviser had been in his or her current post for approximately 6 years 5 months (for first-time advisers, 6 years 3 months). The average age for all advisers was 47 years 5 months (data based on 1,105 out of 1,116 respondents). Given a reasonably constant entry age and a normal retirement pattern, it is likely that the average age will remain more or less constant over the years. This must present interesting training and management challenges. Successful, specialist and experienced teachers enter the profession at about 41 years of age. Almost two-thirds of the survey respondents were in their first post – for the majority, advisory work offers few career opportunities – and the average age was just about 47½ years old. Whatever is offered by way of training and management must take into account this peculiar age distribution and static career structure. These characteristics would appear to present an interesting contrast with the advisers' principal LEA colleagues, the officers.

Professional background: university and current subject match

The advisers were asked to list their main subject at college or university, and Table 3.8 gives the responses for 1,088 of the 1,116 respondents. While accepting that there are difficulties in drawing any conclusions from this type of data (it ignores subsidiary and subsequently studied subjects, as well as assuming some degree of comparability between the like-named subjects from different HE institutions), it does give a reasonable indication of the range and distribution of expertise available. The table shows that English, maths and science, the three 'core' subjects, are well represented and suggests that there has been a change in appointment emphasis since 1974 when PE, music and home economics advisers had a numerical superiority (see Bolam, Smith and Canter 1976). However, Table 2.6 (p. 32) shows chief advisers still reporting that PE exceeds English, maths and science when considering their advisers' 'title' subjects, and is their equal when looking at the full range of subjects they offer.

The analyses suggest that of the 941 advisers who listed subject responsibilities, nearly half had an initial subject which exactly matched at least one of their current subjects (175 advisers reported no subject responsibilities and were thus excluded from this analysis, see Table 2.6). The matching for this analysis was based on the 98 subject categories used for coding purposes, most of which were given in Table 2.6. If a more relaxed subject grouping is applied, with ten very broad categories being used to cover the curriculum (English language, drama, etc.; languages; maths and sciences; humanities; health education, etc.; IT, computing, microelectronics and technical education; sport and PE; aesthetics; and phases), then just two-thirds of advisers have an initial subject qualification in a group that contains one or

Table 3.8: *Advisers' university and college subjects*

No. and percentage of advisers with each subject

Subject	N	%	Subject	N	%
English/drama	143	13.0	Comb./Intermediate Science	17	1.6
Physics ,Chemistry or Biology	123	11.2	Economics/economic history	15	1.4
Mathematics	104	9.6	Crafts	14	1.3
PE	103	9.5	Environmental Science	13	1.2
History	86	7.9	Welsh	8	0.7
Geography/geology	75	6.9	Classics	5	0.5
Modern languages	70	6.4	Dance/drama	5	0.5
Music	63	5.7	Comput,IT Micro	4	0.4
Art	61	5.6	Environmental studies	2	0.2
CDT,design,technology	52	4.8	Business studies/commerce	2	0.2
Other humanities	40	3.7	Textiles	2	0.2
Home economics	34	3.1	Needlework	1	0.1
RE	30	2.8	libraries	1	0.1
			Other*	15	1.4
Total:				1088	100

Note: *'Other' includes a small number of professional subjects (e.g. primary). (Information missing from 28 of the responding 1,116 advisers.)

more of the subjects they now cover; the converse is that a third of advisers were nominally offering subject advice in areas for which they had no *initial* qualification. Given that advisers typically cover several areas of responsibility, it is inevitable that the total areas of mismatch must be larger than this.

But having seen these results, there is a degree of reality which needs to be brought in. First, as has already been suggested, no account has been taken of subsidiary or subsequently studied subjects or of PGCE training in areas other than that of the initial degree. All of these will enhance the match. Secondly, there are a number of 'subjects' which have really only been developed over recent years and their innovation and in-service training have mostly progressed hand in hand. As with the subsidiary subjects, advisers with expertise in these areas would not appear to have any subject training in this analysis, and this includes those most important cross-curriculum areas of equal opportunities, study skills, and so forth.

Having qualified the analyses, there is still the question of the expectations that are sometimes held for there to be initial subject qualifications in the adviser's areas of subject responsibility. These expectations (still) assume the adviser to be the LEA's repository of expert subject knowledge, but they fail to handle the existing conflict of some subjects having advisers while others do not. Chapter 2 raised the idea of some subjects having a more overt importance than others, a concept which is certainly endorsed in the National Curriculum, but this concept only considers the subject's political importance rather than its teaching needs in schools and LEAs. If the expectation of specialist subject expertise is relaxed such that advisers are not necessarily regarded as being the sole repositories of subject knowledge in the LEA, and if their skills are turned towards the more generic aspects of education and teaching, then exact subject match becomes less important as it becomes less necessary. However, if advisers are no longer to be the 'super' subject teachers of these expectations, and if they are no longer to carry out this subject role, then in the place of the subject specialism which is, of course, the training they brought with them from the school, they will need specific advisers' training; and in place of the management that oversaw individuals doing individual work, they will need a management more suited to their new roles.

Professional background: previous jobs and LEAs

The advisers were also asked to list up to eight of their previous jobs. The information from this question offers two areas of analysis, giving 1) an idea of the degree of inter-LEA mobility and the crossover of expertise and experience from one LEA to the next, and 2) an insight into the types of experience advisers brought with them from schools and colleges.

Overall, of the 1,109 advisers for whom we have information, 464 (42 per cent) were appointed to what were their current posts from positions already within their LEAs. Some 245 of these 'internal appointments' (53 per cent) were first-time advisers (internal appointments thus represent 33 per cent of all first-time adviser appointments), while 219 (47 per cent) were second or subsequent adviser positions (internal appointments thus represent 60.0 per cent of all second or subsequent adviser positions). The figure for 'internal' second-time appointments is possibly slightly overstated as it includes any formal job changes the advisers experienced, thus reorganizations, sideways moves and internal promotions will all be listed in this category.

The evidence suggests that the advisory services were fairly static with little movement between them. At the time of the survey, two-thirds of advisers were still in their first advisory job. As far as we can see, for the majority of advisers the first advisory job is also the last

– there is no great expectation of joining the advisory service for an upwardly mobile career. This lack of movement has considerable implications for the cross-fertilization of ideas. Given that in recent years appointments have only just exceeded 200 per annum for all 104 authorities, we can see that the average LEA only receives an 'outside' appointment every other year and, of course, two-thirds of these will be new to the post of adviser and may not be able to bring much experience of the work with them from other advisory services.

The specific jobs held by advisers immediately prior to their current appointments are shown in Table 3.9a. The distribution is very much expected, though much of it is heavily biased towards the specific type of advisory work undertaken. Further analysis (as shown in Appendix Table A3.2 (p. 212)), reveals that the majority of those entering from both schools' middle management (79 per cent) and senior management (65 per cent) went into subject advisory work, whereas the majority of those from headship posts went into primary phase work (56 per cent) with only 22 per cent of ex-heads going into subject work.

This trend demonstrates the significance of the relative salary positions. In salary terms, the move to advisory work is usually beneficial for primary headteachers, but this is not normally the case for those from secondary schools. However, advisory services draw an amount of secondary management experience from the senior management positions of deputy head and senior teacher, that is where the salary differentials can still make the move viable.

Table 3.9a: Advisers' previous employment – the immediately previous job*

	Teaching in school	Middle manager in school	Senior manager in school	Headship	FHE lecturer	Near adviser	Officer	Adviser
N	18	198	77	160	121	132	35	329
%	1.6	17.8	6.9	14.4	10.9	11.8	3.1	29.5

* The job types described here account for approximately 96 per cent of the responses, with 45 (just over 4 per cent) being comprised Schools Council, research, BBC and other educational posts, together with a small number from the professions and industry.

Table 3.9b shows the distribution of up to eight of the advisers' previous jobs. Because advancement within schools effectively follows formal career ladders, virtually all advisers have gained straightforward, non-hierarchical teaching experience (96.8 per cent), with all but three of the remaining 36 coming from FHE. Few advisers, however, entered advising with only classroom experience (1.6 per cent at maximum); two-thirds entered the profession with at least middle-management

Table 3.9b: *Advisers' previous employment – total numbers of previous jobs (advisers holding each job for number of times shown in column 1)*

	Teaching in school	Middle manager in school	Senior manager in school	Headship	FHE lecturer	Near adviser	Officer	Adviser
1	96	348	169	148	159	193	63	240
2	211	287	120	87	79	33	13	99
3	270	96	89	31	33	4	2	20
4	234	22	22	4	6			6
5	146	3	6		3			
6	86	1	1					
7	24	1			2			
8	13				1			

*Number and proportion of advisers with experience of each type of job:**

	Teaching in school	Middle manager in school	Senior manager in school	Headship	FHE lecturer	Near adviser	Officer	Adviser
N	1,080	758	407	270	283	230	78	365
%	96.8%	67.9%	36.5%	24.2%	25.4%	20.6%	7.0%	32.7%

Number and proportion of advisers with no experience of each type of job†:

	Teaching in school	Middle manager in school	Senior manager in school	Headship	FHE lecturer	Near adviser	Officer	Adviser
N	36	358	709	846	833	886	1,038	751
%	3	32	63	76	75	79	93	67

* The analysis is based upon 1,115 completed responses out of 1,116 returned questionnaires.

† Thirty-six advisers did not list any teaching experience and 833 did not list any FHE lecturing experience. However, only 13 listed neither the one nor the other, but from individual inspection of these questionnaires, ten may reasonably be regarded as advisers with teaching experience who simply failed to list their teaching experience. There would thus seem to be only three respondents with no teaching or lecturing experience – two of these entered PSD and heath education advisory work from community health positions, and one entered from computing/IT in industry.

experience, just over one-third with senior management experience and nearly a quarter with headship experience. Experience was also gained from working in FHE and in the 'near advisory' area, for example, as advisory teachers, curriculum consultants/coordinators, teachers' centre wardens, and so forth. Perhaps unfortunately though, only 78 advisers (7 per cent) had any experience of officer work – a figure which hardly represents the amount of time and effort that the case-study research suggested was undertaken for, with and in parallel to officers.

Some 164 advisers had also held jobs outside of the normal LEA education circuit and career paths. In all, some 246 such jobs were recorded, representing 3 per cent of all the jobs listed. These jobs covered a wide field, with 81 being in the education field, for example the Schools Council, the Schools Curriculum and Development Council (SCDC) the Secondary Examination Council (SEC) and education research; 61 in the professions and a further 13 in the performing and visual arts; 40 in the administrative and executive branches of industry and commerce; 20 in manual work in industry; 19 in the armed forces; 11 in the civil service; and one reporting a period of unemployment.

The final comment on the advisers' previous jobs relates to their number and duration. The average adviser reported having held 7.1 different posts before moving into his or her current job, though some of these may well have been internal promotions. As the minimum entry age into teaching is 21, and the average appointment age for first-time advisers is approximately 40, we can see that advisers held their 7.1 jobs over approximately 19 years; this offered a change approximately once every 2.7 years. However, they are unlikely to find any such mobility in the advisory service, though of course by the very nature of the job, it has built into it a considerable degree of flexibility.

The range of adviser work

The difficulty of finding a single answer

Attempts to describe what advisers do are fraught with difficulty. The case studies demonstrated that not only did the advisers' work vary from LEA to LEA, but also within a service from adviser to adviser. For instance, where working hierarchies existed, the individual's work could change with seniority. The case studies showed that middle-management positions tended to have a greater phase or area emphasis, and this was often theoretically coupled with an amount of adviser management. As a result, middle and senior management tended to have fewer subject responsibilities, or at least to have less of an emphasis on this part of the role; however, these tendencies were of course only evident where the hierarchy was functional.

Differences between advisers were also visible in the different types of phase work they undertook. Primary phase advisers had very different tasks and responsibilities from their more secondary-oriented colleagues and, indeed, in many cases the whole adviser–school relationship was basically different. While this may have arisen for a variety of reasons, it might be surmised that it resulted more from the factors of school size and organization than from the advisers themselves. In comparison with secondary schools, primary schools tend to have more integrated curricula, to be smaller in size (but greater in number), to have a seemingly lower status within the LEA and to present greater salary differentials between their headteachers and advisers. All these features might well emphasize a relatively 'powerful', single adviser per school approach for the primary phase as opposed to the use of the many different specialists we are more familiar with in secondary work and which would more closely match these large schools' organization. A similar scale of differences was also visible between secondary and FE phase work, and again the reasons would appear to be more to do with institutional features than adviser characteristics.

Work practices were also influenced by the adviser's particular subject responsibilities. Although the majority of subject specialists might have curriculum and teaching concerns, the case studies demonstrated that there were considerable variations in other aspects of their work. For instance, music and PE advisers tended to have more organizational work than other advisers, with their orchestras, instrumental lessons, peripatetic music teachers, musical instruments, concerts, sports fixtures, gymnastic displays, county teams, etc., all taking up valuable time. On the other hand, science and craft advisers had more involvement in laboratory and workshop equipment and safety concerns, and modern language advisers had responsibility for language assistants and foreign visits. Furthermore, as we have seen in Chapter 2, the number of advisory teachers were also often determined by the subject. Many science, maths and information technology (IT) advisers will have had responsibility for one or more Educational Support Grant (ESG) advisory teachers, whereas other advisers may have had neither the responsibility nor the help afforded by these extra staff.

Beyond these more straightforward considerations there were also the differences that arose between advisers' work because of the way different subjects or curriculum areas interacted with the existing school structures. Thus although the 'main', single-subject adviser may have been able – and indeed was probably expected – to interact primarily with his/her appropriate subject department and departmental staff, this would not have been so straightforward for phase or cross-curriculum advisers. There were rarely the equivalent structures in schools for the work of, for example, the equal opportunities, multicultural, SEN, PSE or IT advisers. Patently, these advisers will be working with a wider range of professionals, frequently including non-teaching staff, and often they will have to work, at least initially, outside conventional school frameworks and with people who have no immediate access to school's management and communication structures – i.e. where there is no departmental structure to accommodate the work. Their styles of work and the tasks they undertake on a daily or weekly basis are likely to differ from those of their conventional subject colleagues.

But advisers also exerted a deal of control over what they did, especially as many were working without job descriptions. Where job descriptions existed, a number of advisers described them in interviews as being wide enough to allow them to 'rattle around inside', and even with the more tightly phrased examples, few were sufficiently detailed to specify day-to-day practice. As a result, beyond all the differences that arose for the structural and subject reasons, there were also those that came about because advisers interpreted their work in their own ways. Quite reasonably, where there was room for manoeuvre, they reported concentrating on those elements they thought would be most successful, although of course success can be seen in many ways.

In essence, the case studies indicated that attempts to produce anything finer than the broadest of generic descriptions of the advisers' role are almost certain to fail. Statements going beyond saying that advisers are involved in educational development and evaluation are just as likely to miss the mark as to be accurate. But it is still necessary to describe the actual work of advisers, to describe what they do. One approach to this problem is to switch from concentrating on the individual adviser and to focus on the areas of their work. In doing this we can consider how many advisers are involved in each area, and where there is evidence of a pattern, to consider which advisers are involved and what lies behind the pattern.

Adviser involvement in a range of predetermined activities

The most straightforward way for the project to examine the advisers' involvement in a range of tasks and activities was to present them with a list made up from the case-study experience and to ask them to put a tick against each activity they had any involvement with. This does not, of course, give any information about the individual's degree of involvement in each activity, a feature which one suspects may have been very frustrating for those completing the questionnaire; however, across the whole population of advisers, it does give a fair indication of the emphases placed on the various tasks and activities.

Table 3.10 shows the frequency with which the 1,101 responding advisers (15 failed to complete the question) were involved in each activity (the question is given in full in Appendix Table A3.3, p.213).

Table 3.10: *The frequency of adviser involvement across a range of tasks*

	No. of advisers involved*	Percentage of advisers involved†
Planning of new INSET arrangements	1,083	98.4
Building design/accommodation	938	85.2
Curriculum development initiatives, e.g. TVEI, etc.	933	84.7
Subject advice: primary	924	83.9
Advice on institutional management	916	83.2
Cross-curricular initiatives, including multicultural, equal opportunities. SEN, etc.	905	82.2
Subject advice: secondary	879	79.8
Formally inspecting, etc.	875	79.5
Assessment initiatives, e.g. GCSE, CPVE, profiling	867	78.7
Appointing secondary staff	864	78.5
Careers advice for school/college staff	805	73.1
Management of advisers and advisory teaching staff	771	70.0
Involvement in redeployment	719	65.3
Appointing primary staff	668	60.7
Attendance at governors meetings	664	60.3
Reorganization (closures, etc.)	650	59.0
Subject advice: FE/tertiary	606	55.0
Appointing special school staff	278	25.2
Appointing FE/tertiary staff	262	23.8

† The percentage was based out of the 1,101 advisers who answered this question.

* The list given in the questionnaire was not primarily intended to describe the full range or adviser work so much as to determine an interface between subject and generalist work. It was thought that several activities were so universal or axiomatic to the job that they did not need including here, for instance, the provision of INSET, preparing reports to the chief adviser/CEO, and so forth. Also excluded from this list, but taken up elsewhere in the questionnaire, were matters concerning the advisers administration of their own jobs and their own in-service education. The case-study experience suggests that the provision of INSET would be at the top, or very near the top, of this list, had it been included.

Perhaps not surprisingly, planning for the new INSET arrangements (i.e. GRIST, etc.) appeared to be the most common activity advisers were involved in, with virtually all of them having some degree of involvement. From the case-study experience and from Bolam, Smith, and Canter's (1978) earlier work, planning and/or providing INSET was taken as being an activity which similarly involved all advisers, and because this was anticipated from the start it was not included in the questionnaire (see note in Table 3.10). Looking right through the list, the planning (and provision) of INSET would appear to be the only tasks which were effectively common to all advisers; for each of the other activities there were fair numbers of non-participating advisers. For instance, the next most frequent activity, 'Involvement in building design and/or classroom and laboratory accommodation', only involved 85 per cent of advisers, – i.e. 15 per cent were not involved. The numbers of those involved was less with all other activities. The problems raised in the introduction to this section of there being few activities common to all advisers are clearly evident.

Since the table shows a predominance of generalist activities (both management and cross-curriculum) at the top of the list, it begs the question of what has happened to the 'pure' subject specialist. There would appear to be few advisers not involved in some generalist activity or other.

Grouping advisers by the work they do – difficulties with conventional headings

In pursuing this issue the project offered the advisers three headings under which they could place their ticks according to which 'hat' they would be wearing when undertaking each activity, that is whether they were acting in one or more of a subject-specialist, phase or generalist capacity (see Appendix Table A3.2, p. 212). The results of this analysis can be seen in Table 3.11 where the activities are listed in descending order of subject-specialist occurrence.

The results demonstrate a number of aspects about the activities that we might have expected, such that the majority of subject (or curriculum area) advice was listed under the subject-specialist heading, while also raising a few surprises such that between a quarter and a third of all advisers listed some subject advice under the phase and generalist headings. Looking down the list, we see that all the 19 activities received some attention under the subject-specialist heading, with the minimum level of involvement being 14.6 per cent. Across the full population of advisers subject-specialist work appears to be an all-embracing category and appears to involve many generalist elements. The same trend also applies to the other two headings, though both have lower maximum and minimum values. It would seem that from asking advisers around the country to describe what happened in practice, we are left with two possible conclusions: either the three categories are very broad and differences are in emphasis rather than in omission or inclusion (i.e. over a period of time the

Table 3.11: *Frequency of adviser involvement across a range of tasks by adviser work type, i.e. subject specialist, phase or generalist work, in descending order of subject specialists' work*

Percentage of respondents undertaking work in each of:

	subject specialist capacity	phase capacity	generalist capacity
Planning of new INSET arrangements	72.5	43.0	45.0
Subject advice secondary	71.5	22.1	29.3
Subject advice primary	65.4	28.2	33.1
Appointing secondary staff	63.6	19.3	38.3
Assessment initiatives, e.g. GCSE, CPVE, profiling	60.1	24.5	30.5
Curricular development initiatives, TVEI	58.9	32.1	34.9
Building design/accommodation	58.2	31.5	28.5
Formally inspecting, etc.	57.0	33.8	37.7
Cross-curricular initiatives, including multicultural, equal opportunities, SEN, etc.	52.3	34.2	40.4
Careers advice for school/college staff	50.2	27.1	40.0
Subject advice FE/tertiary	47.2	11.3	12.2
Management of inspectors, advisers and advisory teaching staff	46.1	26.1	21.9
Involvement in redeployment	38.9	22.8	34.0
Advice on institutional management	38.6	36.7	52.4
Reorganization (closures, etc.)	28.3	22.4	29.7
Appointing primary staff	28.0	23.2	34.6
Attendance at governors meetings	22.8	21.7	35.6
Appointing FE/tertiary staff	17.5	7.1	7.7
Appointing special school staff	14.6	5.8	10.9
No. of respondents	897	622	787
Percentage of total sample undertaking work in each vertical category	81.5	56.5	71.5

Note: The percentage values are based on a total of 1,101 respondents.

subject specialist might cover all the same activities as a generalist, but still differ because he/she spent more time on subject work than the generalist did) or the definitions vary from person to person, and LEA to LEA, to such an extent that we have difficulty in reaching a national consensus.

It can be argued, however, that, to some extent, this result is brought about by the inclusion of so many advisers from so many LEAs with so great a number of different responsibilities. In practice, there would be few advisers who were individually involved in all the activities offered in the list, and the width for any individual would rarely be as large as it might seem for the whole population. However, when the percentages across the three headings are added together for each activity, they frequently exceed 100 per cent and it is evident that advisers were reporting being involved in many of these activities under more than one heading, or, while wearing their different hats'. Thus not only were the headings broad, but many advisers' work embraced more than one heading.

The total number of advisers responding at least once in each column is given at the foot of the columns in Table 3.11. We can see that some 81 per cent of advisers work (for some or all of their time) as subject specialists, while approximately 56 per cent report that some or all of their work is done under a phase heading, and 71 per cent undertook work in a generalist capacity. All in all, this suggests that the average adviser works with just over two of the three headings.

Our experience in different LEAs would suggest, however, that the distribution of roles would be neither uniform within nor between authorities. Thus in one case-study LEA the senior advisers also carried subject, area and phase responsibilities, whereas in another all advisers (bar the chief) were either phase or subject specialists; there was no doubling up of roles. By asking advisers to respond under the three headings this question effectively invited them to give a practice-based answer to the muddy question of whether they worked as subject specialists, phase and/or generalist advisers. Further analysis of this data gives the numbers of advisers answering under each heading and is shown in Table 3.12.

Given all the debate about whether advisers should be subject specialists or subject specialists and generalists, it seems surprising to find that only 16.5 per cent of advisers described themselves as having simply a subject-specialist role. Perhaps less surprising, but possibly only because one normally does not give it as much thought, is the result that only 6.4 per cent of advisers reported being 'pure' phase advisers, and an even smaller 3.6 per cent reported only doing generalist work – these were pure generalists, though as we have seen, this appears to encompass most activities.

Table 3.12b shows the patterns in the advisers' sex, appointment age and salary distributions that we would have expected from the case studies – i.e. except for the 62 'subject and phase' advisers (group 6). On average, the subject specialists (group 1) were paid less than their colleagues and the phase and phase generalist advisers (groups 2 and 5) had the highest concentration of women, a feature which most likely reflected the higher proportion of women in primary work and the

Table 3:12a: *The distribution of advisers between the subject-specialist, phase and generalist categories*

Headings used by advisers (group no.):	Number of advisers	
	N	%
Subject-specialist work only (1)	182	16.5
Phase work only (2)	70	6.4
Generalist work only (3)	40	3.6
Subject + generalist work only (4)	257	23.4
Phase + generalist work only (5)	94	8.5
Subject + phase work only (6)	62	5.6
Subject, phase and generalist work (7)	396	36.0
Total	1,101	100%

Note: Advisers were asked to tick each of the activities they were involved in under the heading that described the role they were fulfilling at the time. The three columns allowed seven possible groupings.

Table 3.12b: *Characteristics of members of the seven groups*

Adviser heading group no.	Number of advisers	Sex as percentage of males	Salary point*	Appointment age (years)
1	182	76.2	8.3	40.4
2	70	62.9	9.3	42.8
3	40	90.0	9.7	45.2
4	257	82.5	8.9	39.5
5	94	61.7	9.3	42.7
6	62	74.2	8.3	40.3
7	396	75.0	9.1	41.4
Total	1,101	1,101	1,028*	1,011

* The salary point is based on the combined Burnham HT and Soulbury scales.

† The number here is reduced because advisers on Officer and Burnham Teaching Scales have been excluded from this analysis.

Within-column differences for sex, salary and appointment age were significant at the $p < 0.005$ level.

high incidence of primary phase work which was coupled with the pastoral responsibility for large numbers of primary schools which thus offered the phase and generalist link. The small group of 'pure' generalists (group 3) was likely to comprise senior advisers since it was more male dominated, offered higher salaries and had older appointment ages, all features which suggest second or subsequent appointments.

The small group of subject and phase advisers (group 6) which failed to fit the case-study observations had very similar characteristics to the pure subject advisers and was quite different to the pure phase advisers. This would suggest that the group principally comprised subject advisers who were giving a loose interpretation to the conventional idea of a phase role. If they were phase advisers who also carried subject roles, one would have expected them to have the 'higher' group's characteristics, but this does not appear to be the case.

Comparing the groupings

The seven groupings were derived directly from the advisers' responses to the question about their involvement in the wide range of activities. In theory, there should be a fair match between these and the advisers' titular groupings derived for salary purposes – i.e. these groupings should reflect the subject and generalist division in advisers' titles. The research looked at the group of advisers formally known as 'General Advisers'. Across the whole 1,116 responding advisers, there were 288 with the word 'General' in their title, but with no senior, area or other structural label attached. There were 474 other advisers who fitted this definition, but who were not called 'General' advisers (for the purpose of the following analyses these two groups will be known as 'General' and 'non-General' Advisers). Table 3.13 gives the distribution of both groups across the seven headings used by the advisers in describing their work. The percentage figures relate to the number of General or non-General Advisers respectively.

Table 3.13: *The distribution of work between 'General' and 'non-General' Advisers*

	General Advisers		Non-General Advisers		Total	
	N	%	N	%	N	%
Pure specialist	10	3.5	138	29.1	148	19.4
Pure phase	7	2.4	18	3.8	25	3.3
Pure generalist	6	2.1	4	0.8	10	1.3
Specialist/general	90	31.2	123	25.9	213	28.0
Phase/general	20	6.9	27	5.7	47	6.2
Specialist/phase	3	1.0	37	7.8	40	5.2
Specialist/general/phase	152	52.8	127	26.8	279	36.6
Total	288	100%	474	99.9%	762	100%

The data show a strong trend for the 'General Advisers' work to be more generalist than that of the others, but it really can only be a trend since 10 General Advisers considered themselves to be pure subject specialists and many non-General Advisers were involved in generalist work. The position is perhaps easier to understand if we consider just those who reported doing some generalist work. Overall, 268 out of the 288 (93 per cent) General Advisers described doing some form of generalist work, and in contrast, only 281 (59 per cent) of the 474 non-General Advisers reported doing any generalist work. The title 'General' adviser thus seems basically to denote a group of advisers who do generalist work, but this is no different to some 60 per cent of non-General Advisers.

In seeking other differences between these two groups we were surprised to find that there were no statistically significant differences in their sex distribution, mean appointment age or the mean amount of time they spent on inspection. However, the General Advisers were paid on average approximately half a point more than their colleagues (9.07 and 8.42 respectively), and considerably more of them (65 per cent) were involved in the appointment of headteachers than their non-General colleagues (37 per cent). Further differences were visible in the groups' views on the specialist/generalist balance. All respondents had been asked to consider what they thought of the specialist/generalist balance of their work with respect to (a) their job satisfaction, (b) their career prospects and (c) the needs of their schools and colleges. Both groups gave responses across all three possible answers ('more specialist', 'stay the same', and 'more generalist') for all three categories. In terms of their personal job satisfaction, the two groups were basically similar and the overall trend favoured maintaining the current status quo. However, when looking at career prospects, both groups felt there should be more generalist work, with the non-General Advisers stressing this the stronger. In contrast, for their institutions the General Advisers advocated on average a move towards more subject specialism, while their more specialist colleagues thought what they offered was about right. Overall, it was felt that the title of 'General', as given to some advisers, no longer meaningfully contributed to our understanding of what those advisers did.

Advisers' reactions to the tasks

Having asked the advisers to indicate their involvement across a range of tasks, we were aware that this told us little about which of these tasks were most time-consuming, which were most difficult, and so forth.

The advisers were therefore asked to choose from the tasks they had already ticked in the first part of the question and then to indicate:

(a)   the three most time-consuming;
(b)   the three most professionally demanding;
(c)   the three which had most increased in emphasis over the last five years.

Finally, they were asked to indicate which out of the whole list were the most important for the institutions they worked with; their answers are presented in Table 3.14.

Looking at these activities in terms of how time-consuming they are produces the third ordering of the 19 activities that we have seen. This one is, though, the easiest to match with the case-study experience and it accords well with what we saw. For instance, although it is evident in Table 3.10 that some 14 per cent of advisers have had some involvement in appointing FE/Tertiary staff, when we see that only 1.4 per cent of all advisers found this to be one of their most time-consuming activities, it seems much nearer the perceived reality of there being very little adviser time actually being spent in this sector. Work on building design and classroom and laboratory accommodation follows the same trend – many advisers are involved, but individually normally only to a small extent.

In interpreting the results in the first three columns of this table there is a need to be aware of a filtering effect. Advisers were only asked to comment on those activities they had already stated they were involved in. For example, as only 262 advisers (24 per cent) initially reported any involvement with appointing FE/Tertiary staff, a maximum of only 262 can report it being time-consuming. However, the first three columns in this table give percentages out of the whole adviser population responding to the question (i.e. 1,101), and thus while it correctly shows that only 1.4 per cent found this activity to be time-consuming, this may not accurately reflect what the smaller population feels. Where the initial percentage involvement is low, there is scope for a considerable mismatch in the first three columns between the impact of what the whole population reports and what the smaller involved population feels. As before with this list, it should be recalled that providing INSET was not offered for comment and its omission should not be taken to mean that it would not appear at, or near, the top, had it been offered.

The second column in the table sought the most professionally demanding of the activities. Formal inspection appears clearly as the most demanding, with planning of the new INSET arrangements and giving advice on institutional management coming second and third.

The third column looks at increases in emphasis over the last five

Table 3.14: *Percentage distributions of advisers' reactions to the tasks listed in descending order of the most time-consuming activities*

Of those tasks you do, which are the three most:	time consuming	professionally demanding	increased in emphasis	Of all the tasks, which three are most important to your school/ college
Subject advice secondary	38.8	23.8	7.1	31.5
Planning of new INSET arrangements	35.6	34.1	34.7	29.2
Subject advice primary	31.3	17.6	9.5	25.0
Formally inspecting, etc.	27.2	40.5	21.3	20.9
Curriculum development initiatives, TVEI	25.8	27.0	37.9	25.8
Advice on institutional management	20.6	29.6	15.0	26.6
Management of inspectors, advisers and advisory teaching staff	16.9	19.0	19.2	12.1
Assessment initiatives, e.g. GCSE CPVE, profiling	16.6	19.5	32.1	12.4
Appointing primary staff	16.5	9.5	5.0	17.4
Cross-curricular initiatives including multicultural, equal opportunities, SEN, etc.	12.2	14.1	20.2	10.7
Appointing secondary staff	11.4	11.3	2.5	22.3
Reorganization (closures, etc.)	9.2	9.4	11.1	3.9
Involvement in redeployment	7.9	10.6	13.4	1.6
Building design/accommodation	5.9	3.6	2.8	3.5
Careers advice for school/college staff	3.4	6.4	5.6	4.2
Attendance at governors meetings	2.9	2.3	4.9	0.3
Subject advice FE/tertiary	2.7	2.8	1.8	2.3
Appointing special school staff	2.1	0.8	0.7	2.8
Appointing FE/tertiary staff	1.4	1.0	0.5	1.9
No. of respondents in each column	1069	1051	912	927
(Percentage missing in each category	2.9%	4.5%	17.2%	15.8%)

All percentages based on a total of 1,101

years (with the five year element causing a relatively large number of advisers to have to decline to answer the question). Two of the advisers' main activities, providing subject advice to the primary and secondary sectors, show little change, while the government's initiatives are clearly apparent in the first three places. There is an interesting second order of new emphases, with inspection, cross-curriculum initiatives and the management of advisory services all coming to the fore.

The final column invited advisers to suggest which three of any of the tasks were the most important for the institutions they worked with; here there were few surprises. Subject advice (secondary) is thought to be the most important overall, and this matches the time priority that the advisers had already afforded it in column 1. This pattern between task and time allocation was also seen with the second most importantly rated task, that of planning the new INSET arrangements: while allowing for the limitations embodied in this list such that inspection was offered but not appraisal, it is interesting to note how the advisers have put 'institutional management' into third position while letting 'inspection' drop into seventh place. At the other end of this list, the advisers appear to be questioning some of the recommendations of the 1977 Taylor Report when so few of them (0.3 per cent) rate attendance at governors meetings to be important for the institution, though there is no differentiation here between clerking meetings and being there to advise on subject or management issues.

Advisers and advisory teachers – phase, pastoral and inspecting duties

Having looked at a wide range of tasks that advisers report themselves to be involved in, and perhaps having presented the beginnings of the picture of what they do, it seems sensible in this section to turn to three very specific functions and consider what we know about them. However, this time the information will, be taken in the main, from the Chief Advisers questionnaire.

Only about a fifth of advisers were specifically reported as carrying any phase responsibilities (21 per cent, compared with the much smaller 2 per cent for advisory teachers). The mismatch between the chief advisers reporting and how the advisers described their work is interesting and suggests problems with terminology. Within the adviser population, phase advisers were paid on significantly higher scale points than those without this responsibility (9.6 compared with 8.7 on the numerically combined Soulbury and Burnham HT Scales).

In contrast to the phase work, two-thirds of advisers were reported by their chief advisers as having been given pastoral work with schools and colleges (67.8 per cent, see Table 3.15). Apart from demonstrating how many advisers have pastoral/general responsibilities, this figure also demonstrates another clear difference between adviser and advisory teacher roles since only just one per cent of advisory teachers appeared to be involved in this kind of work.

Table 3.15:   *The division of pastoral duties: 'does the post involve pastoral duties?'*

	'Yes'	'No'	Missing	Total
Advisers, %	67.8	31.8	0.3	99.9
(N =	865	407	4	1,276)
Advisory teachers, %	1.0	97.4	1.6	100
(N =	12	1,151	19	1,182)
Total numbers	877	1,558	23	2,458

With roughly two-thirds of advisers involved in pastoral work, one-third were not. This raised the question of how pastoral work was distributed: did all LEAs engage in some forms of pastoral work, or did some offer their institutions no pastoral assistance at all? Should we be looking for patterns in the distribution of pastoral and non-pastoral responsibilities between advisers within authorities, or should we be looking at why some schools are perceived as needing pastoral assistance while others are not? A final question arises relating to the use of advisory teachers in this kind of work: even though only one per cent were involved, can we see which types of LEA used advisory teachers for this kind of work?

Of the 64 responding authorities, 19 reported that all their advisers had pastoral responsibilities and only four reported that none of theirs did. In these four LEAs advisory teachers were not used in this role, hence we are not seeing a compensatory factor. Advisers with pastoral duties were paid on significantly higher scales on average than their non-pastoral colleagues (9.1 compared to 8.4 per cent). In those LEAs where a division between subject and other posts is operated, this would possibly reflect the fairly common practice of giving pastoral work to the more senior posts.

The 'right to inspect' produced an equally exaggerated difference between advisers and advisory teachers, with 95.6 per cent of advisers having this 'right' compared with only 1.8 per cent of advisory teachers – (Table 3.16). It is worth noting that some 4.4 per cent of all advisers do not have the right to inspect, and that according to the respondents of the Chief Advisers questionnaire, this figure remains the same whether the adviser is actually called an 'adviser', or an 'inspector', that is, there are 'inspectors' who do not have the right to inspect. One might like to ask what proportion of officers have the right to inspect schools and whether that proportion exceeds that for advisers, but then 'inspecting' might not be the term used.

Table 3.16: *The division of inspectorial duties: 'does the post carry the right to inspect?'*

	'Yes'	'No'	Missing	Total
Advisers, %	95.5	4.4	0.2	100.1
(N =	1,218	56	2	1,276)
Advisory teachers, %	1.8	96.6	1.6	100
(N =	21	1142	19	1,182)
Total numbers	1,239	1,198	21	2,458

In response to the question in the Advisers questionnaire as to whether the advisers had participated, over the last three years, in formal inspections or reviews, although 74.1 per cent (816) of the combined population said 'Yes' (with 26 per cent saying 'No' and 15 failing to answer), there was a small but significant difference between 'advisers' and 'inspectors', with 72.1 per cent of 'advisers' saying 'Yes' compared with 84.5 per cent of 'inspectors'.

Of those 816 'advisers' and 'inspectors' who reported that they inspect, the average time that they spent on formal inspections, reviews and report-writing (but excluding time spent on implementing follow-up work) again showed a small but significant difference, with 'advisers' spending 10.2 per cent of their time inspecting compared with 'inspectors' who spent 12.5 per cent. (Advisers were asked to express inspection time as a proportion of their total working time, and with each working day being reckoned to represent 0.5 per cent of the working year.) If the average time spent on formal inspections for all 1,116 advisers and inspectors is calculated, with those who reported that they had not participated over the last three years being given a zero value, then, on average 'advisers' spent 7.3 per cent of their time compared with of 10.5 per cent 'inspectors'. Clearly, 'inspectors' do more inspecting than 'advisers', but the differences although statistically significant are small. With many 'advisers' inspecting while some 'inspectors' do not, to the outside world, which includes teachers, officers and politicians, the differences in title must often seem most irrational and perplexing.

As with the pastoral division, the right to inspect significantly enhanced the adviser's average scale point – 'inspecting' advisers had an average scale point of 9.0 compared with 7.7 for 'non-inspecting' advisers, a trend that is also apparent in the titles of 'inspector' and 'adviser', with 'inspectors' having a small but significant advantage over 'advisers' with mean scale points of 9.1 and 8.9 respectively. The pastoral role is also important here, in that it might be seen to be used in place of inspection in non-inspecting LEAs, it does, after all, offer an alternative way for an LEA to 'know' its schools. Analysis revealed, however, that non-inspecting LEAs were no more likely to run a pastoral scheme then inspecting LEAs.

There is, of course, a degree of ambiguity in our inspection questions since the terms 'inspecting' and 'monitoring' can have varying interpretations. In the Chief Advisers questionnaire we asked: 'Do you have any *formal* methods of monitoring your educational establishments?' Forty-three of the respondents (70.6 per cent of the 68 replying LEAs) said 'Yes', with 20 chief advisers representing nearly one-third of the sample (29.4 per cent) answering 'No'. The question to advisers sought to use a form of wording which, we hoped, would provide the complementary information. In essence, in the Advisers questionnaire we sought details about practice rather than policy, and thus because there had been industrial action in schools immediately prior to and during the survey, we felt that we had to ask about practice over a reasonable period of time but with a realistic cut-off point to ensure that the reported practice was not too out of date. Therefore, in the advisers' question we asked: 'Over the last three-years have you participated in formal inspections or reviews?' As we have already seen 74.1 per cent of responding advisers (i.e. 'advisers' and 'inspectors') answered 'Yes' and 25.9 per cent 'No'. The positive response to formal inspecting of almost three-quarters of all advisers is higher than we might have expected from the Chief Advisers questionnaire. (The necessity to include the term 'review' in the question arose not because we were aware of any overriding practical or philosophical differences between the two activities, but because during the case-study work it had become apparent that there were political nuances embedded in the terms, and that advisers would reflect these sensitivities by claiming that while they may carry out reviews, they did not inspect, or vice versa.)

One way of revealing any ambiguity was to look at the advisers' responses when grouped according to their chief advisers' responses, – i.e. how many advisers did or did not inspect in each of the inspecting and non-inspecting LEAs. The figures show that while 79 per cent of advisers followed their LEAs' patterns, 13 per cent of non-inspecting advisers worked in inspecting LEAs and 8 per cent of inspecting advisers worked in non-inspecting LEAs (see Appendix Table A3.4, p.214). The results suggest that there is a mismatch between policy and practice, at least in the use of terminology, for one in five of all advisers. However, while ambiguity arising from the terminology may well have influenced these figures, the case studies lent alternative interpretations for what could be happening.

In the case of the non-inspecting advisers in inspecting LEAs, while some may have been appointed too recently to have participated, it was also possible for involvement to vary according to the subject or phase responsibilities carried by the adviser. Not all advisers are always involved in all inspections. Some may never be involved, and in authorities which inspect infrequently some may just not have been involved over the last three years.

The issue of inspecting advisers in non-inspecting LEAs offered two interpretations. First, some advisers might be using a 'weaker' interpretation of the term 'formal', that is their chief adviser might consider that some inspection has been done but not consider it to have been done in a 'formal' fashion, while, the advisers still interpreted it as being 'formal'. The other possibility was observed in the case-study work where, in one instance, although a Chief Adviser stated that inspections were not carried out in that LEA and that this was a policy decision, at least one adviser offered inspections if requested to do so by schools or governing bodies. His inspections came complete with formal reports

Conclusion

In responding to the project's brief, this chapter sets out to describe some of the professional aspects of advisers and their chiefs: it has provided evidence for a national picture of advisory work in 1986. But having provided a number of small pieces for the picture, it is now worth stepping back and briefly considering the whole. There appear to be three main themes which emerge from this picture.

First, there is no single generic adviser. Both the case studies and the surveys clearly showed that apart from local conditions, advisers' work was highly influenced by subject, phase and seniority considerations. Advisers, as a whole, do not do the same work. Beyond the planning and provision of INSET, there were no 'adviser' tasks common to all advisers. It would seem helpful for planning and communication considerations if the idea of a mythical generic adviser disappeared and comments were now targeted at work-related groups, for instance, primary phase advisers and, science advisers, advisers with advisory teachers, or even inspecting advisers.

Secondly, there were still a number of just recognizable residual traditions and historic behaviour patterns within the services. At some stage in the past it appears that there were some fairly clear concepts about what advisers did. There were phase, subject and general advisers and, by definition, they did different things. But now, while these underlying beliefs are still visible, the distinctions between the groups have blurred. For instance, there are few (exclusively) subject specialists left, and not all 'inspectors' inspect. However, the problem would appear to be not that there are local influences or that there have been changes over time, but that the extent of change has not been recognized. There was a strong suggestion throughout the work that while advisers were working with a new set of tasks and demands, the people they came into contact with – both managers and clients – had expectations for the old set of roles. The mismatch was neither profitable nor comfortable.

The third and final theme in this picture reminds us that advisers, who represent a most valued resource within education, are severely overworked – they do too much. The reasons for this are presumably many and varied and this research could only touch on a small number, but even so, a number of points are worth making. As we will see later, many advisers would like their workload to be rationalized. A complete fulfilment of fewer and more appropriate tasks must surely be better, more useful and more satisfying than the partial fulfilment of a larger number. But if the individual's work is to be rationalized for all members of the service, then there could also be a rationalization of the service's work, and here we come back to closing the gap between expectations and reality – many of the old tasks advisers were expected to do still lie within their remit. Advisers have been given new tasks without the old being set aside.

But rationalization alone cannot solve the problem. Advisory services are also ridiculously short of administrative and secretarial assistance. It surely cannot make sense to pay someone £20,000 to type letters slowly and badly. This frequent failure to offer sufficient administrative support, together with an overall lack of emphasis on management and a general shortage of personnel all adds to the problem. Of course, all these elements require money and this, in turn, requires the services and work of advisers to be valued, an issue that will arise again when the organization and structure of the services are considered in Chapter 4.

4 Understanding the Differences between LEA Advisory Services

Introduction

Visitors to their first local education authority advisory service may be forgiven for assuming that all such services might be organized on roughly the same basis – after all, on the face of it, advisory services exist to perform the same basic functions. Similarly, any teacher, head, adviser or officer who has worked only in one authority might also be tempted to hold the same views. In practice, however, these assumptions are far from correct. While there may be many similarities between one LEA advisory service and the next, there are also the following differences:

(1) what is done in one authority by one adviser is not necessarily done by the similarly titled adviser in the another;

(2) indeed, what is done in one authority might not even be done at all in the other; and,

(3) the meaning of certain words in one authority is no guarantee that they mean the same in the next, for instance, the terms 'adviser', 'review' and 'pastoral' all have varying but locally consistent usages.

This situation required some exploration, and since so many of these differences were thought to be centred on the LEA itself, it seemed sensible to explore what it was in the LEA that gave rise to them. In effect, we were interested in how it might be, for example, that two teachers applying for what appear to be identical jobs in two neighbouring authorities could find themselves working in very different conditions, doing very different things and having considerably different career prospects.

Framing the research

But in looking at these differences our inquiries needed to take note of the LEAs' historical and political backgrounds. These, we were constantly reminded, not only helped to demonstrate the enormous changes that have been, and are still, occurring in LEAs, but they also explained some of the differences. It was felt that authorities could not really be seen in a single 'snap shot'. We needed mechanisms that could compare them in a context of change: mechanisms that could describe how an advisory service was working whatever its stage of evolution. For the case-study research, we took the following factors to be salient, though they are not presented here in any order of priority:

(i) The aims and perceived roles of the service, the methods employed to achieve them, and their degree of communication to schools and colleges.

(ii) The rationale behind the deployment of personnel within the service.

(iii) The status of the advisory service in terms of its access to policy decision-making and its 'position' within the LEA as a whole.

(iv) The management and organization of the service.

The starting-point for the research was to investigate each of these factors in some depth, and to this end, they were pursued in the 12 LEA case studies. In the interviews with the CEO or Director of each LEA, his or her perceptions of the roles and functions of the advisory service were sought along with information about the four factors listed above. Similar information was also collected from the chief adviser, and to complete the picture, detailed descriptions of advisory work were gained from advisers, and schools and colleges were asked to give their localized perceptions of the service and how it assisted their task.

In making comparisons from one authority to the next it was recognized early on that it was most unlikely that just one model of the advisory service would emerge. Similarly, it was felt that attempting to refer back to a single position from which all LEAs had developed would be equally inappropriate since they appeared to have very different histories. In essence, we accepted that any full description of an LEA and its services needed to take into account the effects of at least three major 'historical' influences which individually and collectively bear upon the LEA as we see it today:

(i)   The effects of local authority reorganization in 1974.

(ii) The effects of the character of an LEA in terms of its socio-economic setting, geographic size, recent history, politics and the educational philosophy of the past and current Education Committees.

(iii) The effects of the demands for change stemming from central government legislation.

This chapter thus sets out to explore those elements in the 12 case-study LEAs' backgrounds, make-up and practices which varied significantly from one to the next and which are thought seriously to affect advisers' professional work. With such an overt emphasis on history and change, it is inevitable that the chapter moves straight into tracing developments which have occurred over the last few years before leading to the current debates over the role of the advisory services. This is followed by a brief look at the differences in practice between services (pp.90 *et seq.*). We concentrate on the role of the chief adviser in running the service and the different structures that are adopted to enhance the work of both the individual and the team. The chapter ends by considering the reactions of advisers, headteachers and heads of department to the role and organization of the advisory services.

Influences on LEAs (1974–87)

In the autumn of 1987, LEAs were preparing themselves for legislation aimed at securing a National Curriculum and programme of testing. Since 1974 local authorities have been required to respond to a considerable number of significant Education Acts which have covered a wide range of innovations, the implementation of which has often necessitated departures from previously accepted philosophy and practice. Throughout this period of change there have also been significant shifts of emphasis in the control and funding of curriculum initiatives and their INSET provision. The scale of these initiatives has had considerable impact on the interactions between central LEA personnel, that is officers and advisers, and school and college staff. Table 4.1 offers a brief review of the main legislative and thematic changes since 1974.

Table 4.1: *The main educational legislative and governmental changes since 1944*

1974	ROSLA (Raising of the School Leaving Age to 16)
1976	Education Act requiring comprehensive reorganization
1979	Education Act to repeal the 1976 Education Act
1980	Education Act: parental choice, governors
1981	Education Act: special educational needs, Statementing and integration
1986	Education Act: governing bodies, appraisal, sex education
1988	Discussion documents and Education Act: governing bodies; open enrolment, national curriculum

Note: During this time four major themes also emerged:
(i) the Manpower Services Commission became a major source of power and influence in education;
(ii) the control and funding of INSET has radically altered through TRIST and GRIST;
(iii) a new tier of personnel, the advisory teachers and project staff of various kinds, took over large areas of adviser work; and
(iv) central criteria for examination syllabuses have been imposed through the inception of CPVE and the GCSE examinations.

Responding to these explicit demands for change was made difficult for most LEAs by constraints which arose from other directions. In the main, these constraints may be traced to three sources. First, and perhaps foremost, education had been subject to a financial recession which started in 1973 and peaked at the end of that decade. For some LEAs this has turned into 'rate-capping' – not only was money scarce, but central government has taken over a greater control of what there was. In many cases these financial cutbacks led to the contraction of advisory services at a time when there was no reduction in the demands being made of them. Thus having gone through an expansionist epoch in 1974/75, by 1981 adviser numbers were back to their pre-1974 size (DES, 1982), and more recently average growth in the advisory services has still been limited. From 1983 to 1985 there was only about 1.3 per cent growth per annum (DES, 1985, 1986), and it has only been in 1987 that a return to 1974 figures has been realized (see Chapter 6). Secondly, some LEAs had such extreme falling rolls as to require officers, and in many cases advisers, to give almost full-time attention to school closures, amalgamations and teacher redeployment. And thirdly, over the years, and particularly following James Callaghan's Ruskin speech in October 1976, the curriculum had moved into a more public and political arena. This, accompanied by the growth in demand for accountability, management training in schools, appraisal and the growth of the perceived power of parents and governors, required LEAs to respond in new directions and shift some of their traditional emphases.

With all these issues and constraints in mind, these interviews with CEOs and chief advisers showed there to be basically seven major common influences upon advisory services and their LEAs: the reorganization of 1974, the recession, falling rolls, the accountability movement, the increasing centrality of education, the Education Committee and the growing use of advisory teachers. These are now presented over the following pages as separate issues.

Coping with the 1974 reorganization

While it had been anticipated that the first of these influences might have related back to the impact of the 1974 reorganization, it had not been expected that in some LEAs the unsettling effects of this change would still be reverberating some 12 years later, yet more than one authority described how they were still trying to combine the different historics resulting fium strained amalgamations in 1974!

The difficulties were particularly pertinent in LEAs where there had been different or even opposing philosophies about the purpose and approach of the advisory services, and one CEO described the now combined personnel from three old authorities as still being very partisan. Similar difficulties were apparent in LEAs which were formed by bringing together strong traditions of inspection and prominence with those used to a much less conspicuous and lower-key image – the type of amalgamation that might have occurred, for instance, when the 'old' city and county authorities were brought together.

The new LEAs were also affected by differences in the pre-1974, LEAs' working practices. It appeared that there were difficulties in getting schools used to the new styles and levels of service and in reducing differences in the various teaching staff's experience of curriculum development. One CEO reported that after reorganization he had felt it necessary to put considerable time and effort into lifting the morale of schools in one half of a new union where previously, as he described, there had been no advisers and little money spent on curriculum development.

A particular difficulty faced by two of the case-study LEAs after reorganization arose from the need to share one or more advisers with neighbouring authorities. Although this practice was almost uni-versally disliked by both those in charge of the services and the advisers, the subsequent financial cutbacks meant that some LEAs have experienced difficulty ending it, and even now it still continues to a small extent. In one authority, however, the sharing of a specialist senior adviser was seen as a means of developing curriculum and policy strength through the involvement of a consortium of LEAs and hence the practice has been kept on.

For all these difficulties, there were some authorities which experienced few or no problems either because reorganization barely touched their 'central' administration, or because the changes were so large that the authority used them to build itself anew. In the reorganization of one group of old LEAs, the existing advisers were all required to apply for the new posts in the new, smaller, LEAs. In one new LEA those advisers selected were placed into a strong organizational structure devised by the already in-post chief adviser, and, according to the CEO, all their key personnel were appointed in that year. That structure remains to this day, and it may be considered to be fairly resilient to the subsequent demands made upon it.

Financial recession

There is little doubt that the contraction in educational spending from the mid-1970s onwards was a major influence in many advisory services. For some the lack of finances exacerbated the difficulties they were already experiencing following the local government reorganization of 1974, but this was not the only area where the recession was felt. One chief adviser described the fairly common problems of vacant posts being 'frozen' and remaining unfilled, and in other authorities adviser posts were simply cut or advisers were persuaded to move into alternative posts. There were also difficulties arising from the relatively high cost of advisers. One chief adviser spoke of this particular problem when he commented that a Group 10 salary was necessary to buy the quality which was needed for developments, and that as such advisers were expensive and his authority could not afford to enlarge the team. Unfortunately, not only were advisers expensive, but their returns were not always sufficiently immediate and visible to persuade Education Committee members of the need to increase or even maintain their numbers. The case was made that if cuts were to be made, county hall staff should go first. Of course, arguments were then put forward (see, for example, Fiske, 1977), but the damage was done. Not only did the recession reduce numbers, it also reduced job security and morale.

Developments within the advisory services were also reported to have been blocked by the recession. In a number of cases LEAs reported that the consequences of the recession and its resulting shortages was insufficient time to consider, plan and implement any desired changes. In a parallel fashion, it was reported that the recession had also created difficulties for the implementation of educational initiatives themselves and, in particular, several authorities reported difficulties in trying to meet the requirements of the 1981 Act.

Falling rolls

The most frequently reported single 'local' influence to have affected advisory services over the last few years was the decline in the pupil population – falling rolls. While this could be described as a national phenomenon, its effects and the political, philosophical and practical approaches taken to ameliorate them varied so greatly from one LEA to the next that they are better seen in a local perspective. In many advisory services falling rolls brought a large shift in emphasis in the work of some or all of the advisers with increased involvement in the contentious issues of school closures, school amalgamations, teacher redeployment and major reorganizations of the LEA provision as a whole – e.g. where middle schools are brought in and then later removed. In many ways these changes can be seen as giving advisers a higher profile and shifting subject emphases towards generalist roles.

Perhaps surprisingly, although nobody welcomed the addition of redeployment work, many of those advisers involved in it commented that they would rather it were done by someone who knew the teachers to start with than someone who did not. Given it had to be done, they were pleased it was they who were doing it. Furthermore, their involvement in such major reorganizations within the system, though time consuming and possibly frustrating, was taken up quite positively in a number of LEAs since it was argued that only by their involvement could the advisers become prepared for the changes, as well as making good contributions to their development.

Greater accountability

The fourth influence concerns the increasing demand for accountability which has had effects both on what advisers do and what they are called. In one LEA it was reported that the response to the accountability movement had brought changes in the advisers' roles and they were now heavily committed to formal school inspection. In another, the chief inspector described the accountability movement as being 'the thrust for accountability, evaluation and testing', which accompanied 'the loss of public confidence in education and educationalists'.

Somewhat significantly, he then added that he would have liked to change his title from inspector to adviser, but that was not the politic thing to do. This raises the issue that some degree of public accountability appeared sometimes to be met simply by calling advisers 'inspectors', a move that was not necessarily accompanied by any change in role.

Increasing centrality

The recent centrally inspired curriculum initiatives and centrally controlled grant funding have attracted a range of reactions and have significantly influenced advisory work with promises of greater changes to come. One chief adviser talked of the Manpower Services Commission (MSC) as being:

> 'an overwhelming influence, shifting power to the centre. It is a powerful financial factor. It is a style of management which is unfamiliar to Local Government, but which may have been overdone. It may be seen as a move away from amateurism to management.'

Two CEOs were rather less ambivalent in their attitudes but expressed somewhat opposing views. One said, with something of a caveat about the dangers of over-centralization, that the intervention of central government and the MSC had been very good, that the extra funds available had been a great bonus and that bidding for money was extremely stimulating and had acted as a great catalyst in the inspection of curriculum. He thought it made people think ahead and to cost carefully. In contrast, the other CEO was more concerned about the 'external edicts' about curriculum, and he said that his authority had chosen on a political basis not to be a TVEI authority. His chief adviser then talked of how the increasing centralization and 'interference' in curriculum was eroding the autonomy of LEAs and schools; he went on:

> 'I am sympathetic to some curriculum initiatives but others are dubious in terms of motives. In 1979 the government listened uncritically to industry's views on education – hence MSC and the industrial model of appraisal. We have a far greater involvement in curriculum reforms and improvement. This is positive organic development and there was not the need for the centralized direction which has happened.'

In other LEAs more emphasis was placed upon the direct impact of the centrally directed initiatives on the advisers' roles. One senior adviser commented that the job was now very different because of having to respond to national demands and being involved in national initiatives, both aspects which determined the advisers' development. In another authority a CEO again referred to the change in emphasis in the tasks undertaken by advisers. He suggested that the last two years had been almost entirely concerned with responding to central initiatives. 'Some of them', he said, 'are very worthwhile, but the preparation of submissions can take an inordinate amount of time especially when they have to be converted into "MSC-speak".'

Not surprisingly, when we asked advisers about the time spent responding to government initiatives, out of the wide range of possible tasks we offered, this task was described as having increased the most, though attending meetings and administration were described as having increased by nearly the same amount. The activity which was reported as having declined the most was work in classrooms (see Chapter 3).

The Education Committee

The influence of the Education Committee entered the case-study interviews on many occasions. One major element concerned the working relationship between the advisory service and the Education Committee itself and/or subcommittees, and in some authorities it was reported that considerable subtlety was necessary to balance the need to keep the Education Committee sufficiently informed to secure support with the need to maintain the service's managerial independence.

One CEO warned that advisers themselves must become more aware of the implications in this balance; he continued:

'Advisers can be very naïve about political involvement at County level. They need more experience of involvement with the Committee. The reduction of Committee influence in senior staff appointments must come from convincing them of our professional credibility and advisers must learn this.'

But Education Committee involvement in the activities of the advisory service has not necessarily remained constant over the years. One chief adviser described increased political activity at Education Committee level as a national phenomenon, and added that in 1974 managers were left to manage. 'Now', he said, 'members wish to manage. We are not professionally compromised, but we have to justify ourselves more.'

The influence on the Education Committee was also significant in the advisory service's activities through its hold on the funding. In some LEAs the relationship between the Education Committee and the advisory service appeared to revolve around the amount of financial support made available, and this was reported as depending upon how well the advisory service could justify its existence. One chief adviser referred to the need to convince the Education Committee of the advisory service's 'usefulness' and he described how, with this in view, he had raised the advisers' profile and ensured that their work was now more visible. He thought that during the 1970s the low profile was thought a good way to avoid being cut. Now, he suggested, the overt approach was more appropriate. However, as one CEO argued, overt status could be reached through title changes alone:

'The service became an inspectorate some years ago and this was a deliberate decision on my part. The way to increase the service in terms of numbers was to call them an inspectorate – it worked. The present Education Committee wants them to become advisers again; and I am not averse to this. I am not sure that the last change was that well understood in schools.'

From comments like these it became increasingly evident that some of those we interviewed felt that Education Committees have had to be convinced of the usefulness of their advisory services, and that a concerted effort has had to be made to secure that conviction. This was quite forcibly underlined by one chief adviser who commented that there was a growing recognition by the Education Committee that advisers have a role and were not just parasitic.

Of course, part of the difficulty for chief advisers stems from the frequent changes in the Education Committees' political composition. Only three of the 12 LEAs referred to any political stability since 1974. Overall, the research encountered a fairly universal picture of stop–start development in advisory services, where the implications of nationally imposed financial constraints were made more complex by the varying degrees of support of Education Committees whose dominant political persuasion could (and often did) change.

The growing use of advisory teachers

As has been described in Chapter 2, the number of advisory teachers was rising rapidly, with some 37 per cent being directly funded to some greater or lesser extent by central government. This has three main effects on advisers. First, most of this funding will have had to be 'bid for' by LEAs from central government. Many advisers will have been involved in this, and they will have had to spend considerable time preparing these bids. Secondly, once the advisory teachers were in-post, much of their support and management will have fallen, if anywhere, to advisers. Through the Advisers questionnaire we learnt that 62.6 per cent of the responding advisers (698) reported being responsible for advisory teachers and other educational support staff. These 698 each reported on average, a responsibility for 6.6 advisory teachers – a responsibility which cannot be taken lightly.

The third effect concerns the advisory teachers' impact on the work done by advisers in schools and with teachers. As far as we understand, the major input from advisory teachers was in giving subject advice in schools and colleges, and in providing INSET for teachers, although conversations with advisory teachers have suggested that their roles are still evolving and that there may well be a movement towards their having a broader brief in the future. We, therefore, asked the chief advisers to describe how advisory teachers were used to provide curriculum support and how they complemented or supplemented the work of advisers. We also asked if there were any noticeable changes in the advisory teachers.

Sixty-six chief advisers listed a total of 153 tasks undertaken by advisory teachers. The majority of these tasks were obviously associated with giving direct curriculum advice to teachers in schools (95 entries) and with the provision of INSET courses (28 entries). Three other areas involved giving advice to schools in a phase capacity (nine entries), providing materials for teaching (eight entries) and running teachers' or specialist centres (six entries). In addition to the more unexpected duties of interviewing and giving management advice, as shown in Table 3.1 (p.48), in one LEA advisory teachers were involved in the monitoring of schools and in another they undertook the supervision of probationary teachers – it should be noted, though, that our category of advisory teacher included a number of advisory headteachers.

Twenty of the 66 responding chief advisers reported that there had been noticeable changes in the roles of advisory teachers and they offered 26 examples. Seven of these were associated with what might be regarded as changes in the 'traditional' advisory teachers' role and basically described greater involvement in curriculum support in schools. The others, however, demonstrated a broadening of the role as can be seen in the following comments from different chief advisers:

> 'Advisory teachers have had to become more autonomous in areas where there are no advisers.'

> 'Their role has become important as Soulbury advisers have less time.'

> 'They are being drawn into appointments.'

'More involved in trouble-shooting.'

'There is a tendency to move away from classroom-based work into INSET and advisory work.'

'In future their role will be broadened to possibly include [responsibility for] probationers and evaluation, with closer management.'

For the individual adviser, advisory teachers can be a mixed blessing. Certainly, they provide extra curriculum support but they also bring in extra managerial duties, more form filling, more administration and often, an amount of evaluation. The use of advisory teachers is moving the advisers' role towards a more generalist position.

Arguments about advisory service roles

Having considered these seven major influences and being aware of the geographic, socio-economic and political differences between LEAs, it is perhaps not surprising that there should be variations in practice from one LEA to the next. However, when these variations occur in the most fundamental aspects of advisory work, for example, in inspection, in the degree to which advisers specialize in subject roles and in appointments, and when the variation between LEAs can be extreme (with inspection, for instance, taking up from 0 to 90 per cent of individual advisers' working time), then it seems appropriate actually to ask what roles are being fulfilled. In effect, because the local variation in practice is so substantial, we are questioning the assumption that advisory services use a single, national set of roles and instead suggest that they might be using a multiplicity of different sets of roles.

The chief education officers were asked what they saw as the main functions of their advisory services. Like the Secretary of State's Draft Statement (see Chapter 1), all 12 CEOs stressed the importance of the advisory service. This was one of the few real points of agreement, though some of the other differences between them were more to do with interpretation than strict matters of principle.

The centrality of the service in the authority

One CEO believed that the advisory service was a major and fundamental part of the education service and that advisers' roles could not be undertaken by education officers or lecturers from higher education. Another concurred by stating that advisers should play a full part in the running of the education service with administration colleagues. A third, however, wanted them to maintain a relatively low-key and entrepreneurial role, and one which would inevitably divorce them from some of the administrative and executive functions of the authority. In other words, there was a range of views with the advisers' roles varying from being indispensable and totally central to the LEA's thinking on the one hand, to being seen as associated with schools rather than with the 'office' on the other hand.

One of the difficulties faced but not resolved in this research is that of attributing any causal relationship between intentions and practice. In one LEA where advisers were very much involved in the running of the authority, this did not appear to have been the intended outcome – indeed, the advisory service had not been considered important for years. However, the recession and various Education Committee policies had so seriously reduced administrative and executive personnel that the few advisers who were left were now totally central to what went on and had thus acquired a high profile. At the other extreme, in another LEA, years of success as subject specialists had left the advisers in a poor position to change their role. The change from autonomy to teamwork was proving difficult and prickly for all concerned and as a result they were being bypassed.

Which way to face?

Inevitably with the issue of advisers' roles, we managed to evoke the spectre of the 'Janus complex', which has been seen by many as inherent in the role of the adviser (Bolam, Smith and Canter, 1978). It is felt that the adviser has to face both towards the LEA executive – i.e. to the CEO, officers and Education Committee – and towards the teachers. While there must be obvious difficulties in working with and mediating between these potentially conflicting interests, the roles are neither necessarily equal, nor necessarily diametrically opposed. For all this, the conflict still attracts attention and there is a degree of tension at both interfaces with all three parties describing difficulties in their interactions. For instance, advisers do not always appear comfortable being seen as too integral a part of the LEA's decision-making team. On more than one occasion the researchers heard advisers dissociating themselves from the executive and administrative branches of the LEA while actually talking to teachers within the Town Hall. However, one CEO argued that the first priority of an adviser was as an LEA professional who must not identify too closely with schools. He felt that the advisory service should not 'act autonomously to an improper extent as an independent body within the LEA'. Also he was concerned about the definition of the term 'adviser' – which he described as dangerous – since he questioned to whom they actually proffered advice. He was worried about them *advising* education officers as opposed to his preferred idea of their *reporting back* function. While other CEOs did not appear to have the same qualms and difficulties with this double role, quite frequently the point was made, in interviews with education officers – the second and third tiers in the department seemed to be more sensitive than the first.

Eyes and ears and monitoring

The 'collection of information', which is a somewhat broader definition than that of just monitoring, attracted a range of views. Five of the 12 CEOs commented that advisers were primarily the eyes and ears, or, as one phrased it, the 'antennae', of the education service and emphasized the advisers' responsibility to collect information and report back to education officers. One CEO specifically stated that advisers were a major source of information to the Education Committee and others regarded advisers as the officers' first line of inquiry in resolving complaints from parents and others.

The CEOs were also divided on the issue of the advisory services' role in monitoring schools and colleges and whether advisers should carry out formal inspections. Interestingly, having stressed the growth in the accountability movement, and having all agreed that a prime function of an advisory service was to know what was happening in schools, none of the 12 freely advocated a formal inspection programme. Indeed, inspection seemed to be advocated only in a very circumspect fashion. The more pro-inspection of their responses are offered first:

> 'Advisers have two functions, namely inspection and advice. Being called "advisers" does not diminish their inspectoral function'.

> 'There must be inspection as part of the role, but it should overlap comfortably with the advisory role'.

> 'We use inspection if something is going wrong or if there are signs. We do not use inspections to get to know our schools'.

> 'They need to know what is happening in schools but the intrusion should be unobtrusive'.

'I deliberately play down the inspectoral role – they advise schools and they advise me'.

'We used to have informal inspections which produced formal reports. We have abandoned these in recent years'.

'The advisory input is emphasized. The inspectoral function creates suspicion in schools and creates conflict'.

'I don't want a high profile to be equated with inspections and reviews which frightens schools and is mimicking HMI. Working in groups in schools is different to this'.

'Advisers should not be seen in a judgemental fashion. Inspecting is for HMI'.

Although the debate is often phrased in an 'inspect vs advising' context, it could more properly be viewed as selecting the best combination of the many means constantly to monitor schools and to meet both the LEA's and the school's need to know what is happening.

Subject specialist or the authority's generalist?

The CEOs' views of the advisers' roles with respect to schools were also somewhat diverse, particularly in terms of the corporate image they wished them to project. Several CEOs put forward a centre–periphery model, in that the service should keep schools appraised of LEA and central government policies and ensure their implementation. To achieve this some CEOs advocated the subject-specialist approach to encourage development in closely defined areas, while others emphasized a more generalist/pastoral role where the adviser acts across a broader front as the major source of communication between the school and LEA.

Similar diversity was seen in how the CEOs perceived the growing overlap between advisers' and officers' work. Some saw advisers' involvement in school closures and redeployment as a positive unification of adviser and education officer functions, where a 'united front' was presented to schools. However, others saw it as an impediment to what advisers should really be doing and argued that advisers' needed to be independent from any executive role. Whatever stance was taken by the CEOs, the duality of the 'Janus complex' was always evident, though that is not to say that there was always a conflict. Conspicuous by its absence from these discussions was the part advisers might play in helping to formulate the policies that they are required to take to the schools.

One or many sets of roles?

Looking back over the considerable variations in the CEOs' perceptions of their advisers' roles, we see that there is little evidence for
there being any commonly accepted set of roles or tasks for LEA
advisory services. To build on such a premise, as we saw being done in
the introduction, ignores so many other factors that it invalidates the
exercise for both descriptive and planning purposes. However, having
said this, we were also aware that many changes were taking place
around the country. For instance, the debates of 1974 which often
focused on whether to inspect or not and whether to be general or
not, have now moved on to how best to monitor *and* promote
improvement, and to ask which elements in the general role best
promote what is wanted in schools. Thus the fact that it would be
difficult at present to fit any common set of roles to the 104 advisory
services does not negate the chance of this being possible in future
times. If there is a desired single, national set of roles, as for instance
advanced in the Draft Statement, it does not seem unreasonable to
float the ideas and persuade movement towards them. It is less useful,
however, to offer such a set of roles as a prescriptive factual statement
which is then taken as evidence for their existence.

Variations in organization

Differences from one LEA to the next were not simply confined to the
perceived roles and the work undertaken; they also included the
management of the post, the support that was offered and the level of
communication between colleagues. Advisory work under the 1974
single-subject model effectively praised the virtue of advisers being
individuals. The 'lone furrow' they talked of needed a lone plough-
man and, in some LEAs, this concept still existed into the mid-1980s.
In other authorities, however, the need for change in schools had
been associated with the need to change how advisers worked, and
not only was the nature of the workload changing, but also the
manner in which it was being approached. The management and
accountability emphases being applied to schools were also now
being sought in both advisers and advisory teams, and it was thus of
interest to the project to look at these developments. To do this we
looked at two features, the role of the chief adviser and the service's
organizational structure. Obviously a caveat must be offered about the
value of discussing these issues divorced from the other personnel

and issues in the education department – but even so, they offered some clear ideas about what was, and what could be, happening.

The chief adviser

The different titles given to those who carried responsibility for the advisory services gave an insight into the status and nature of their posts in terms of their functions, the time spent on duties other than managing the service and the postholder's access to decision-making at CEO and Education Committee level. The different post titles and the character- istics associated with them fell into three broad groups. The first group (the Chief Adviser group) comprised the Chief Advisers and any principal advisers. In this group they reported spending most of their time on advisory service duties with little or no time being spent on specific officer or ordinary adviser-type functions. The second group (the Officer group) comprised education officers for whom managing the advisory service was only one of several tasks. The third group (the Adviser group) was made up of full-time senior advisers who had a 100 per cent adviser load as well as having varying degrees of whole-service responsibility.

Although respondents in both the second and the third groups had responsibilities other than the management of the advisory service, it was the third group which reported the greatest difficulty in reconciling any conflicts in their multiple roles. First, they reported having too much work to do with the two roles of advising and managing, and secondly, there was a perceived lack of status which could be argued to make the management job more difficult. They expressed concern about this lack of status and commented that it led to poor access to decision-making and to a lack of allocated time to bring unity and cohesion to the service.

There were two instances of services being led jointly by a senior primary and a senior secondary adviser. In each case the questionnaire was completed by the senior secondary adviser and both independently commented on the need for a full-time chief adviser to be appointed. They also drew attention to the problems that arose in the service with the pupil-related age divisions that split their services into two camps, problems that they argued were exacerbated by the dual leadership.

Lines of responsibility and the status relationship

The status of the person in charge, and thus also the status of the advisory service itself, was felt by a number of CEOs and others to be linked with the status of the person to whom they are responsible. The Chief Advisers survey showed that in the majority of cases (83 per cent) the chief advisers reported directly to the LEA's chief officer. However, in ten cases (nearly 15 per cent) the chief adviser, and hence implicitly the advisory service as a whole, reported to a second- or third-tier postholder, and obviously this has ramifications for the status of the service, its ease of communication within the LEA as a whole and the status of the advisers in the field. (In one case the chief adviser reported being responsible to the Education Committee directly.) Perhaps surprisingly, the chief adviser's direct access and responsibility to the CEO was seen as contentious by second-tier officers in at least two of the case studies; and certainly, with the combination of this issue, plus salary differentials, one is aware of a deal of friction just below where the two services formally meet.

Management and other roles

But having been given a management role, rarely did we see chief advisers having enough time – as was evident in Chapter 3, the job of chief adviser most often came with a package of other tasks. We therefore asked the chief advisers about the proportion of their working time they spent off-task on non-advisory service tasks. Fifty nine chief advisers reported spending from 0 to 95 per cent of time off-task, with 15 respondents saying *no* time was spent on other duties in contrast to six who only had 30 per cent *or less* time left to spend on the service, – i.e. 70 per cent or more of their time was spent off-task. Overall, the respondents spent 26.4 per cent of their time on tasks *not* associated with the advisory services.

The amount of time off-task was found to vary significantly, according to which of the three 'title' groups the respondent belonged. For the Chief Adviser group, those advisers or inspectors labelled with only the terms 'chief' or 'principal', the average time spent on tasks *not* related to the advisory service was 19 per cent. In the officer group, that is those with the terms 'deputy CEO', 'assistant CEO', or 'principal'/ 'senior education officer' in the title, the average time off-task was 43 per cent. In the third group, the senior advisers with a full-time advisory role in schools, all except one stated that no more than ten per cent of their time was spent off-task, but then while their low position in the hierarchy would keep them clear of many extraneous LEA or officer duties, their 100 per cent advisory responsibilities would have severely eaten into the rest of their time.

Throughout the case studies and questionnaire work it was very evident that those in charge of advisory services were permanently very busy – so much so that many were kept too busy to conduct any real management and planning. After many interviews and discuss-ions, it seems reasonable, if not contentious, to suggest that in some cases at least, being (kept) overtly busy, being at everyone's beck and call and working grotesquely long hours was a good defence against having to manage those who did not want to be managed. But this was not seemingly how the chief advisers wished it to be when asked about their priorities. The 66 respondents to this survey question listed a total of 189 individual priorities which could be categorized in seven broad areas, as shown in Table 4.2. In contrast to the amount of time respondents seemed to be able to devote to managing the service, the responses in Table 4.2 clearly show that they saw management as one of their most important roles, with all but two of them listing it as a main priority.

Table 4.2: *The most important aspects of chief adviser's role*

Aspect of post	No.	No. as percentage of number of respondents %
Managing/coordinating the advisory service	64	97.0
Involvement in policy-making	40	60.6
Organizing provision of support/advice to schools/colleges	25	37.9
Advising in schools/colleges	16	24.2
Ensuring provision of INSET for schools/colleges	13	19.7
Ensuring maintenance of standards in schools/colleges	10	15.2
Liaising with other departments/services	5	17.6
Other	16	24.2
Total aspects	189	
No. of respondents	66	66

The second most frequently listed aspect, with just over 60 per cent of respondents giving it, was the need to be involved in policy-making, and again this was an area where the desire to be involved probably exceeded the degree of involvement at the time of the survey. (The case-study experience suggested there were two types of policy involvement: curriculum and general. Advisers' involvement in their subject area was often more likely than in general matters, though their work did not necessarily follow this division.)

Apart from just counting the responses, it is also worth while looking at a few individual statements. One group of the chief advisers' responses focused on the priorities they saw surrounding the management of the service with respect to Education Committee and council members:

'Securing political support for the objectives of the service'.

'Bridging the credibility gap between the service, schools and members – both ways!

'To affirm the independence of the Inspectorate'.

For the 'advisers group' of chief advisers, those for whom leading the service was possibly additional to their primary function of being senior adviser, management functions had to remain somewhat peripheral. Perhaps the essential conflict can best be seen in the words of one senior adviser for secondary:

'At present, although I have no defined management role, the most important aspect is managing the advisory team'.

It could be that the managers of the advisory services themselves need help to rationalize their own roles, so that they can carry out the tasks they perceive as most important, but then, of course, there is the problem of time – i.e. time to manage the service on a day-to-day basis, time to plan long-term and personnel management and time to do all the other required tasks.

As has already been stated, the different Chief Adviser groups reported spending different amounts of time off-task: those with 'Chief' or 'Principal' only in the title spent about one-fifth of their time off-task, whereas their 'officer'-titled counterparts spent over twice this time on non-advisory service duties. This titular split between the officer and adviser elements of the chief advisers' roles was important in other respects, too. When viewed nationally, (see Chapter 3) there seemed to be an ambivalence as to whether the person in charge of the advisory service should be an adviser or an officer. Where the adviser title is emphasized, the majority of incumbents came from advisory service work, though some came straight from headship posts. On the other hand, where officer or deputy director elements are empha-sized, the majority came from officer jobs. Few of those answering our questionnaire had both officer and adviser experience. Obviously authorities and members view this post very differently.

A number of CEOs suggested that the status of the service within the education department as a whole depended upon the officer tier to which the chief adviser reported. In the majority of cases, this was to the CEO, and as has been suggested, this was not always without feelings of resentment from one or more of the deputy CEOs. It was suggested that one solution to the antipathy was for the chief adviser to have the title of deputy director, and thus without a job change this would immediately give the service the status it required and possibly alleviate the difficulties perceived by deputy CEOs and others of having lower than second-tier officers reporting directly to the CEO.

This title change was also advocated for salary reasons. Until recently the differentials between adviser and officer pay scales were such that in small(ish?) authorities advisers and chief advisers could easily exceed second-tier officer salaries unless either an artificially low ceiling was imposed or the chief adviser put on to a proportion of the CEO's salary as is accepted practice with second-tier officer posts. The difficulty had arisen because one pay scale (Soulbury for advisers) was nationally based while the other (for officers) was dependent upon the size of the LEA. Unfortunately, before it is assumed that this mechanism has resulted in the differences between 'adviser' and 'officer' chief advisers being only titular, it should be recalled that only few of the chief adviser respondents had experience of both branches of the department – the solution of giving adviser-derived chief advisers an officer-style title has only happened rarely.

The final issue in this section considers advisory service communication and input to policy-making, and here we should consider the channels that exist for all 38 members of the average advisory service. There are, or perhaps should be, three channels routed upwards through the chief adviser to the CEO:

(1) A channel for conventional subject information for subject policy-making, curriculum guidelines, etc.

(2) A channel for inspection and monitoring reports on the state of specific schools, teaching, education, etc.

(3) A channel for those areas concerned with all the other work undertaken by advisers but for which policy-making may yet have to be opened up, for example, in the implementation of initiatives, the stance on redeployment, personnel, early retirement issues, and the development of governor and adviser roles.

It is difficult to be objective and to quantify matters here but several respondents clearly suggested that direct access to the CEO and membership of the LEA's senior management team enabled better communication than might be the case if communication were routed through second- and third-tier officers, and even if it were not, in a status-conscious world, the direct access to the CEO lends status to all adviser activities. The position of the advisory service and its chief in the education department's hierarchy clearly affects the work of the advisers.

Different organizational structures − ten hierarchical models

As has already been suggested, attempts to present a single, definitive model of the LEA advisory service are impractical for a number of reasons, not the least being that it does not appear to be possible. The various contexts and philosophies from one LEA to the next are so different that a whole range of solutions has been sought to meet national expectations while still being sensitive to local considerations. One of the most significant ways LEAs have chosen to differ lies in how they have structured their services, for instance, who is responsible for what, how important is the idea of middle management and what stress should be placed on setting up channels of communication.

The research showed that the LEA advisory service management structures varied enormously and that to achieve true descriptions of the full range would require an individual description for each separate LEA. However, to a large extent, the crucial and visible organizational factors appeared to involve just a few elements: the amount of the chief adviser's time available to the service, the presence or otherwise of a middle management tier of senior advisers and whether the chief adviser was a member of the senior management team. As such the research can offer a tentative indication of what was happening with a breakdown into ten models − see Table 4.3.

Although these are described with a numerical ordering, care must be exercised on two counts. First, there is no necessary linearity or unitary division across the ten models since the three factors, the amount of chief adviser time available, the presence of middle management and the chief adviser's membership of the senior management team, which are all taken to work in the same direction, cannot be gauged quantitatively. Secondly, although the models are based on real LEAs, there will be many variations upon these themes, and there are other factors at play which will interact with them to change the overall emphasis on management. Placing LEAs into individual categories and determining cut-off points between one model and the next cannot be done with greater certainty.

There are four of these other factors which should be mentioned here, since they would influence an LEA's position in the table. The first relates to whether or not an authority adopts an area basis for its advisory service since this almost inevitably requires elements of hierarchy to be built in. However, by delegating power away from the influence of the central 'authority' can decline and in parallel, that of the area or divisional education officer can increase − strong team cohesion and fully functioning area structures do not normally seem to go hand in hand. Thus while the area system might seem to offer a strong central, hierarchical model on paper, in practice it might represent little more than two or three separate services working more or less in tandem.

The second factor influencing the management emphasis concerns the overall status of the advisory service within the LEA. Elements like the centrality of the service to the department, the role of the advisers in the workings of each school and the status of the schools vis-à-vis county hall can all make a serious difference.

The third factor concerns the integration of adviser and officer work within the LEA. Where this happens in a serious way, for instance, where individual advisers' skills, experience and time availability are more important considerations in the issuing of work than which team they belong to, then the advisory service structure will effectively blend into the larger education department structure. Obviously this has 'dangers' for the advisers if in losing their structure, they are not given compensatory places in the broader management of the department. On the other hand, though, if an integration of the work is desired, it possibly makes more sense to do this without the handicap of historic and now artificial barriers.

The fourth and final factor concerns the size of the advisory service. When the number of advisers in each LEA was correlated with its structural model number (see Table 4.3), there was a small but significant association ($r = 0.33$, $p<0.005$) between the nature of the structure and its size. In effect, the larger the service, the more likely it was to adopt a hierarchical organization, but size must still be regarded as just one small factor.

With these caveats, as described, the 68 chief advisers' descriptions of their service structures were used to place each LEA into the hierarchical model and thus to give each a number from 1 to 10. The frequency with which each model number occurred is shown in Table 4.4.

For all the difficulties with this type of analysis, an interesting picture still emerges. For instance, while four out of five of the responding LEAs had clear Chief Adviser posts (a figure which may be slightly inflated due to the difficulties faced by non-Chief Advisers in completing our questionnaire), nearly one in five authorities did not – at least 19 per cent of the services were being run without full-time managers. As we have already seen, even where there was a chief adviser, many LEAs still required the postholder to undertake other responsibilities as well. The analysis also shows the variable importance afforded to the middle management role with almost half of the LEAs without it.

Table 4.3:   *The ten hierarchical models*

---

1. *Clear chief with full hierarchical structure.* The model incorporates a functional middle-management system where nearly all communication is through the line manager. All subject and pastoral issues relating to individual schools are handled by the appropriate area (middle) manager. The Chief Adviser functions within the CEO's senior management team and has few non-advisory service tasks

2. *Clear chief with relaxed hierarchical structure.* This model has defined middle-management responsibilities but access to Chief Adviser through line manager is not overemphasized. Responsibility for subject work may rest directly with the Chief Adviser – i.e. the middle management role is somewhat relaxed and is often concerned only with pastoral work. The Chief Adviser functions within the CEO's senior management team

3. *Clear chief, but with a 'vague' hierarchical structure.* In this case, advisers often report directly to the Chief Adviser and middle management is bypassed for a variety of reasons. The Chief Adviser functions within the CEO's senior management team

4. *Clear chief, no hierarchy.* In this model all advisers are responsible directly to the Chief Adviser. There are no intermediate positions between adviser and chief. The Chief Adviser functions within the CEO's senior management team

5. *'Part-time' chief combined with other senior post.* The chief adviser can allocate only a proportion of his/her time to this task. No other hierarchy; all other advisers are equal. The Chief Adviser functions within the CEO's senior management team

6. *Visible but temporary part-time chiefs – one member of a group leadership.* The post of special responsibility for managing the advisory service is attached, possibly on a rotating basis, to one of a group of senior advisers. The attachment gives access to CEO's senior management team but does not usually reduce original workload

7. *Part-time leader or chairman – hardly visible.* No post of Chief Adviser *per se:* one of group of senior advisers act as part-time Leader or Chairman, sometimes on a rotating basis. Nominated leader does not function within the CEO's senior management team. Original workload usually still applies

8. *No individual chief, but a group of senior advisers with joint responsibility.* No representation on CEO's senior management team. Lack of any chief coupled with senior advisers working on a phase or area basis can be divisive

9. *Virtual 'flatarchy' with a just functioning 'voluntary' leader.* Here the leader has no extra remuneration, title or reduction in other duties. Little time is given for the managerial role. The 'Leader' has full adviser duties and has to fit leadership role into spare time. All advisers are equal. Leader does not function within the CEOs senior management structure and has little authority/responsibility over adviser colleagues

10. *Flatarchy – no leadership or executive management.* Here all advisers are equal and the service is *administered* by an executive Education Officer, sometimes in a different building

---

Table 4.4: *Distribution of LEAs across range of organizational structures*

Model No.	Description of structure	No. in each category	%	No. wishing to change
1	Total hierarchy, Chief Adviser is member of senior management team	13	19	2
2	Relaxed hierarchy, Chief Adviser is member of senior management team	22	33	13
3	'Vague hierarchy', Chief Adviser is member of senior management team	12	18	8
4	Clear chief, no middle hierarchy; chief is member of senior management team	8	12	5
5	Part-time chief with other duties; chief is member of senior management team.	4	6	2
6	Part-time temporary/rotating chief with membership of senior management team	3	4	3
7	Part-time leader or chairman, no Chief Adviser *per se;* no membership of senior management team.	1	1	1
8	Leadership through group of senior advisers, no Chief Adviser *per se;* no membership of senior management team	2	3	2
9	Virtual 'flatarchy' – little leadership, no direct contact with senior management team	1	1	1
10	'Flatarchy' – no leadership, no direct contact with senior management team	2	3	2
	Total	68	99	39

Reactions to these models

Advisers

Although the case studies did not cover the full range of the ten models, it is possible to put some 'colour' on some of them by describing one or two examples where the evidence exists; this can be enhanced by then considering the advisers', heads' and heads of departments' reactions to the models. One example of a Model 1 structure may be seen in Figure 4.1, which depicts a metropolitan borough which adopted an area structure.

The 13 subject advisers had a whole-LEA remit for their subjects. Before starting work in a school, however, each would liaise with the

Figure 4.1: *Example of a Model I structure*

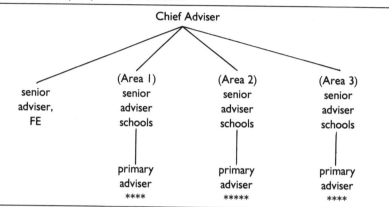

Chief Adviser

	(Area 1)	(Area 2)	(Area 3)
senior adviser, FE	senior adviser schools	senior adviser schools	senior adviser schools
	primary adviser ****	primary adviser *****	primary adviser ****

Note: The asterisks represent the 13 subject advisers who also carry pastoral responsibilities.

appropriate primary or senior area adviser. Subject work was thus coordinated on an area basis, as was the distribution of any funds the subject adviser might wish to distribute. Each subject adviser was also responsible for a pyramid of schools within his or her area, and this included all phases and special schools. For this work they reported to the appropriate senior (area) adviser. The senior adviser, FE covered the whole LEA. Overall, this was a highly structured service, with a most significant element being that the senior area advisers were responsible for both the pastoral and all the subject work in 'their' schools. In effect, all lines of communication went through them.

When interviewed about this structure, the advisers were for the most part, positive about its effects, though they stressed various different elements and some raised a number of difficulties:

'I came in as a senior adviser. Line management is very clear. The Chief Adviser expects senior advisers to be knowledgeable on schools and they (the senior advisers) depend on advisers to supply information. We are desperately overworked. I have easy access to the Chief Adviser, but not for long.'

'I like the area basis since it gives you close contact with a group of advisers who know a group of schools well. The service does inform well. There are regular fortnightly meetings and circuits of bumf to be read which need noting, signing, dating and passing on. It is a well chosen close-knit group.'

'Despite the fact that it has been very carefully thought out, there does still seem to be some confusion over the roles of the senior/pastoral/primary advisers. I am not sure if we are well enough organized for whole-school approaches, for instance, who provides the cross-curricular INSET?'

'It is quite hierarchical, and this is to do with the nature of the people in it. I find it quite constraining and it doesn't encourage individual initiative, though I can see its purpose in filtering information and providing a point of contact. A great deal depends upon personality, and it could lead to whole team involvement – it can be a barrier to communication. We seem to be moving towards greater direction which can stop creativity and flexibility. We could all become rather colourless and depend only upon the creativity of our leaders.'

'It's hierarchical, – information always seems to go upwards – downwards is edicts. Not enough consultation.'

If we look at LEAs in Model 2, we see a relaxed form of Model 1, although how far the relaxation of the middle tier was intended or just happened is not considered since it is accepted that any structure can only function as well as the people within it, and for all their ingenuity and flexibility, the people can only effectively operate within the bounds allowed and encouraged by the structure. Subject advisers in Model 2 LEAs are directly responsible for their subject work to the chief and not to the senior or area advisers. As before, all subject work is county-wide, the exception to this being where there are two or more advisers in the same subject. In essence, advisory services which fit Model 2 tend to work in area teams for pastoral and general work and in central teams for subject work, a pattern that may well encourage a tension which is not evident in the first model.

Some advisers appeared to appreciate the slightly relaxed features of the area-based county LEA they worked in, whereas others emphasized the difficulty with area and central control:

'I think the way in which we operate works well. With the area system, there is a hierarchy, but it is a happy working hierarchy and it helps to pave the way to get things done.'

'How do you relate to the area education officers? We have meetings with them once per term, but they are mainly giving information to us about policy changes, closures, and so forth.'

'The chief adviser is not too happy about the autonomy of the areas – coordination would be better on a central basis.'

Comments received during the research appear to suggest that the area-based office structures were possibly on the decline in contrast to the centrally based area team structures, which appear more secure.

Apart from cost, the issue touches upon communication within the team, and communication between the team and the rest of the LEA personnel. The centrally based office was felt to have many team, status and communication benefits over the area office.

The case studies involved four LEAs which fitted the Model 3 pattern, that is with a clear Chief Adviser but an ineffectively functioning second tier or middle management. One Model 3 LEA, without an area structure, based its hierarchy on a phase and subject basis and had what, at first, appeared to be a fairly straightforward structure, as is shown in Figure 4.2. However, towards the end of the case study its structure appeared more like that in Figure 4.3.

In this authority, there were 11 senior subject advisers. However, not all subjects had senior advisers, not all seniors had juniors and nor were there any senior advisers for those advisers with cross-curricular responsibilities (the latter being ultimately responsible to the senior secondary adviser). All advisers had generalist responsibilities but it was not clear to whom they reported in the carrying out of these duties.

Looking at the advisers' reactions to three of the four Model 3 LEAs we see clear patterns. First, in respect of structures and communication, advisers from the three different LEAs all made the same basic point:

'Our structure at the moment is not what the hierarchy thinks. We all do our own thing – no coordination between senior and other advisers, no teamwork and too much trivia in meetings, but in a way this is our strength since we work very hard. The chief adviser is so busy that structuring does not get done.'

'There is a clear need for a line management structure. At present all advisers work directly to the chief adviser. There is wasteful duplication. There is not sufficient accountability in a non-line-management structure. Subject specialists should not remain isolated.'

'We have been left to be individualists. This works if good people are appointed. Some changes are necessary because the chief adviser cannot do everything he is expected to do now. Everyone is directly responsible to him. I need the opportunity to work and relate more to colleagues for advice and support.'

'At present, we are a 'team' of 38 individuals – there is a great deal of 'ad hockery.' One manager cannot be responsible for and manage 38 people – decisions are not made. The proposed restructuring is necessary, even though it is more hierarchical. It will lead to better decision-making, more teamwork, flexibility of approach to problems, better career prospects.'

Figure 4.2: *A Model 3 structure as first perceived in one LEA*

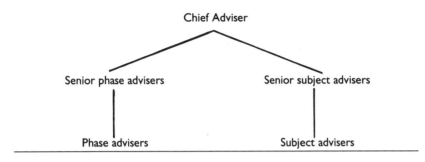

Figure 4.3: *The actual structure in that LEA as seen after close observation*

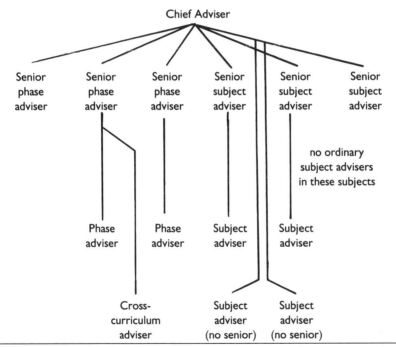

The lack of team communication and imbalance in representation raised curriculum issues in a number of LEAs. Of the examples offered here, the third comment is probably far more generalizable and significant than its author envisaged:

> 'We have 20 county advisers, three senior advisers and a chief adviser. A fairly logical arrangement except that the primary

phase is not represented among the recently appointed senior advisers. It should also be mentioned that the primary team were not allowed to apply for the senior posts.'

'It's hard in the present structure to give enough time to developing a coherent curriculum policy. There is a need for someone to frame curriculum design in a more sophisticated way.'

'This service is modelled on secondary school structures and we have the same constraints as schools in bridging cross-curricular links.'

On a different tack, but still in Model 3, a fourth LEA had only recently gained a Chief Adviser. Not that long before the research its advisers had worked in an area-based 'flatarchy', which was spread over an enormous geographical area. Their comments about the recent changes were most significant and reiterated much of what was discussed in earlier sections on the role of the Chief Advisers:

'I think having a chief adviser is good and so, too, is the bringing together of a group – we feel we are members of a team.'

'The structure has improved a lot. As a team, it is a friendly team and we all have more or less the same philosophy. Very important.'

'Much improved in recent times since more subjects have been covered and the presence and position of a chief adviser has helped. We know more about each other because of it, and teachers know more about us. The administration has not reduced, but on the whole, organization is better – less things are *ad hoc*.'

'The only change that there has been has been from "no structure" to "structure". If I wanted a meeting earlier, I called it and we met. Now I don't need to as we liaise closely. We get on very well together: there is much cohesion in the team. Once you have a chief adviser, he creates a structure consciously or otherwise. Before we had a chief adviser, there was no clear line of communication – it creates an identity, but it also distances us from the other officers. The advisory body may create differences of opinion within the LEA, but it also allows them to be communicated.'

The fourth hierarchical model relied on just two tiers, the Chief Adviser and the rest, and almost inevitably this ruled out any area-based systems; to some extent, one might expect to see it mainly in smaller LEAs. One of the case-study LEAs operated this system, but because it required the Chief Adviser to carry a deputy-CEO role, it reduced his impact as Chief Adviser, both in terms of how much time he could devote and in his not being seen as an adviser so much as an officer. One adviser's comment on this structure needs little explanation:

> 'I am not over-worried by the absence of the Chief Inspector, however, there is not really any structure.'

But this advisory service did not completely lack a Chief Adviser, and his partial presence may have been significant in raising consciousness about the issue and thus in producing a polarized set of comments, as follows:

> 'I think the appointment of a Chief Adviser might constrain me. I enjoy the freedom and status. I enjoy being everything – I can't say no.'

> 'It's difficult without a senior adviser. We tend to all do our own thing. It's nice to have the freedom, but there is no one with overall oversight over all our visits and over all the development.'

> 'We need some kind of effective structuring. We need to have understood priorities. The Chief Adviser will protect our roles from being infinitely extensible.'

The possibility of a full-time Chief Adviser had certainly been mooted, and in a way, one suspects that these comments already reflect a position half-way towards accepting such a structure. One particularly fascinating comment clearly picked up on the role of this putative or potential chief adviser:

> 'A couple of years ago we were asked to write how we saw the service developing. I said that the service wasn't giving value for money and I suggested a hierarchy, a leader (deputy-CEO), four general advisers, subject advisers and advisory teachers. The CEO does not see the chief adviser's role as having enough authority unless they are at least a deputy CEO. The person in charge must oversee advisers, INSET and TVEI, and have a wider authority than just that of the advisory service. For instance, he must be able to ensure compatibility of IT equipment across the LEA.'

As has been mentioned, the case-study LEAs did not cover all the ten models, and in creating the series we had to rely upon our knowledge of other authorities and upon the information supplied in the Chief Advisers survey. However, one case-study LEA fitted well with Model 9. What had once been a group of 17 advisers with a well-defined structure, was now reduced through normal attrition and non-replacement to a nominal ten, with only seven or eight of these being active in the field due to TVEI, secondment, illness, etc. In what was left of this group, all were on the same pay scale but one adviser undertook a chief adviser role (without title or status) in what little was left of the waking-day after carrying out his other responsibilities. Two of the advisers endorsed the problem:

> 'When we had a structure I thought it a very reasonable one. At present, it is a very hand-to-mouth existence. It needs a long hard look taking at it, but any moves the CEO might make have been pre-empted by all the other support services that now exist.'

> 'In effect, he is fulfilling the chief adviser role, though he does not do it in name. We need the time to coordinate more.'

One, however, expressed the strongest anti-structure argument of all the advisers we encountered:

> 'I can see no advantages in having an advisory team – there would be little in common between a nursery and FE adviser. There should be close working within phases but not necessarily between phases for the advisers. I would break down officer/adviser barriers, but officers in offices spending time on politics would have problems with educational specialisms.'

Headteachers

In the case-study LEAs, a small and perforce unrepresentative number of headteachers were asked to comment on the organization of their LEA's advisory service. In general, the few comments they addressed to organizational matters tended to endorse the more structured approach. One question asked them about what they perceived were the constraints, as follows:

> (From an authority where there was no chief adviser.) 'I think there should be a senior adviser who takes responsibility for the service – i.e. a senior member of the team should take the chief adviser role.'

> 'There is also a need for adviser meetings and for a chief adviser.'

> 'They used to have very individually autonomous roles but now the LEA wants changes. The advisers just don't have the structure to absorb it.'

'I am not quite sure how they are organized, if indeed they are organized – do they have staff meetings to discuss issues as we do here? How do they know of the issues? I do not know how they spend their days. I think I would be happier to receive visits from more and different advisers, each with his own specialism – the patch adviser cannot be the focus for all wisdom, though it is good to have personal contact.'

'They need to get together as a team.'

'I have mixed feelings, really. If there was a team, it would generate its own identity and influence. Schools' sovereignty has currently been eroded considerably and any team would further erode this sovereignty, but this is within the current atmosphere – not from the advisers themselves, just that with all the current pressures, if you added an advisers' team, it would all be too much.'

'I think their (Model 2) structure is a good one. I am quite impressed with the advisory service here. The leadership from the advisers is of a high standard.'

In the main, heads, like their heads of department, restricted their replies to those areas where they had direct experience of advisers and their work. In response to a question about constraints upon the service, in all 12 LEAs the advisers' lack of time and finance were stressed and there was very little of the old argument that the money would be better spent providing teachers and materials in the classroom. Many suggested there should be more advisers, although their reasons for this varied from stressing the difficulties of working with an overburdened team to the problems of the teams being unable coherently to plan ahead:

'They have not got a lot left to cut, but cuts have reduced their services – they have too much work at present – you can never get hold of them and then they attend courses! It is difficult to get hold of them for nitty gritty things. It took four phone calls last time.'

'This advisory service has not been a fully staffed service for too long. This has led to crisis management reacting to demands rather then being involved in forward planning. The advisory service should be proactive. Too many changes in the way advisers have been deployed covering gaps.'

'They have to do far too much. There is conflict between their general and specialist role. The job is not clearly defined and heads do not know exactly what advisers do or are supposed to do.'

'Not enough of them. They are still looked upon as inspectors because they don't spend enough time in schools.'

'Too little time to do what is expected of them. Some are unable or unwilling to keep up with the massive recent curriculum developments. The gap is widening between knowledgeable advisers and those who are out of date.'

'Lack of money and time. The advisers are not able to provide any financial support – very frustrating – but they also have no executive clout. This is a shame.'

'They come for particular issues only and often don't have enough time to deal with these thoroughly.'

'The advisory service here is superb compared with my last authority, but I would like to see them much more often. They spend too much time in the office.'

Many heads were concerned that as a result of the plethora of recent initiatives, advisers and their services were not taking a sufficiently independent and planned approach in what they implemented or in their own management. There was a feeling of a loss of control, as follows:

'Too *ad hoc*, no cohesive policy, lacking in direction. For instance, INSET should not be left to teacher choice to attend. It should be school-based and compulsory.'

'They respond too easily to demands from central government and the LEA tries to make schools implement the impossible. They should be more political and stand up to certain issues.'

'Responding to central government issues inhibits the team working together and breaks the continuity of what they have been doing. Too much short-term planning in education.'

'All new circumstances are de-skilling. Advisers are facing many new circumstances, probably too many, – i.e. external pressures, conflict of inspectorial roles – resulting in antipathy from teachers.'

As has been suggested in some of these comments, some heads thought that the widening of roles placed a constraint on the quality of the work of individual advisers, though it is difficult at times to tease out whether this is seen as resulting from the reduced time they can give to old areas, or the problems of taking on new areas where they have little experience.

Finally, in commenting on the services' constraints, the heads' last group of comments related to the individual skills and personality

traits that they thought were necessary but not always present; two of
the heads commented, though, that there was not always the management support to help advisers with this:

> 'The personality of the adviser is important, if you don't have a
> good relationship with the head you can't get much past him
> or her.'

> 'It depends largely on the chief adviser. Ours is a thinker and
> not a doer. There is not a lot of action to back the philosophy.'

> 'One of the constraints is that some advisers do not have
> enough management skills and have problems establishing
> priorities – too many of them chase paperwork.'

> 'There is a lack of adequate instruction on how they should use
> their time and a lack of clarity in our own perceptions of their
> roles and how we could best use their advice.'

> 'There is a lack of in-service training available to them.'

Headteachers were also asked whether they would like to see any
changes in the advisory services' organization. Once again, the majority of heads ignored the generalized issue of structure preferring to
concentrate on roles, workloads and the range of work undertaken. A
small number raised the type of issue that suggested advising was not a
professional task in its own right. One head suggested that he would
like to see some advisers and inspectors (HMI) actually doing some
regular and difficult teaching, and another commented that the tenure
of advisory posts should be five years. Behind both these suggestions is
the idea that advisers improve through gaining or renewing 'hands on'
experience in the areas where they help teachers and heads. This view
can still be heard throughout education as a whole and is often
associated with the concept of credibility, that is you cannot be a good
adviser unless you can walk into a school and teach a class of children
without notice. These sentiments clearly assume that advising and
teaching lean on the same skills.

As can be imagined, many of the heads' comments about desirable
changes matched those they had already given when considering the
constraints. In wanting more advisers to be appointed, however, they
offered a range of tasks for them to undertake:

> 'The service should be brought fully up to strength, – i.e. all
> curriculum areas should be covered.'

> 'No particular changes – it would not worry me if they
> disappeared altogether! But if we are to have them, then we
> should have a complete set.'

'They need another primary adviser, especially when there are so many new heads.'

'The job they do is too much. They spread the cream too thinly. I would like to see more advisers, but there is a cost. They need more time for us to feel any advantages and for them to receive satisfaction.'

'I think the greatest potential growth area is for advisory teachers, though there are great cost implications.'

'To pump more money in would be the only way to improve things, but as they leave, some of them are not replaced.'

Having considered the prospect of more advisers, a number of heads also advocated a greater efficiency in their work. Three ways were suggested, as follows.

1   Advisers should be allowed to concentrate on educational matters:

'It would be nice to have advisers who were concerned with the curriculum and teaching methods, etc., and not being 'Jack-of-all-trades' in buildings management, etc.'

'The peripheral functions – the administrative tasks – should be reduced considerably. They should spend as little time as possible in County Hall – the width of their individual briefs should be reduced.'

2   Advisers' roles should be protected from being too large:

'They should have their own patch of about 30–40 schools and get to know them well.'

'Their role and the amount they have to cover are too big – they need areas of experience, they must not be wholly general.'

3   Advisers should have some method of prioritizing their roles:

'I don't know what the range of functions is, but they should be reduced or prioritized.'

'The current system is a bit of a jumble – phase, subject, area – some role confusion, needs to be clarified. It needs more well-defined roles, and not quite so many different strands. Perhaps more senior or area advisers should be allowed to concentrate upon being senior without other responsibilities such as subjects.'

'I would like their role to be enhanced. I would like subject advisers to advise on subjects, and area teams to concentrate on general matters. But I see them all on an equal plane.'

Despite all the resistance that is reported about the pastoral role, the interviews across the 12 LEAs suggested that the majority of heads were in favour of it. However, it did appear that there was more enthusiasm for it where pastoral systems were already in existence and the heads understood what was meant. Not unreasonably, heads looked for a high level of expertise in the area, and once again, we touch upon the unsuitability of the term 'general' for a highly specialized range of skills. Among the following comments, the last is especially interesting, in that it balances school needs with advisers' needs:

'I would like to see the whole team strengthened in terms of their pastoral team, but they don't necessarily have the expertise the head needs – they need to go on managerial courses so they can gain this expertise. The pastoral idea is good, but they must match it. Their role needs to be upgraded and the amount of administration reduced so they can get on with the real work.'

'I would like to see an adviser allocated to each school.'

'I would like to see the return of the generalist adviser, preferably someone with headship experience. The generalist should be senior to the subject adviser, who does not have the status that is needed.'

'I had a general adviser as a new head. Even as an experienced head, I feel the need for a general adviser. No one has an over-view of any school. I need help on strategies, managing people, etc. No one gives that. Generalists need to have senior experience and be knowledgeable to be of help.'

'The team should be strengthened by having more of them. It should be large enough to have general advisers who are not subject specialists as well. But general roles do make subject specialists go into schools they otherwise would not enter (or could easily avoid!)'

Equally immediate in the mind of several heads was the difficulty of gaining access to advisers and the difficulties then of maintaining the contact:

'They need to be more available. We only contact advisers in emergency. They are so busy you are brainwashed into only contacting them when it is vital. They have a lot to offer and should be used more positively.'

'A school builds up professional bonds with the many and varied professionals (ed. psychs, social workers, therapists, doctors, etc.) but the special needs adviser does not have time to build up these vital links – organization of service should allow for this.'

'I would like to see advisers turning up regularly to [school] departmental meetings, if that means they should be more involved in schools, then we need more advisers. I would like to feel I had someone helping me make certain I was doing well.'

Of course, for some heads the system was fine, or if not quite that, at least they seemed to accept their lack of knowledge about it amicably and passively, though that in itself is a reflection on the service. One head commented that it was 'difficult to say "really know" what the organization was', and another simply commented that 'the service changed a year ago and thus it was impossible to comment'.

The project, finally, asked heads how they thought they could help their advisory service. Some commented on the value of advisory teachers and secondments, – i.e. enhancing the advisory services from the staff in schools:

'The ESG advisory teachers are a great help and are providing another level of advice – but advisory teachers must have credibility and not be seconded for wrong reasons or on low pay scales.'

'A headteacher has been seconded for one year to organize the INSET for a specific curricular project. He is excellent and badly needed for its success. I would like to see the LEA extend headteacher secondment to the advisory service for specific curriculum issues such as this – especially when they could bring their more recent school experience to it.'

Others felt that headteachers and schools were able to offer a considerable pool of expertise, that could help with INSET, working parties and evaluation, though not all felt that this resource was well enough used:

'Not nearly enough use is made of expertise among headteachers. This is partly the result of headteachers being reluctant to allow a colleague to help.'

'This school has a head and two deputies with advanced qualifications in educational management. None has been approached to help with LEA INSET. The advisory service offers no management training – they do not have this expertise. They are beginning to be aware of this.'

'We already contribute a great deal. The senior staff of this school have done a great deal on INSET for the LEA, TVEI and the Oxford Certificate of Education Achievement (OCEA) in place of the advisers.'

'Heads could run in-service courses, particularly using Open University materials.'

'Heads can help in management courses and in the evaluation of other heads bringing in self-evaluation courses.'

'I think the time will come when experienced heads in redeployment situations will be able to offer their expertise especially in evaluation, appraisal, etc.'

Headteachers also saw themselves as facilitators and supporters:

'I can facilitate, mediate, introduce and present the human side of advisers to the staff so they do not see them as inspectors *per se.* I pass feedback and draw attention to the advisers of those with career possibilities or problems. I also point out staff who could help advisers.'

'Schools should have development programmes. These would help advisers focus on where advice was needed. There is too much short-term planning in education.'

'By getting advisers into staff meetings, explaining his role, getting the barriers down.'

'If we can get several schools together, then it makes their visits more worth while.'

'There could be a self-development group for headteachers.'

'By making them welcome in schools – not to feel that his [the head's] duty is to protect his staff from them – staff should feel comfortable with advisers and vice versa.'

'One is appreciative of the tremendous workload they have. I try to hold on to some capitation for curriculum development. I offer sympathy with respect to their lack of executive power.'

'Sometimes they come in very depressed, so I offer tea and sympathy from time to time. We all need encouragement and it is a partnership.'

And some also felt they could assist in an administrative fashion:

'We could write to them to visit schools more often and we could follow up our invitations to make sure it happens. But one tends to work well with those who give a good response –

but the staff get worried if they see too many advisers, they perhaps fear too much innovation. You could have too much and too varied an input.'

'We could monitor the number of times we could do with talking with them and then ring up and ask how often they could come in. We have lost the habit of asking for advice.'

The final group of positive suggestions offered a political and influential role:

'Heads could, as a group perhaps, apply more pressure on the LEA to provide a better advisory service.'

'We heads in infants schools need to ensure that advisers take infant education more seriously.'

Some headteachers were, however, more negative, or perhaps just more honest. To the question of whether there were any ways schools could help advisory services, some gave a straight 'No' and others said they had never given it thought. One group gave some reasons for their not helping the services, as follows:

'We have never been asked into a consultation about the way we work or how the education service works.'

'I am sure we can, and that we ought to, help the services. I am equally sure that we probably don't (won't) – we have a certain inbuilt arrogance that might prevent this. Perhaps I ought to involve advisers more. It's not that I am averse to accepting advice, but I take it from senior members of staff.'

'We are supposed to consult them before we do various things, but I have been a head for 21 years. I try to consult them, but it is difficult when you have to ring round the schools they are in – when they come here they always get two or three phone calls. Perhaps we should bother them less, but primary heads are frightened of them and so they daren't move without permission.'

Heads of department

Secondary heads of department constituted the third group whose reactions to the advisory service organization we sought, and some 44 were interviewed during the case studies. One question asked whether they would wish to see any changes in the functions of advisers and/or the methods of operation of their service.

In light of the often reported view that teachers are cynical about advisers, it was interesting that in only two instances were the responses negative. In the first, a head of department with many years experience in a 'reluctantly' reorganized comprehensive school harked back to grammar school days when he claimed heads of department would not have needed them. He questioned why he should need them now, and he concluded that advisers would be better off teaching! The other 'negative' head of department referred to a personality clash between him and his subject adviser, but was not negative about advisers in general. In contrast to these two, there were positive comments, for example: 'I think I am lucky with the RE adviser – he is helpful and constructive, he does not interfere, but will support when necessary.' Overall, however, few of those interviewed claimed to see enough of their adviser(s) to be able to be satisfied with the service, and as outlined below, for most of them, the basic problem was just that – a shortage of advisory time.

In just over half the interviews the heads of department stressed the advisers' lack of time or excessive workloads. Their comments ranged from a straight need for an adviser in the specific subject to wanting more subject time where the post already existed; for instance:

'We would just like an adviser!'

'I would like to see an adviser, both for business studies and for equal opportunities! How can I really start an equal opportunities programme without any real status, width of knowledge, etc? Without an adviser, there is too great a reliance on teacher initiative and goodwill over and above our daily work.'

'Our problems are geographical. We are a long way from County Hall. We feel isolated. We need more visits to keep in touch with what is happening in other parts of the county.'

'My impression is that they have too much on their plates and live at the wrong end of the LEA.'

'I would like to see them more often. Advisers should not be appointed to a subject, but to a number of staff who teach the subject within the LEA.'

'My adviser has too great a range of functions – she has been given "active tutorial work", etc., and now she appears not to have time to do anything thoroughly.'

'The administrative load is too great to allow them into schools. They respond to requests to visit more than initiating visits. Therefore it is perhaps necessary to be pushy and express your needs. There should be more advisory teachers – teacher resources not used enough.'

But having described a shortage of adviser time in school, two further major elements in the department heads' comments became apparent. First, in a quarter of all responses, dissatisfaction was expressed about the heads of departments' lack of knowledge about what advisers did, though much of this dissatisfaction was aimed at not knowing those areas other than the subject work:

'It is difficult to know what their exact brief is – they are only seen when *they* wish to see the head of department on specific issues. Their full role is not seen by us: advice on wider issues is not easy to ask.'

'Teachers are not aware of the width of functions and their time-consuming nature. Wearing too many hats is as dangerous as over-specialization. There is a need for rationalization.'

'I would like to see more teachers knowing who the advisers were and what the advisers did – it should be publicized, including committees. Teachers feel they are remote. We are too isolated in this London borough as members of staff.'

'I don't really know what the functions of an adviser are. Is he a policy instigator or what?'

Secondly, again in about a quarter of the responses, the department heads expressed the wish that advisers' work should be more teacher and teaching focused. There appeared to be some resentment about advisers having work to do at (or for) county hall, and a desire for them to be agents of the class teacher, as follows:

'The adviser needs to work more closely with the head of department, and department staff. There are 24 schools in our authority and the advisers should spend one week with each school maths department. This would be better than running/attending courses. Advisers tend to become advisers to the authority rather than to teachers.'

'I would like to see him come in more frequently. I have been told it is a compliment. I would like him to come in for one day per term – they have good ideas, the courses are good, and when he comes in he is good. But he is in an impossible position – he needs an assistant, a seconded head of department.'

'I would like them to have more power to act for the things we want. They give us money, but I would like more help reducing group numbers. I would like him to point out the dangers of secondment for schools to his superiors, – i.e. again, he needs much more power.'

'I would like to see them more in charge of the fabric of the room and new equipment.'

'They have lots of ideas and opinions of resource facilities – they should do more finding out and contacting places for us – they have more time.'

Although, at first, this appears to contradict earlier sentiments, if advisers' time and mobility are compared with what time teachers have left after their teaching commitment, then it is easy to see how this view arises. As with headteachers, it is notable that although the heads of department were invited to comment on the organization of the advisory services, it was the delivery and the interface between the school and adviser that they chose to comment on.

Conclusion

The rate of change

During the case studies it became apparent that LEA advisory services differed in both practice and organization, a result that was matched by the findings from the project's later surveys. This chapter has set out to explore some of these differences and to try to understand some of their causes and consequences, though obviously in this kind of work few direct causal links can ever be established.

Throughout the case studies we were constantly reminded that current LEA practices were very much influenced by recent historical (and often non-educational) events acting in conjunction with the effects of the enormous amount of educational change imposed upon education over the last few years. The research identified seven major influences on LEA practice over and above those arising from the legislative changes. The first of these relates to the major local authority reorganization of 1974, when the majority of LEAs were changed to their present size and shape. For all the enormous impact of this reorganization, it is none the less surprising that some of the pre-1974 influences were still operating in 1986 and that a degree of local partisanship was still visible.

But there has been another influence from 1974 that has been even slower to disappear. A number of older advisers have described what seemed to be a fairly clear consensus of the role of the 1974 advisory services. They described a situation where, in many LEAs, the secondary school subject ruled supreme and advisory services were built around a range of secondary subject specialists whose main if not entire responsibility was for the promotion of their subject within secondary schools. Primary work was the responsibility of a disproportionately small number of primary phase advisers, and any non-primary general work that was undertaken by the advisory service fell to a small number of secondary phase advisers who might also have carried senior or area positions, or to one or two subject advisers who took on a more general role. In the main, these advisers have described there being little emphasis on school management, 'general' advice, pastoral assistance or cross-curriculum work. Furthermore, there appeared to be little crossover between the roles of officers and advisers. Advisers were given an amount of subject funding to give out and basically were expected to fill their time working alone on promotion of their subject.

To be able to fulfil the requirements of this model the advisory services were considerably enlarged in 1974, with many of the appointments coming from secondary heads of department. While this surely must have been the heyday of those employed to 'plough their own furrow', it also represented a considerable change from the prevailing conditions beforehand. This was, perhaps, the first time that there were advisory services available in all parts of the country. Given the scale of the changes that hit education immediately following this reorganization, it is really quite surprising that this 'secondary school' model of the advisory service has survived so long.

Almost as soon as the new LEAs were finding their feet, the oil crisis occurred and a recession followed. The expansion of the advisory service ended and cuts were imposed in education, and if cuts were to be imposed in schools, it was demanded that they should equally be imposed on county hall staff. The effects were dramatic and during the mid-1970s to early 1980s advisory service numbers fell by some 20 per cent. But as numbers fell, other changes brought an increase in the advisers' non-subject workload, for instance, falling rolls brought about the need for officers and advisers to organize school mergers and closures, and staff redeployment and early retirement. With the increase in these general and administrative tasks, the time left for subject work began to decline.

In parallel with these events came a growing dissatisfaction with state education and a demand for greater accountability. The curriculum became politicized and was taken into the public arena. What had mostly belonged to teachers and advisers was now public property. Officers and members started talking about curriculum, and central government began to take an active interest. By 1977, complaints were already being expressed about the extent of central government intervention in education (see *Education*, November 1977, referring to intervention by the Labour government) and since then both educational and financial intervention has continued to grow and to affect local government remorselessly.

With government intervention, there came also the offer of targeted money to help buy advisory teachers. Over the last few years their numbers have grown considerably such that they now almost equal those of the advisers and may soon be expected to exceed them. While advisory teachers may help some advisers with their classroom and curriculum load, they unfortunately need support and management, and as such they create for them an additional administrative load. As the advisers' administrative load increases, for this and other reasons the advisory teachers' directed work in the classroom can be seen to replace some of that which used to be done by the adviser, and once more, the 1974 concept of the subject-oriented adviser is further eroded.

Varying practices and roles

Since each LEA responded to the demands for change individually, often in an *ad hoc* fashion and always from a different starting-point, it is not surprising that their practice now varied so greatly. But in looking at the differences in LEA practice, it soon became apparent that we were focusing upon some of the most fundamental aspects of advisory work – e.g. the monitoring, pastoral support and appointments procedures. As such it is likely that it is the advisers' roles that varied, not just their interpretation.

The project asked CEOs and chief advisers about their advisory service's roles. Four related elements emerged which seemed crucial to determining practice, as follows.

(1) *The degree of centrality of the advisory service in the authority.* How important and involved was the advisory service in the running of the authority? How 'near' were the advisers to the nominal locus of decision-making? How near did they feel themselves to be? What was their relationship with the members, and how different was the status schools afforded officers from that they afforded advisers?

(2) *The way the service was required to face in the 'school vs LEA' debate.* Was the official officer stance really neutral (and is there any reason why it should be), or was the advisory service required or encouraged to face one way more than the other?

Put another way, if the authority encouraged advisers to promote their subject, or become involved in the pastoral support of 'their' schools, how much did the executive arm of the authority then look down on them for not presenting a 'balanced' view? Conversely, having demanded advisers give a balanced and objective view, how much were they then criticized for not becoming sufficiently involved in their schools? While this may be a somewhat jaundiced analysis of affairs, and professional staff should, perhaps, be able to find a balanced position for their work, many officers complained that advisers were too school-centred. This was almost the opposite line to that taken by most heads of department!

(3) *The method and importance of monitoring in the LEA.* This offered a range of views about the value of inspecting which were then greatly tempered by (a) the 'adviser/inspector' argument, which contends that the inspectorial approach does not favour good advisory relationships in schools and vice versa, and (b) a sensitivity that suggested that inspecting schools during the teachers' dispute may not have been too profitable an avenue to pursue.

(4) *The local outcome of the subject specialist vs the (specialist) generalist debate.* This has not only the obvious differences in role effects (as discussed in Chapter 6), but also is thought to affect the advisers' centrality in the authority. The generalist role was seen as putting the adviser in the position of the authority's representative. In contrast, the subject-specialist role offered more independence and required the necessary 'distance' for advisers to be able to be critical of the executive arm of their authority. This raises the question of how advisers might best influence the executive arm. Are they more influential as generalists acting from within and agitating at frequent intervals, but without the 'freedom' to be freely critical, or are they more effective as independent agents producing possibly stronger reports but from a greater distance. This can be seen as the same argument as that of whether school monitoring and development are best approached from the active pastoral attachment or from the occasional inspection or review.

These four elements can also be seen as continua with attitudes determining where an advisory service is placed on each one: all of them are associated with how the decision-making part of the authority values the various functions of their advisers. But this value can arise in different ways. Where an authority was badly affected by the financial cuts and lost considerable numbers of central staff, then what is left of the advisers' services might be seen as being more useful in terms of general functions than in specifically supporting subjects – the officer and adviser roles might merge through necessity. On the other hand, there are those authorities where the advisers' value is in no doubt, where strong and independent teams have been encouraged and where these teams' opinions are sought prior to decisions being made. In contrast, there was the CEO who felt it improper for an advisory team to act autonomously within the LEA, and there are those advisers who are still encouraged to work alone on the promotion of their subject while their officers run the authority.

Like the advisory service's roles, its organization and position within the authority can similarly be viewed as being influenced or even determined by these same attitudes. The research looked at elements of organization by starting with the role of the chief adviser in terms of his or her lines of communication to the CEO, the emphasis on managing advisers and the other roles given to the post. The first difficulty for the research, though, and presumably also for teachers and advisers in these authorities, was that in many authorities the title of the person in charge of the advisory service was not helpful in indicating that they carried this role. Furthermore, there were some LEAs where no one was clearly in charge of the service at all.

Where there was someone in charge, the amount of time they were given to manage the service varied from as little as five per cent to the full working-day. Patently, the fact that someone had responsibility for managing the advisory service did not mean they had been given the time to do it, but the actual titles gave some clue here. In essence, there were three groups of chief advisers. In the first group there were those with 'Chief Adviser' as the title (without other parts being written into it), and on average they only spent about one-fifth of their time off-task. The second group comprised those with combined 'officer' and 'Chief Adviser' titles, or with 'officer' titles only, and these spent approximately twice as much time (40 per cent) off-task. The third group comprised full-time advisers who had been given (part-time) responsibility to manage the service. While this group had few non-advisory service tasks as such, we can see that they were left with even less time to manage the service than those in the other two groups. All in all, it would seem that there are many authorities where advisory service management is not deemed to be particularly important.

Structures

With such a variation in attitudes towards the advisers' role and so many different influences over the last few years, it is not surprising that we also found very different organizational structures within the services. The project looked at the chief advisers' descriptions of their structures and produced a ten-part model by loosely using three elements, the visible amount of chief adviser available to the service, the presence and use of a middle-management tier and whether the chief adviser was a member of the LEA's senior management team. This model covered structures from the tightly hierarchical systems on the one hand, to the basic 'flatarchy' or 'pancakes' on the other – though it has to be emphasized that in reporting 'flatarchies' and 'pancakes' there is no question of decision-making being consciously pushed out from the centre to the periphery. It would be fairer to say there was little conscious decision-making at all in these cases. While the majority of services employed some or all of the more hierarchical aspects we were looking at, there were still nearly 20 per cent with little emphasis on management. (It is worth noting that Bolam's (1978) three 'types' of advisory service structure fit into this new scale, with types 1 and 2 both being seen as similar versions of our model 4, and type 3 relating well to our total hierarchy model 1.)

Reactions

Having produced this kind of analysis, we were interested in the advisers' and headteachers' reactions to these different approaches, but caution is necessary, for the majority of them will have worked under only one system, and as such their reactions cannot have the comparative edge one might like.

Advisers' reactions to their services' organization tended to favour greater organization, and it is only at the higher levels of management that 'teams' were described as actually working. The case studies included two rural authorities which were placed at position 3 on the scale, since while they had strong chief advisers, they also had 'relaxed' middle-management structures that hardly appeared to function. In the one, which had been like this for some time, the 'relaxation' brought a fair deal of frustration and criticism – some of the advisers felt the system blocked their work and that decisions took too long to be made. They argued there was too much work for just one person at the centre of the service. The other LEA, however, had only just gained a chief adviser, and the move towards a structure and a degree of organization from a diffused area-based 'flatarchy' was greatly welcomed.

The tighter structures were not completely without their detractors however, and some felt excessive organization constrained their work while others were critical of an apparent tendency in these systems for edicts to flow downwards. In the case-study authority where the possibility of a chief adviser post was just beginning to be discussed, the comments revealed a welcome for the new structure, but with the qualifications one might expect with the uncertainties and change the new position would bring if implemented.

Although heads and heads of departments were invited to comment on the organization of their advisory services, perhaps not unreasonably, they tended to ignore management structures and concentrate upon the advisers' roles and deployment as they saw and interacted with them. The heads almost universally reported a lack of advisers and adviser time which, they argued, led to poor long-term planning and poor resource deployment within the service. For the individual adviser, they claimed, it presented difficulties with access, with finding the appropriate balance of tasks and with completing jobs properly. Their criticisms were, in the main, addressed to the lack of resources and not to the role of the adviser. In most respects, the heads expressed considerable support for advisers, indeed more so than one might have expected after the comments made in the late 1970s.

The question about how heads and schools might help advisers in their work provided responses across three areas: (1) the provision of curriculum and/or management expertise which was present in schools and which some heads felt LEAs were slow to capitalize upon; (2) an enhanced facilitating, introductory and administrative role by heads which would make advisers' school visits easier and more effective; and (3) a political role using the headteachers' 'voice' within the authority to develop the advisory service in the direction they wished. However, one or two of those we asked were taken aback at the question and clearly had previously not given it any thought. This leads to the question of how passive schools should be in their workings with advisers.

The heads of department we talked with were similarly concerned about the shortage of advisers and advisory time and generally seemed to welcome (the prospect of) seeing an adviser. The departmental heads raised two other related points. First, many suggested that advisers should spend more time and effort with teachers in the classroom and in dealing with classroom and curriculum matters. The heads of department seemed to be suggesting that advisers ought to be doing more work with them, and less with county hall personnel. To those working at county hall level this may seem a naïve statement, but it was very real in our conversations and it perfectly reflects the real pull both on advisers' time and loyalty. Furthermore, it highlights the problem that arises with the heads of departments' second point of not really knowing what advisers do. Not only is there not enough adviser time available, but contact and communication is made even more difficult by teaching staff not fully understanding the adviser's role and expectations. It would seem that there is scope here for an effective 'PR' exercise to be carried out.

A concluding heresy

In concluding a chapter such as this, the question arises of how far one may dare to jump from the known to the risky and hypothetical. We know that the vast changes in education have caused disarray in LEA planning and organization and that the cuts have reduced many of the best ideas to skeletal ghosts of what was intended. We also know that advisers are relatively expensive, and that with such a broad role, difficult to defend to cost-conscious Education Committees. But for all that, why do some LEAs regard the management of the advisory service as no more than an 'also-ran' on an already busy person's job description, while other LEAs appoint a chief adviser only to give him (or rarely her) a whole list of advisory and non-advisory tasks to do apart from running the service? Where is the logic in allowing only half a manager to run the service? Beyond this, why (as we have seen in Chapter 3) do some authorities appoint chief advisers who have no actual advisory experience? Is it, and here comes the jump, because some do not yet rate advisory work to be sufficiently important to spend money on its proper management? Alternatively, is it because there is still a lurking suspicion that advising is not a real, specialized and professional job in its own right, and as such not only can it be done by non-specialists, but it needs neither training nor management? When we see some authorities operating levels of management many times more sophisticated than others, when we hear the 'clients' in schools asking for better-organized deployment and communications, and when we hear advisers themselves recognizing that their role needs managing, what other conclusions can be drawn?

5 Liaison and Communication

Introduction

There is little need here to labour the point that fundamental changes in education over the last decade have accentuated the need for advisory services to examine their individual and collective working practices. Throughout this research, the evidence has consistently painted a picture of advisers doing most of their work on their own and being almost exclusively concerned with what went on in their own subject or phase domain. But this was not the case with all advisers and all services, and it suggests that for some at least, the possibilities of change have been realized. A number of advisers have described the difficulties they found with the traditional work practices and have suggested alternative solutions, including the need for more teamwork and directed leadership. Similarly, a number of chief advisers have talked of the approaches they have tried, or would like to try, to help advisers overcome the difficulties of meeting current needs with inappropriate strategies. The pattern was completed in the case studies with the headteachers who said they would welcome more of a team ethos in the work of the advisory service. A few heads went further and argued that they actually wanted the product of this greater teamwork and cross-fertilization of ideas; that is, they wanted advisers to have both broader remits and broader experience, elements that the heads felt would more closely reflect the schools' working practices and needs. Overall, it would seem that the encouragement of teamwork and improved communication within the service might be one of the better ways to equip advisers and their services with the skills, experiences and work practices that are argued to be more appropriate to meeting today's demands.

Given the importance of this area, a large part of the project's research was directed towards looking at the nature of advisers' working relationships with schools and colleges, with advisory colleagues and with other LEA personnel. The project was keen to explore the opportunities for advisers to meet and work together, to broaden their horizons and to contribute towards decision-making. This chapter thus sets out to describe the advisers' working relationships with colleagues, the formal communication channels open to them within the LEA and the opportunities for their teamwork. As before, the information is taken both from the case studies, which offer a detailed insight across a broad range of personnel in a small number of LEAs, and from the Advisers and Chief Advisers questionnaires which offer more of a national picture.

Teams and teamwork

Feelings of team membership are difficult to research with any accuracy and objectivity and, in the end, they tell us little about the nature of the membership or the team. They do, however, give some indication of the advisers' working life. The section was introduced in the Advisers questionnaire by asking the advisers whether they felt any sense of belonging to a team. Of the 1,102 advisers who answered this question, just under three-quarters (788) said they felt they worked as a member of a team, while just over a quarter (314) felt they did not. This result was not found to be related to the adviser's sex, age or salary. However, significantly more 'inspectors' (86 per cent) said they felt themselves to be members of a team than 'advisers' (67 per cent), and of the seven self-reported work styles described in Chapter 3 (the 'pure subject specialist', the 'phase' role, the 'generalist role' and the four various combinations of these roles), all were close to the overall mean except for the subject specialists, of whom significantly fewer reported feeling they belonged to a team (53 per cent). As one might expect, working practices can affect the advisers' feelings of team membership.

It was also possible to consider the advisers' responses to this question by the LEA they worked for. In most cases, advisers within LEAs showed a mix of responses – some felt they belonged to teams and others did not. However, a number of LEAs showed a very high sense of membership with all, or nearly all, of their advisers being of one accord; while in contrast, a small number of LEAs had as few as one-third or less of their advisers feeling they belonged to a team. (This analysis only drew on LEAs with a total of ten or more responses.) From inspection of the individual LEA results there appears to be a small but positive relationship between an emphasis on a managerial structure in the service (as coded in Chapter 4) and the percentage of advisers saying they felt themselves to be members of a team. The stronger the management emphasis (as portrayed by the service structure), the stronger the sense of team membership.

However, knowing that some advisers felt themselves to be part of a team tells us little about what sort of teams these were. The advisers who felt part of a team were therefore asked, first, to say whether their 'team' comprised the whole group of advisers or just a part of it, and then, if they belonged to a sub-group, to describe it. Of the 795 who felt themselves to be a member of a group, nearly half (47 per cent) belonged to the whole group of advisers, a further 8 per cent belonged both to the whole group and to one or more sub-groups and 44 per cent belonged only to subgroups.

Advisers described the nature of 535 of these subgroups. The groups fell into the five main areas that one might expect: phase groups (179 entries); area or divisional teams (109); single-subject groupings, – e.g. a maths group or a science group (90); working parties and various task-oriented groups (79); and cross-curriculum groups – e.g. SEN, TVEI and equal opportunities (28). Apart from a few other rather small groups, there was one other group of specific interest which amounted to a self-selecting mutual-interest group. Twenty-four advisers reported belonging to such a group. (The frequencies of the ten most popular subgroups are given in Appendix Table A5.1 page 214.)

The advisers' thus fell into three groups: approximately 40 per cent felt they belonged to the whole group, the team; approximately 38 per cent felt they belonged to a subgroup, though not necessarily the subgroup their managers intended; and 28 per cent felt they were members of no group at all. Of course, not all advisory services might aim for a whole-group membership, especially where the service is large or where the team is spread out over a large geographic region. In these instances, the area, phase or subject-based grouping might be more appropriate.

In the case studies the frequent lack of team ethos was mentioned by both headteachers and chief advisers, but both groups tended to see the problem more as a need for more teamwork (a 'good thing') than as a need to reduce the advisers' isolation *per se*. If implemented, most of their remedies look as if they would attack both problems, though the respondents were acutely aware of the financial difficulties that would also apply.

The heads offered a range of comments, of which some are presented here. The difficulties are given, first, and examples of possible improvements and solutions then follow:

'They are not seen together in schools, only on courses. They tend to plough their own furrow. They are not seen as a team.'

'I couldn't envisage them coming as a pair. They are only seen in an individual subject context and there is little team ethic.'

'I perceive there to be an advisory service comprised of a number of individuals. They have always worked alone. There is scope for development. We have still not got a service.'

'There is a danger we won't see them at all. If they came in twos, we would only see them half the time.'

'Normally they work as individuals – there would be benefits from them working together because there are links between subjects – especially in the process mode of the curriculum.'

'It would help enormously for cross-curricular themes if the advisory service were seen more as a team.'

'It has to be a corporate activity. Whilst they have separate specialisms, they must work together.'

'Apart from inspections, I think there is some scope for them to work together – e.g. maths and computing, English and computing, maths and science – this all relates to how we link all our teaching together.'

'Teamwork is increasing a little as a result of things like modular technology.'

Many chief advisers were aware of what heads were saying and expressed a wish for greater commonality and teamwork among their advisers. However, moves to create such ideals were patently not that easy:

'Searching for some ways to bring about a team ethos. This is a real issue. We have used the curriculum document as one method – we are about to initiate some consultancy training for the advisers and that should enhance the team.'

'Various strategies have been tried:
(1)   a faculty structure did not work;
(2)   the *ad hoc* groups were not terribly successful;
(3)   the introduction of new teams with designated hierarchical leaders should be more positive.
(4)   the first full school evaluation proved to be the most successful example of teamwork. This would suggest that teams need specific tasks and a time limit.'

'We have three area teams and so there must be some commonality about the way we operate. Recruits to the service come expecting to work in a team – this is in the descriptions sent out to applicants. We hold regular team meetings and have an induction programme that encourages team ethos and is seen as a team effort to induct a new colleague. Teams should make things happen, not just wait for them to happen'

'I try to give people the opportunity to do things together, to think as a team and to get them to recognise themselves as individuals within a team. We need to raise their perceptions of themselves and of how they can contribute to the whole.'

The issue is not, therefore, what is the way forward, for this seems to have been clearly enough spelt out by those we talked with – greater teamwork appears to be the desired route for advisory service improvement. Really the issue is to do with how to get there. In this vein, the project continued to look at the various processes and practices that might encourage the desired improvements in teamwork and communication.

Attendance at divisional and/or full-team meetings

The project used the Advisers questionnaire to ask about the number of divisional and/or full-team meetings the advisers had attended over the last 12 months, that is to the autumn/winter of 1986. The 1,064 responding advisers recorded approximately 18,700 divisional or full-team meeting attendances over that period, with an average of 17.9 meetings per annum each; this represents just about one meeting every three weeks. However, as the results in Table 5.1 show, there was a wide range of attendance patterns, with some advisers attending between 80 and 90 meetings per annum, while at the other extreme a small number reported attending none, though this could include one or two advisers who were relatively new to the service.

With such a variation in attendance, the possible causes for it were sought. The number of meetings attended was not significantly related to sex or age. However, for advisers on the Soulbury pay scales, there was a significant trend for those on higher salaries to attend more meetings than their less well-paid colleagues. Attendance was also work related. With the self-reported styles of work, there was a significant difference ($p < 0.001$) between the numbers of meetings attended by the 'pure subject specialists' (14.2 meetings per annum) and by those coupling the generalist and subject specialist roles together (20.5 meetings per annum) (see Chapter 3 for definitions of these roles).

Table 5.1: *The number of divisional and/or full advisory team meetings attended by advisers over 12 months*

No. of meetings attended	No. of advisers	%
0	9	0.8
1–10 (inclusive)	340	32.0
11–20	398	37.4
21–30	159	14.9
31–40	96	9.0
41–50	40	3.8
51–99	22	2.1
Total	1,064	100
(52 missing)		

Differences also occurred between LEAs. The most 'minimalist' LEAs were reported to hold no more than six or seven team and/or divisional meetings per annum (average value as reported by ten or more advisers), whereas other LEAs had up to as many as 40. For all the potential influence of the LEAs' size and structure on the number of meetings, one cannot help but suppose that there was at least a policy or leadership element entering in here, with some LEAs encouraging or even requiring more meetings than others.

Involvement in working parties and the like

Teamwork and a collaborative working style were also argued to be promoted through the use of working parties and other task-oriented groups. It was thought that as well as meeting their overt purposes they could promote communication, broaden horizons and get people working together. One chief adviser described it in the following way:

'Advisers wish to work more as teams. We are looking towards functional teams which would look at specific curriculum areas and initiatives – i.e. teamwork which has purpose and focus, then the team will disband and other teams will form.'

The Advisers questionnaire asked advisers about the nature and number of working parties they had been involved with over the last year. As is shown in Table 5.2, the vast majority of advisers had been involved in between one and ten working parties, with only five per cent involved in none, and just under nine per cent in more than ten. The 1,025 advisers reported approximately 5,300 working party involvements, with an average individual involvement in 5.2 each.

Table 5.2: *The number of working parties advisers were involved in over 12 months*

No. of working parties	No. of advisers	%
0	55	5.3
1–10 (inclusive)	876	85.0
11–20	75	7.3
21–30	12	1.2
31–40	3	0.3
41–50	4	0.4
Total	1,025	100.1
(91 missing)		

The advisers' age made no difference to the number of working parties they were involved in. However, sex was significant, with men being involved in a significantly higher average number of working parties than women (5.4 to 4.5 respectively, $p < 0.05$). As before, the adviser's self-reported work role was important with 'pure subject specialists' being involved in significantly fewer working parties per annum than the 'specialist/phase/generalists' (3.5 and 6.0 working parties per annum respectively: $p < 0.001$). The number of working parties attended also significantly increased in a virtually linear fashion with Soulbury salary – the average number of working parties the adviser was involved with approximated to just over half his/her Soulbury scale point!

As usual, there was a variation between LEAs, with the advisers in some LEAs reporting an average attendance of almost 11 working parties per annum, while in others it was as few as only 2.6 per annum (where the number of advisers was equal to or greater than 10). If those authorities with few team meetings were using working parties in their stead, one would expect a negative correlation between the numbers of meetings and the number of working parties advisers reported being involved with. However, the correlation was found to be insignificant which would suggest that, on average, LEAs were not compensating the one with the other. Similarly, the correlation between working party involvement and team meetings on an individual adviser basis was very small (+0.08), which suggests, once again, that across all the authorities there was very little relationship between the number of team meetings attended and the number of working parties an adviser is involved in.

Our experience in the case-study LEAs had demonstrated the varying significance, from one LEA to the next, of officer involvement in these working parties. We were also interested in working parties as a channel of communication between officers and advisers. The project thus followed this line of inquiry. Those advisers who reported any working party involvement were asked to state how many of their working parties had involved education officers. Respondents were then asked to give examples of the subject-matter of their working parties under two headings: (a) where there was officer involvement, and (b) where only advisers were involved.

Advisers recorded 5,292 working party involvements. Of the 970 advisers with involvement in one or more working parties, 22 per cent were only involved with adviser-only working parties, 16 per cent were only involved with officer and adviser working parties (they only met in groups which always included education officers), and 55 per cent (532) were involved in both officer and non-officer types of working party (7 per cent failed to complete the question).

Table 5.3 shows the grouped subject distribution for all 3,078 working parties where subjects were given. The second part of the table considers the information given the 532 advisers who worked in both types of working party and splits the distributions according to whether officers were present or not and shows if the LEA differentiated between the subject content on the basis of who attended.

Table 5.3 shows the working parties to cover a wide range of topics and demonstrates, as before, the width of adviser involvement across the whole education field – less than 14 per cent of their involvement was in single-subject working parties, though by the way in which LEAs are structured, one might not expect advisers to involve their subject in many working parties anyway. In line with earlier results, we see that INSET, TRIST and GRIST seem to have been the most demanding areas and that, once again, adviser management and other adviser issues (inspection, adviser appraisal, working practices, and so forth) fail to get into the top 11 categories.

When we look at the differences between the two types of working party in LEAs that operate both types, that is those working parties with both advisers and officers in them, and those with only advisers, the picture becomes more interesting. The two types of working party appear to be more or less equally common in respect of INSET, cross-curriculum initiatives, assessment, phase work, school management and health education. On the other hand, single-subject work, as we might expect, appears to be an area that officers shy away from, whereas matters to do with school staffing appear to be more in their domain. The reason for more officer-type working parties, in the equal opportunities and multicultural fields, seems less certain, unless it reflects the political sensitivities of these issues, while in the SEN area, the frequently complementary role of the SEN officer to the SEN adviser could create this characteristic.

Table 5.3: *The subject areas of adviser working parties*

Main subject areas:	A All WPs		B Adviser + officer WPs		Adviser only WPs	
	N	%	N	%	N	%
INSET, TRIST, GRIST	439	14.3	132	13.3	142	14.9
Single-subject curriculum groups	416	13.5	79	8.0	168	17.7
Cross-curriculum areas and initiatives, TVEI, CPVE, IT, Modular Technology, etc.	415	13.5	132	13.3	135	14.2
Assessment and examinations	260	8.4	72	7.3	98	10.3
Phase work (whatever phase)	254	8.2	75	7.6	77	8.1
School staffing levels, building, planning, reorganization, etc.	239	7.8	138	13.9	27	2.8
School management, school staff training, staff development, teacher appraisal	174	5.7	45	4.5	67	7.0
Multicultural and equal opportunities	148	4.8	62	6.3	30	3.2
Special education needs	131	4.2	60	6.0	33	3.5
Health education, drugs, child abuse	120	3.9	36	3.6	39	4.1
Resources, libraries etc.	76	2.5	29	2.9	16	1.7
Other	406	12.3	132	13.3	119	12.5
Total	3,078	100	992	100	951	100
No. of advisers reporting	798		515		480	

Note: A, for all 3,078 working parties for which information was given.
Note: B, for only those 1,943 working parties described by the 532 advisers who had experience of
working parties, both with and without education officers on them.

Overall, it is perhaps surprising that the differences are not greater. Here
we are looking at LEAs where there are both officer and officer and
adviser working parties, but except in a small number of cases, the
authorities do not seem to have particularly channelled their
employees' work into adviser-type or officer-type work. We could be
seeing here an uneconomic overlap of work, but then it is also just
possible that we are seeing the implementation of an officer and adviser
integration policy.

Communication

We thus have the position, as seen in the case studies, of advisers generally working alone, even though the potential exists for them to work together in the provision of INSET, in inspection and indeed in the cross-curricular and managerial aspects of ordinary advisory work. Although it appears that collaboration has been encouraged in all three, it seems only to be really seen in the first two; ordinary advisory work in schools and classes remained very much an individual activity. In the advisers' office collaboration can also be encouraged through team meetings and working parties, and here the research showed a wide variety of practice. But teamwork and collaboration can also be encouraged in the normal day-to-day interactions of office work, and three areas of interest arise here: the methods of communicating between a static office and a mobile and distant workforce; the centrality of the advisers' office within the LEA; and, the value of open-plan offices.

Difficulties with the first area of communications, those between the office and the advisers 'in the field', arise because much of an adviser's day is spent away from the office. But the communication and administrative support systems devised for their offices seemed to have been designed for ever-present static personnel working a 9 to 5 office day. Given the cost of both the advisers and those they work with, and the importance of the work they do when carried out effectively, their office communication systems appeared highly unsuited and inadequate. Several heads reported spending hours trying to contact advisers before having to give up, and a good number of heads and teachers referred to the telephone messages they left being answered too late. Contacting advisers was not, apparently, a simple or easy matter, and only rarely was there evidence of it being improved by the provision of clear and comprehensive information to schools about who did what and how they might be readily contacted. New teachers were seen to be given full guides to the LEA, and many INSET officers and/or advisers and teachers' centres published annual and sometimes termly guides to forthcoming events, but how often was there a simple advisers' information sheet sent to school staff-rooms?

Advisers had problems, too. Schools are only open for a limited part of the advisers' day, and teachers are only accessible for a much smaller part if lessons are not to be interrupted. Advisers seemed to spend much valuable time simply in the process of just trying to contact teachers. Furthermore, in terms of written communication, many advisers reported having to use their cars as mobile offices, writing notes and letters at night or early in the morning, and frequently having to face a backlog of messages when at last they got back to the 'official' office.

With only two exceptions known to us, advisory services were not making use of the available information technology. With electronic mail, personal computers and effective word processors, none of these problems were really necessary. The new systems have the potential to keep advisers comfortably in contact with their offices and schools. They could improve advisers' accessibility without there being any need to interrupt sessions in schools or to require school secretaries to go chasing after them. Apart from the ability of this type of communication to improve the effectiveness of their work and their value to all concerned, it could also serve to keep them in closer contact with their chief adviser and other colleagues. It could have an impact on the team ethos. Inevitably there would be a financial cost, but one suspects that the introduction of such systems would soon pay for themselves in the improved effectiveness of the advisory service.

The second area of interest in this field concerns the physical centrality of the advisers' offices within the LEA. Advisers were asked in the questionnaire about where they worked from. Table 5.4 presents their responses, arranged in order from the most individualized to the most centralized; for the most part, the five categories are self-explanatory. Our interest lay in their impact upon advisory team communication.

Table 5.4: *The advisers' bases – where they work from*

Working base	No. of advisers	
	N	%
Home	13	1.2
Teachers' centre	62	5.7
Area education office	155	14.1
Central Advisers' Office separate from the main education department	113	10.3
Central Advisers' Office within the main education department	753	68.7
Total	1,096	100
(missing from 20)		

Advisers who work from home potentially suffer enormous communication problems. The difficulties for the adviser can include the day-to-day problems of managing to be in the right place at the right, time with the right papers, the medium-term difficulties of keeping one's work in line with that of the rest of the team, and the longer-term difficulties of keeping abreast of changing goals and working practices. There are also difficulties for the service manager and, to a great extent, one might suppose that team-building may be a pointless activity in these situations. In this context, working from home is only being considered from the communication and team-building point of view. There may well be other considerations which outweigh these aspects, and the introduction of home-based computers which are linked to the office could well assist in making this a more viable alternative to long distance commuting and noisy offices. Working from home need not, of course, be seen as an all or nothing solution – it is, after all, where most advisers work in the evenings and weekends!

Those working out of area offices (such that the advisory team is split into three or more small and geographically remote units) face potentially similar difficulties, although presumably to a reduced extent compared with those working from home. If the advisory service is split into several groups, it can present difficulties for its manager in maintaining any whole-team cohesion and in balancing the central and area demands upon the advisers. It also exposes them to undue absorption into the area education officer's concerns.

But another factor can also damage the team cohesion, and this also applies to those advisers based in teachers' centres and advisory offices any distance away from the main education department. Inevitably, if the advisory service is separated from the main education department, then the advisers' involvement in policy-making and the central running of the LEA is reduced.

For all these reasons, the chief advisers interviewed in the case studies were clear about their liking for advisory offices to be stationed in the middle of the education department, as the following comments demonstrate:

'It is easier for me [the chief adviser] to contact them personally.'

'It has made it easier to begin to establish a team ethos and to establish the new general role.'

'Schools have a single point of contact.'

'It makes communication much easier. It enhances the status of the advisory service to be working alongside other people. It makes them more visible. We are real people.'

'Advisers are more likely to be consulted by management before decisions are taken.'

'We are tied in tightly to education officers and administrators. This helps coordination and cooperation.'

'Advisers are centrally involved and therefore become part of the service.'

Given the importance of their offices being in the middle of what is going on, it is gratifying to see in Table 5.4 that over two-thirds of advisers are centrally placed. But having an office in the middle of the department is not all that counts. A number of the advisory services in the case-study LEAs were in open-plan offices, the third of our areas of interest. Although there were some criticisms of such offices – a lack of privacy, where no interview rooms were provided and the potential for too many interruptions from teachers and officers who would pop in too easily – the chief advisers seemed generally in favour:

'It eases possible tensions between education officers and advisers and makes for good communications. Ability to work this closely has worked particularly well in redeployment issues. I am totally for the centralization of the education department.'

'They [the advisers] sit between the various departments and sections [of the education department] and close to the executive.'

'Open-plan areas are good for communication.'

The only cautious note that was offered related to the danger of assuming too much of informal communication alone. One chief adviser stressed that one could not fully count on informal communication networks and formal systems still had to be devised. But there is also a note which should be raised here relating to the sentiment, raised above, that teachers can 'pop in' too easily. With the difficulties of communication between teachers and advisers, the encouragement of a point of contact might well seem sensible, and, perhaps greater accessibility should be sought, even at the expense of some office efficiency.

Knowing the rest of the team

The degree to which many advisers still worked in relative isolation from some of their colleagues was revealed by their answers to the question: 'Are there any advisers within your whole team who you rarely meet except at formal team meetings and on working parties?'

Of the 1,109 respondents, nearly three-quarters (815) said 'Yes', with only a little over a quarter replying that they actually met all members of the team outside formal meetings.

The interpretation of this result is not easy. At the one extreme, it could suggest that little communication and mixing occurred in advisory work, even though the advisers shared the same offices. At the other extreme, there are the obvious communication difficulties facing those with different subject or age range specialisms, who work out of distant area offices under different line managers. There are, however, some clues here since the numbers who said 'Yes' vary according to a range of factors which, for the most part, reject the geographic interpretation and favour the difficulties of communication arising from within the shared office. For instance, women advisers were significantly more likely to say 'Yes there were those in their team who they did not know' than their male colleagues (79 and 72 per cent respectively) and, in line with the previous analyses, the self-reported 'pure subject specialists' appeared to be more isolated (to be more likely not to know all the team) than their more generalist colleagues (pure subject specialists, 85 per cent 'Yes', compared with 67 per cent for 'subject specialist/phase/generalists' – see Chapter 3). Furthermore, for those on Soulbury salary scales, the higher the salary, the less likely they were not to know the whole team.

For all these factors there was still considerable variation between the LEAs' mean answers when there were ten or more respondents. Several LEAs, of which the majority but not all, were geographically large, had all their respondents saying there were some advisers in the team who they rarely met. In contrast, there were other LEAs where less than one in ten of their responding advisers said this, that is the vast majority of their team knew the whole team.

In pursuing this question, (and being aware that its meaning was fairly vague), we asked those who had answered that there were some that they did not meet to give an indication of how large this number actually was: was it just one or two colleagues who they rarely met, a quarter, half or even more than half of the team? The average response for those who had answered 'Yes' was that they rarely met between a quarter and a half of the advisers in their service. That is, very nearly three-quarters of all advisers rarely meet between a quarter and a half of their colleagues in their advisory teams, except in formal meetings and working parties. There would appear to be ample scope for extra measures to be brought in to enhance teamwork and collegiality. These figures would also appear to make good sense of one chief adviser's remark that he was even trying to increase the time they spent socializing together.

Communication and contributing to policy-making within the LEA

One important aspect of belonging to a team relates to the existence of the channels of communication necessary to facilitate the team members' ideas being heard and responded to. Communication channels encourage the feeling of being able to contribute to the planning and policy-making of that team, or indeed of that LEA. In the case studies the project encountered a range of experiences with some advisers feeling that they played an important role in the LEA's policy-making, while others felt totally ignored. An example of this can be seen in how LEAs handled their responses to the government's request for curriculum statements in the DES Circular 6.81. A small number commented that they had played no part in the formulation of their LEA's curriculum response; others described submitting papers which more senior advisers or officers then pieced together and edited, and yet others described playing a full role in this area with the writing of finished papers and the participation in consultation meetings, and so forth. The differences between the advisers' responses appeared to lie in how enthusiastically the LEA embraced (a) the idea of creating a curriculum policy statement, and (b) the idea of doing it through a process of consultation.

It seemed from the case studies that there were two main areas where advisers could contribute to the LEAs' policy-making, and that both these varied considerably. First, as we have seen, there was the area which concerned advisers' sector or subject specialism, and in this there were many who felt they made some form of contribution. The other area concerned the management and staffing of schools and education in general, aspects which advisers cover in their generalist roles and for which they were rarely allowed to make much contribution to LEA planning. Perhaps the most striking example here occurred where advisers were greatly involved in redeployment and early retirement, yet for all their work in implementing the LEA's policies in these areas they reported virtually no input to the decision-making processes that led to this work.

The questionnaire did not differentiate between the various areas in which the contributions could have been made, and advisers were simply asked whether they felt they had the opportunity to contribute towards the educational policy-making within their authority. Overall, 76 per cent felt they had this opportunity, a figure which was not significantly influenced by the advisers' age or sex. However, the 'pure subject specialists' were almost three times as likely to have said 'No' than the 'generalists' (34 and 12 per cent respectively – see Chapter 3), and for those on Soulbury salary scales, the higher the pay, the greater the feelings of being able to contribute. Again, the questionnaire reflected the case-study experience in reporting an enormous variation in feeling from one LEA to the next. In some LEAs (where the number of respondents was ten or greater) all the responding advisers felt they could contribute, whereas in others the average figure dropped well below 50 per cent.

However, being provided with an opportunity to contribute towards policy-making is not necessarily synonymous with the contributions being received, considered, channelled in the appropriate direction or even acted upon. Therefore, advisers were asked to consider their experiences across a range of possible communication channels and to indicate which of these channels, if any, were: (a) open to them in the expression of their ideas and opinions on LEA policy, and (b) effective. Their responses are shown in Table 5.5. Given all that has been said so far, it is perhaps surprising to see how positively advisers seem to regard these channels. The top five categories, all those that occur within an office structure, were all reported by the vast majority of advisers as being open for communicating their ideas, and indeed just over nine out of ten advisers believed team meetings to be open to them for channelling their ideas. Governors and Education (Sub)Committee meetings fared less well, but then they served to meet other purposes than adviser communication with the leadership.

Table 5.5:   *Advisers' reports of open and effective channels of communication*

| Channel of communication | Number and percentage of advisers reporting each channel to be: | | | |
| | Open | | Effective | |
	N	%	N	%
Participation in advisory team meetings	1,014	91.0	596	53.5
Written reports or documents	932	83.7	583	52.3
Discussions with chief adviser or equivalent	898	80.6	612	54.9
Discussions with immediate line manager	888	79.7	621	55.7
Discussions with education officers	885	79.4	617	55.4
Attendance at governors' meetings	450	40.4	220	19.7
Attendance at Education (Sub)Committee	272	24.4	136	12.2
Total no. of advisers responding (missing from 2)	1,114	479.9	1,114	303.7

The effectiveness of these channels of communication had a similar pattern to their openness but revealed a more cynical interpretation. The five main channels were once again grouped very closely, but only just over half the respondents regarded them as being effective. To be open does not guarantee their usefulness.

By adding together each adviser's responses across the seven potential channels in Table 5.5 it is possible to gain a different insight into what is going on. The average adviser reported 4.9 channels to be open, with men offering a significantly higher number than women (5.0 to 4.7 respectively). Surprisingly, although the number of reported open channels was found to increase markedly with Soulbury salary scales, it was found to decrease with age – it may be that older advisers are more disillusioned, cynical or even honest, or that being older they have been in the service longer and, perhaps, bring different interpretations to this question. As ever, the self-reported 'pure subject specialist' came out badly, with fewer channels being reported as open than for the 'specialist/phase/generalist' (4.4 to 5.1 respectively).

As usual in this area of communication and liaison, there was a considerable variation between LEAs, with some being reported as having almost twice as many 'open' channels than others. (The maximum and minimum average value for LEAs where the number of responding advisers was ten or greater were 6.0 and 3.2).

If the same treatment is applied to the effectiveness column, then a similar set of results emerges. The average adviser felt that just over half of the seven channels we offered were effective, with men being slightly, but still statistically significantly, more positive than women (3.6 to 3.2 effective channels per adviser). This time age was not influential, but the 'pure subject specialists' again reported themselves to be less well off than their more generalist colleagues, and Soulbury scales were once more influential, with those on higher scales reporting more channels as being effective. Differences between LEAs were still marked, with the maximum and minimum average values for LEAs, where the number of responding advisers was ten or greater, being 4.5 and 2.5 respectively. It would seem that not only does the number of channels vary but also their effectiveness at communicating the advisers' thoughts.

Contacts with advisers from other authorities

So far this chapter has concentrated on communication and teamwork within the advisers' own authorities. However, many authorities have only one of each 'type' of adviser, perhaps only one science adviser and only one language adviser, and thus in considering their professional development and how they managed to keep up to date with their subject or phase responsibilities, the project was interested in their various working and professional contacts with advisers from other authorities. The case studies demonstrated that most advisers had some such contacts and the Advisers survey clearly reinforced this point: 92 per cent of advisers reported external working contacts – see Table 5.6.

Table 5.6:   *Advisers' working contact with advisers from other authorities*

Context of working contact:	No. of advisers	
	N	%
Membership of regional bodies/committees	780	70.0
Membership of professional associations	688	61.8
Membership of subject associations	639	57.4
Joint INSET programmes	619	55.6
Membership of national bodies/committees	572	51.3
Working parties with neighbouring LEAs	482	43.3
Membership of examination boards	175	15.7
Total	1,114	355.1
(missing from 2)		

Of course, membership of a body gives little indication of how much contact there is, the type of work involved or even how beneficial that contact might be. However, the case studies were more informative and we were given many examples of the type of cross-LEA work being undertaken, and of how much it was appreciated. In the main, most of the national involvement seemed to be concerned with developing national courses, contributing to these courses, sitting on advisory training committees and working on various national curriculum or examination development projects. Unfortunately though, along with the descriptions, there also came reports of advisers currently being unable to find enough time and money to be able to continue with this kind of work. With the very obvious pressures within the LEA, it is easy to see how it becomes difficult to find the time to see people outside, and indeed there were reports of some LEAs offering a hostile attitude to this type of work. There was evidence, though, that regional work, that is where groups of LEAs work together, was not so badly affected.

The questionnaire missed one category that received a fair number of responses in the 'others' column. It seems that although we were seeking information about overt working contacts, advisers also wished to tell us of their informal contacts with friends and colleagues in other authorities. It would seem that these informal contacts can be just as useful as working contacts, and that they should be regarded as such.

When the individual advisers' responses across the seven activities were tallied, advisers had, on average, responded to 3.5 of the offered categories, with sex, age and Soulbury salary scale making *no* significant difference to this figure. For once, the self-reported 'pure subject specialists' came out of the analysis quite well, and this time it was the 'pure generalists' and the 'phase/generalists' who had significantly lesser amounts of external contact; this might have arisen because there is a broad range of professional subject associations for advisers, the project was unaware of any association that specifically catered for general adviser work and skills.

As before, there was considerable variation between LEAs with the better off having average figures (from ten or more responding advisers) of up to 5.2 out of the possible 7.0, and the less well off reaching as low as 2.2. Inspection of the individual LEA results suggests a strong geographical component in the differences – the metropolitan LEAs are smaller both in geographic terms and in the number of advisers they employ, and distances to neighbouring advisory offices are much smaller than is often the case with the shire counties. External working contact must be easier where distances are smaller. For all the time-consuming nature of these contacts, with very limited job mobility between LEAs, it would seem essential that it be maintained.

Conclusion

Within advisory services, levels of liaison and communication seem inextricably entwined with working practices, shortages of time and money, and a reluctance to give team and individual adviser development any real priority. To be fair, the demands upon advisers have a great immediacy about them, and the shortage of time and money are for the most part outside their individual control. It does not seem unreasonable therefore for advisers to bow to the pressures of the work for which they are being paid and there is often an undeniable element around advisory services of: 'let's get out there and do something rather than sit around talking about it!'

But is this fair to the adviser, and in the long term, is it cost-effective? As the previous chapters have demonstrated, much of current advisory work is still based upon a 1974 mould. But schools, teachers and LEAs appear to need a different set of skills – the emphasis has turned towards a cross-curricular approach, the facilitating of demand-led INSET and the necessity to develop and support school management practices which can accommodate and thrive under such innovations as teacher appraisal, local financial management, national curriculum and testing policies, and GCSE examinations.

All this appears to set up a conflict. Advisers are busier than ever, both time and money are short. But advisory work needs to evolve to meet the new demands, and in the one or two case studies where it was evident that some advisers were not involved in meeting these new demands, they became marginalized as the authorities' developments took place without these advisers' involvement. Over time their roles became less important and more isolated; the prospect of change appeared to become more difficult. It has been argued that there are two solutions which could help ease the advisory services' transition. The first is through the development of the team approach with improved communication both within the service and between the service and the rest of the education department. The second solution matches this and encourages more joint working – the bringing together of people's expertise to resolve problems and the broadening of advisers' individual expertise and remits over time. But both these solutions require time, the one thing the services are short of.

Against this background, the project looked at a range of facets to do with communication and teamwork, including the numbers of team meetings, working parties and ways advisers could express ideas to the authority, where the advisers' office was based, and the scope for working contact with advisers from outside the LEA. Both the case studies and surveys produced a wealth of information, and while it is difficult to know whether any individual result is good or bad, the variation in practice certainly suggested that some were better at it than others. One theme that appeared consistently in the first three of these facets was that pure subject advisers, women and those on lower Soulbury scales, all came out worse with less of each facet than other advisers. Over and above these structural differences, there were also consistent differences between LEAs. Some LEAs were more active in this area than others, and we might conclude that teamwork and cohesion have varying priorities from one authority to the next.

As well as looking at these more tangible aspects, the project also inquired about the respondents' feelings of team membership, about how many of their colleagues they did not really know and about whether they felt they were able to contribute to LEA decision-making. The results supported what we had been told in the case studies. The more team meetings that were held, and the more likely that the respondent was to know all the members of the team, then the greater the feelings of team membership. There are, however, two interesting caveats: involvement in working parties does not appear to increase feelings of team membership, and although knowing the whole team tends to increase team membership feelings, there were still 255 advisers, or roughly a quarter of the sample, who knew the whole team but still did not feel themselves a member of it. Feelings of team membership were also significantly and positively related to the feeling of being able to contribute to the LEA's decision-making.

Looking back across all these elements, they are in many ways just straightforward aspects of accepted good management practice. It comes as no surprise, therefore, to find there is a small but positive and significant statistical link between the feeling of belonging and the presence of a more hierarchical management structure as recorded in the previous chapter – as management structures are emphasized, and thus opportunities for better management encouraged, then the team spirit seems to benefit.

6 Advisers' Professional Development and Change – Entry to Departure

Introduction

Previous chapters have described advisers undertaking important work in helping schools, colleges and authorities adapt to new ways of thinking. The changes have been many, their requirements have gone to the heart of education and the lead times have often been monstrously short. In many cases the advisers have borne much of the brunt of this work, and both of the project's surveys have shown the focus of advisers' work to have changed since 1974. Not only has the vocabulary changed but we now have tasks and demands that were undreamt of when many of today's advisers were appointed. But change, in itself, need not be seen as a bad thing or even as a problem. It can act as a stimulus and as a growth point – a mechanism for enhancing both individual and institutional development, though, of course, not all changes are brought in for educational reasons and their goals may not always be perfectly apparent.

Two issues emerge as a result of all this emphasis on change. The first, which has already been partly addressed, concerns how the management of the service and the deployment of its teams and individuals have been adapted to meet these new demands. Questions about developing the ever more essential support and communication systems within the LEA have already been raised and will be returned to in Chapter 7 where, in concluding this report, the chief advisers' experiences of change and of trying to develop the advisory services will be considered.

The second issue concerns the individual adviser. It relates to the question of how someone coming straight from a position in school is

initially expected to achieve all that is asked of
Furthermore, it concerns how over time he/she is
develop with the job, given that both the job and th
changing constantly. Further difficulties arise in the
occur. For the most part, it appears that while re
skills, presenting extra work and undermining confidence, the
that are made to advisers' workloads are implemented without there
being any any real notion or even recognition of the job having
significantly changed. It could be the case that unless the significance of
the changes is recognized, the ensuing training needs will also go
unrecognized.

This chapter, therefore, concentrates on four elements: (1) the
selection criteria for appointing advisers; (2) induction and induction
training; (3) advisers' needs and the INSET they have experienced; and
(4) appraisal as part of the adviser's professional development and the
service's management of change.

But perhaps before entering into these areas, it is as well to consider
some details about advisers. The average adviser was 40 years old when
first appointed to an advisory job, and approximately four out of five
advisers entered the service straight from school or college posts, while
virtually all the others entered through intermediate or alternative
routes – advisory teachers, Schools Council work, research, education
officers, and so on. (Of those who are now in their second or third
adviser jobs, we may again assume that initially some four out of five of
them came straight out of school or college.) The research showed that
two-thirds of advisers were still in their first advisory post (see pp. 50 *et
seq.*) and that the annual entry to the profession in 1986 nearly reached
ten per cent of the total adviser population – probably the first time
since 1974. For all this, what has not been considered is what happens
to advisers – how many stay in-post until retirement, how many move
on to other jobs and what is the annual departure rate? To resolve these
questions the project asked chief advisers about the advisers who had
left their services between 1981 and 1986; their responses are given in
Table 6.1.

The results show that for those 375 advisers who left during this
period, approximately 70 per cent effectively stopped work when they
left advising, with retirement (in one form or another) accounting for
the largest individual group. For the majority of those appointed to the
advisory services the job they were joining at 40 was a 15–25 year
terminal post with only about one-third of them moving on to other
positions before leaving the service.

The results contain three other interesting elements. These 65
responding LEAs employed approximately 1,280 advisers at the time of

Table 6.1: *Chief advisers' reports of where their advisers went (1981–86)*

Cause of Leaving	N	%
Early retirement	145	38.7
Normal retirement	79	21.1
Transferred to other authorities' advisory services	56	14.9
Made redundant	23	6.1
Returned to teaching or lecturing	23	6.1
Appointed to HMI	16	4.3
Died	16	4.3
Joined education administration	5	1.3
Other*	12	3.2
Total no. of advisers leaving	375	100

* Other typically included ill-health, maternity leave and secondment and permanent attachment to national projects, TVEI, GRIST etc. Information provided by 65 LEAs.

the survey (see Table 2.1, p. 17). The results therefore show that only 4.3 per cent of all advisers had moved to other authorities over the five-year period. That is, assuming for the moment that this number had been constant since 1981 an inter-LEA transfer rate of less than one per cent per annum – a figure that, one suspects, is much lower than for most other professions, for education officers and particularly for teachers between schools or LEAs. The number of advisers joining the HMI is even smaller, just a quarter of one per cent per annum, and for entry into LEA administration, out of 1,280 advisers, just one person per year on average!

In the light of this level of job mobility, the case-study chief advisers were asked to comment on the career opportunities their services offered advisers. Many were quite blunt about this and used expressions like: 'very limited', 'cul-de-sac' and 'financial imprisonment'. One commented that: 'you have to be highly mobile to be a serious contender for promotion. You cannot afford to be selective geographically.' Another, however, phrased his reply as it might be seen from an LEA perspective:

> 'We want people to be in the job for a fair number of years – this is good for the LEA. It takes time to get to know the authority and the teachers. Career prospects are limited, but it is a very satisfying and interesting job.'

One cannot help but wonder whether apart from the LEA's self-interest in keeping advisers, there might also be a tendency to see advisory work as a vocation. As such, any element of advocating that the intrinsic rewards might override the difficulties might well be suggesting a passive acceptance of the problems. By disguising the problems in this way it could be making development more difficult.

A final point from the table relates to the whole adviser population. The 375 departures over the five-year period represented just under 30 per cent of the 1,280 advisers in the 65 responding authorities at the time of the survey. If departure rates were stable across time and across the country (an unfounded supposition), this would give an average departure rate of approximately 5–6 per cent per annum. Nationally this represents about 120 advisers per annum, a not unreasonable figure given the estimate of the full population being about 2,200 and the average age of entry being about 40. However, looking back to Table 3.5 (p. 54), if the departure rates had been constant over the years, then with such a rate of loss, 1985 and 1986 would have been the first years since 1974 when the services would have actually grown in absolute terms. If, on the other hand, the annual departure rates had been uneven, and 1981 and 1982 had perhaps taken a larger share than later years, then 1983 and 1984 may have just managed a slight increase as well.

However, far from being constant around England and Wales, the departure rates varied drastically from one authority to the next. Some authorities lost up to 50 per cent of their current complement of advisers between 1981 and 1986, whereas in others there were no departures at all. There is, of course, a problem with stability; LEAs may be storing up their future changes. One chief adviser commented that as virtually all his advisers were of a similar age, his authority's great changes were all coming up in about ten years time.

The selection criteria for the new intake

In the 1974 model of advisory services, the subject adviser's job was in many ways a straight extension of the head of department's role. Chief advisers described seeking subject and teaching expertise combined with a flair for innovation and the right personality. The large numbers of heads of department in schools thus offered a large pool of expertise from which new advisers could be selected. A similar position existed in the primary field where advising was again seen as an extension of existing skills and experiences, in this case, of headship qualities. Again, a fair pool of expertise existed to meet demand. In both cases, if advisory work was considered to be an extension of existing expertise, it is easy to understand, if not approve, the practice of providing little training – after all, authorities were appointing the almost complete adviser, and these advisers were appointed one day to take over a role and its responsibilities the next.

However, by the mid-1980s many advisers were having to learn to use different experiences and skills in order to accommodate education's changing needs. The project was therefore interested in any changes in what was being sought in the new intake and in whether the prospective pool had changed in any way.

The chief advisers' views

The case-study chief advisers expressed a range of views about what they looked for in prospective advisers. For all this range, however, they said that virtually they were primarily seeking a good and broad record in education which included senior management experience in school (or college for FE appointments). On their own, head of department experience and years of teaching were now unlikely to be sufficient. One chief adviser described himself as having a holistic but not a rigid view – he believed there was a wide range of qualities which could be put together in different ways and proportions – he just looked for the best combination.

Four respondents commented on how their criteria had changed over the last ten years. One chief adviser suggested that he was now more aware of what he was looking for and that he now wanted good educationists rather than subject specialists. Another commented that broad views were now what he sought first; an interest in the whole age range second; and only then came the subject specialist criteria. The third considered that advisers' salaries had improved over the years and consequently he was now looking for more seniority. The fourth, however, said there had been no change, but then he had been seeking generalists all along.

The headteachers' views

Perhaps not surprisingly, headteachers saw advisers in a different and more task-oriented light than the chief advisers and the necessary characteristics they described mainly concentrated on the advisers' work in schools. However, even with this focus, their emphasis on subject-specialism and classroom expertise was less pronounced than had been expected. Only a third of the 47 interviewed overtly stressed subject specialism as a prime requirement, with almost as many emphasizing the importance of a wide range of experiences whether that be experience with different ages, responsibilities, schools or LEAs! For many, the right personality was also an important ingredient.

To stress individual elements, however, gives a false picture since many heads offered several essential criteria as they recognized that the posts require a range of skills:

'Advisers need to have a wide base of education and not just a subject specialism. They need knowledge of curriculum development across the board. They also need expertise in helping people with their careers, particularly when career prospects are bleak. The ability to stimulate people in their own subject is important but counselling is equally important.'

'Advisers should have very solid experience of teaching – i.e. head of department. They should have exhibited flair, imagination, intellectual ability and an ability to communicate an excitement to sceptics. They should have recent relevant experience, otherwise they lose touch with reality.'

'I do not know what the full role of the adviser is: we are not told. It is therefore difficult to say what qualities they should have. They should be someone with primary headship and successful teaching experience. Someone who is prepared to listen and give constructive advice.'

One headteacher raised the important question of whether LEAs had really made their minds up about what they wanted:

'LEAs have to decide whether they want advisers, administrators or inspectors. This affects recruitment – are they looking for all these things? I think that advisers are going to be increasingly involved in assessment and appraisal – they must have the qualities to do it. More women are needed, for the teaching profession generally career prospects are bleak enough for women.'

Heads of department's views

During the case studies 44 secondary heads of department were interviewed about advisers. Their replies very much centred on two aspects: they felt advisers should have both a good deal of teaching experience and subject strength. The majority of these heads of department were stressing criteria which were basically concerned with those areas in which they came into contact with advisers – they sought strength in advisers in class and school work. However, as we have noted in Chapter 4, heads of department frequently and justifiably complained that they knew little else of advisers' work. The following comments express their common feeling about teaching experience:

His [*sic*]teaching skills must be seen to be respected – an ideas person is not enough. I would not want to be appraised by someone who has not taught recently.'

'You need someone who can relate to people well. Someone who is seen to be doing a worthwhile job. Someone who has done what you have done and gone through the career structure of the school. A good teacher, not someone who has escaped the classroom.'

Three other selection criteria were raised by this group, but far less frequently. They felt advisers should have (a) a realistic and practical view of teachers' workloads; (b) the right personality – they should be approachable, enthusiastic, innovative and energetic; and (c) an extensive range of management skills.

The heads of department were further asked whether they wanted to become advisers. Of the 44, four vacillated, just over half said, 'No' and just under a third 'Yes'. The most common reason for saying 'No' was a desire not to leave the classroom and teaching, but this was also echoed by several of those who had said 'Yes' and then qualified their answers by saying they would only like to do so if there was a teaching component in the job. Three heads of department volunteered an attraction towards advisory teacher instead of adviser posts, but there was some confusion among others as to exactly what were the differences between advisory teachers and advisers – a confusion that is most understandable! One head of department's comment raises the significant issue of the discrepancy between the pay scales:

'I would like to be an advisory teacher, but this depends upon the salary. I think advisory teachers should be better paid. Advisers appear to be overpaid for what they actually do in schools.'

A final point to emerge from their comments was that many of them felt advisers should not be allowed to stay away from the classroom for too long. Several suggested that advisers should hold three-year second-ments from teaching posts while a number of others thought five years more appropriate. One argued that it was 'too easy for someone to get into the advisory service and just stay there' – again, their comments reflect a single focus on the conventional school and classroom elements of the advisers' jobs.

Retrospective adviser memories

The other side of the coin must relate to the advisers' own experiences and memories: for instance, what were they seeking when they applied to join the service? Surprisingly, there was often bemusement when we asked this question – almost as if, in an interview about advisers and advisory work, the question of why you wanted to become one was either totally irrelevant or totally unconnected with the actual job. Once past this stage, we encountered a wide variety of responses, with at least a quarter of those interviewed claiming to have more or less fallen into the job without a great deal of thought. For one reason or another, they were looking for a new job and advisory work was just one of a number of possibilities – it just happened to be the possibility that became real.

A further quarter or so described how they were teaching in school and had not given advisory work much thought when they were approached, usually by an adviser, and either left with the suggestion that they might like advisory work and why not look around for a post, or more directly had been told that there was a specific post coming up and that they should apply for it.

A third quarter described how they were already half out of the classroom (as advisory teachers, INSET providers, secondees to the advisory service, and so on) when the issue of becoming a full adviser arose. For many of them, taking up the full role was just a small but natural progression from where they were, and indeed quite a number must already have been doing a virtually full adviser job for their new posts were either created around them or they were given the job without having to apply.

With three-quarters of our case-study sample arriving at their posts via the routes above, this only left a small group of advisers who were positively seeking advisory work. Typically, having been heads of department, they wanted promotion but did not want to leave their subject and/or did not want to become deputy heads. One adviser described this position:

'I had become a head of department in a secondary school. The next move to deputy head was all to do with measuring hem lines of girls' skirts and I wanted a curriculum job!'

Although the examples given have so far related to secondary posts, similar paths were described by primary advisers, except that the 'jump', whether planned or by chance, tended to arrive after one or more headship posts.

Overall, the advisers' recollections of why they wanted the job suggested little in the way of well-thought-out plans and career structures. For a small number there was a particular aspect about advisory work that attracted them, for others it was an extension (or recognition) of what they were already doing. For many it was simply a job they could do at a time when they were looking.

Matching the perspectives

Three different perspectives about adviser appointment criteria have been considered and juxtaposed with the recollections of those in-post. Several issues arise both within and between these perspectives. First, even within the small case-study sample, where the number of new appointments will have been fairly limited, it appears that there has been a shift in the selection criteria over the past few years. Thought is being given to different characteristics which in many cases appear to give more emphasis to generalist and educationist skills than to pure subject expertise. It looks as if the new set of skills more closely matches the current demands described by advisers. However, whether this change came about because individual chief advisers became more experienced the longer they were in-post and the more appointments they made, or whether it was because there was a growing recognition of the new demands is uncertain.

What is certain, however, is that this trend was less well recognized in schools where the more traditional aspects were still strongly emphasized. Heads of department, and to a lesser extent headteachers, still basically drew on just one aspect of advisers' work, their teaching work in schools – they wanted advisers to be strong in the areas that concerned them, they wanted advisers to have vast teaching experience and very sound subject knowledge. This is hardly surprising, however, since we saw few attempts to provide schools with an accurate and useful picture of what advisers actually do nowadays. The traditional view is still assumed to be extant and the broader, more generalist areas of advisers' work are basically unrecognized. Had we wished to present a comprehensive picture of the necessary criteria, it would have been better, perhaps, if we had sought recommendations from the full range of those with whom advisers work: in effect, the selection issues should also have been put to advisory teachers, officers and members. What is being suggested therefore is that each individual 'client' group feels as if it has a special right to the advisers' time and expertise: views on adviser appointment criteria thus reflect the constituent groups' individual needs rather than the overall balance.

Quite how advisers are expected to cope with this conflict of interests and the inevitable dissatisfaction that results is difficult to see, though one answer must lie with advisory services being more informative about the full range of demands that they set out to meet. But there is another important issue here. If advisers' work has moved away from reflecting subject and classroom needs, is there a large enough pool of that type of expertise naturally available in schools? The advisers' recollections of what motivated them to apply for adviser jobs suggests that for many teachers the prospect of entering advisory work and the possibility of gaining pre-advisory experience have never been seriously considered. We also know that LEAs have so far spent little effort on consciously increasing either the size of the pool from which potential applicants are eventually chosen or the level of residual expertise within it. This may have been fine when advisers were wanted with skills which were extensions of existing jobs. It cannot be so good when they need a broader range of skills.

Induction procedures and training

The case for providing new advisers with induction training often seemed stronger than the practice that was described to the research. Three advisers used the back page of the questionnaire to comment on induction training, and in so doing, gave a useful insight to the problem.

'An adviser's job is a strange one and it should not be assumed that senior management work in schools prepares people in any significant way for a job with completely different demands:
1   a new work pattern, no set holidays, bells, periods, etc.
2   a new strange work environment (office);
3   wider but less significant influence;
4   jack of all trades, master of none;
5   would it matter to children if advisers disappeared?;
6   no significant feedback;
7   no loyalty to an institution;
8   involvement as an authority officer, redeployment, unions, etc.
9   sense of inadequacy to 'control' education development, cf. the head of school who can shape education for 1,000 pupils – few advisers can shape education for an authority;
10   increasing contact with political masters;
11   continuing struggle to keep abreast of all educational developments from primary to tertiary – you can be asked to help everywhere and anywhere.'

I have been in the post seven months. I don't really understand what is expected of me. It is totally different from what I had expected. I have no way of judging whether I am having any effect, making progress, etc. I feel overwhelmed by the number and range of different skills which I am expected to employ without any training. Although I am not unhappy, I find it impossible to answer the two most common questions asked by teacher friends: 1) What do you do? 2) Are you enjoying the job?'

'Coming from industry, I had little understanding of the educational system or jargon. I had no induction and learnt to work in areas I had no experience of – e.g. course design, INSET, discipline, adult education and youth service. The pressure of this nearly killed me. The authority, having appointed me, had not thought out how to use my industrial and work-related expertise.'

These and many of the ideas expressed elsewhere in the questionnaires suggest that starting a new job is a serious step which requires the two elements of induction and induction training. The first element affects all those who start work in a new place or system: they need to know who is who and how the various idiosyncratic operations are handled in the new system. The detail may be mundane, but attempting to work without this information is difficult, frustrating and inefficient. The second element concerns the necessary professional training needed to allow someone with one set of skills successfully to take on a job which requires another. While both elements encourage the new entrant to become effective as soon as possible in practice, however, they often seemed indistinguishable since the first element was often effectively all of what was offered.

Amounts and types of induction training given and received

Advisers were asked whether they had received 'any significant induction training' during their first year of advising; 82 per cent of the 1,116 respondents answered 'No'. In contrast, when chief advisers were asked whether they had an induction programme for advisers, 75 per cent replied positively. Part of this discrepancy must lie with language used: advisers were asked to respond only to 'significant' induction experienced, whereas chief advisers could count any induction programme in existence. A further difference would have arisen because chief advisers were describing the position at the time of the survey, while advisers were describing the situation when they were appointed, and this could be some years ago.

Overall, the amount of 'significant' induction training appears to have increased in recent years; 27 per cent of first-time advisers appointed in the five years up to the survey reported receiving significant induction training in contrast to only 12 per cent of those appointed more than five years before (significant at the p<0.0001 level). However, even if the 27 per cent figure has further increased since the survey, it could still be considerably short of the ideal figure of 100 per cent of all new entrants – even then, we were not asking whether 'significant' meant satisfactory.

The answers given by chief advisers and advisers allow us to look at the types of provision to which they were referring, and this information is given in Table 6.2a and b. Table 6.2a gives the main elements of the induction programmes described by 56 chief advisers – a further three had no programmes and nine failed to answer this question.

Many of these programmes can be seen to rely upon various schemes for new advisers to work alongside their more experienced colleagues coupled with short residential induction courses (as basically provided by NAIEA and CAID). Examples given by chief advisers in the case studies describe the typical types of programme where they existed – three of the case-study chief advisers (excluding the first example) described having no induction programme at all:

> 'No, there is no induction programme. I try to break them in gently and to arrange some kind of induction, but they are really thrown in at the deep end.'

> 'We have a one-year induction programme. New advisers have a mentor for the first year and for the first half-term they are attached to their area adviser. They are also sent on carefully selected courses (e.g. COSMOS, DES). Before starting, they attend a three-day pre-service awareness course in county hall, – i.e. they are shown the ropes.'

> 'It is a team effort. There is no specific blueprint, but there is a definite programme. The new adviser is eased in and encouraged to listen. Their load is lightened in the first year and they do not run their own INSET in this time, instead, they work with other colleagues. During the first two weeks they go out for a day with every adviser. They will also see me and the senior adviser frequently during this period.'

> 'Our induction programme has evolved – it is a list of activities and things they should know, it is the responsibility of an area inspector. Every member of the team takes the newcomer out for a day – visiting is essential. Courses? We sent newcomers on NAIEA's new advisers' course and any other courses they ask for. They have considerable freedom in the first year. They also attend the new heads' course.'

Table 6.2a: *LEA induction programmes, as described by 56 chief advisers*

Types of induction	Chief Advisers %*
Accompanied visits; attachment to senior colleagues; observation of interviews, etc.	71.2
Residential courses and workshops, NAIEA, CAID, CCDU	47.0
LEA-based tours; explanatory talks and observation; introductions to heads and department heads	36.5
LEA-based induction courses, e.g. talks on role, etc.	12.8
Team meetings, meetings with other advisers, the previous incumbent, other new colleagues, etc., informal discussions with colleagues	10.5
Regular review meeting with chief adviser and/or senior education officer	7.3
Total no. of responses	96
Total no. of respondents	56

* Percentages based on number of respondents.

Table 6.2b: *Significant elements of induction training, as experienced by 219 advisers*

Types of induction	Advisers %*
Accompanied visits; attachment to senior colleagues; observation of interviews, etc.	58.5
Residential courses and workshops, NAIEA, CAID, CCDU	75.5
LEA-based tours; explanatory talks and observation; introductions to heads and department heads;	13.2
LEA-based induction courses, e.g. talks on role etc.	22.6
Team meetings, meetings with other advisers, the previous incumbent, other new colleagues, etc., informal discussions with colleagues	5.7
Regular review meeting with chief adviser and/or senior education officer	5.7
Total no. of responses	406
Total no. of respondents	219

* Percentages based on number of respondents. (897 advisers reported having received no significant induction training and therefore did not respond to this question.)

Given the imprecise nature of the language in this field, and that we do not know how long individual LEA programmes have been in existence, it is difficult to interpret fully the information. But for all this, the position still does not seem good. Over 80 per cent of advisers recorded receiving no significant induction and, in the next section, many advisers described this lack of induction training as presenting major difficulties in their first year. It seems reasonable to suggest that in many LEAs adviser induction training is probably insufficient to enable advisers to fulfil their roles efficiently and effectively.

Advisers' in-service needs and in-service training experience

As with induction training, ordinary in-service training for advisers attracted a good number of free comments on the Advisers questionnaire:

'I am passionate about initial and continuing training for advisers – you need to have time at the beginning to sort yourself out when schools are appraising you, and then later on, you need to stop 'giving out' and 'take in' for a bit, to have a breathing-space and meet others, etc.'

'Too many people – officers and elected members – appear to believe that advisers have no further need of training once in-post. If the team structure is vague and imprecise, there is no way that either the specific or general needs of the individual and team can be precisely identified and met. There are so many initiatives from all sides that it is essential to have time to study them and to weigh up their implications and methods of implementation. There should be an element of further training built into advisers' job descriptions and provision allowed in their workloads – the funding and provision of such training should be regarded as a priority for the central authorities.'

'I consider that there is insufficient time given to professional training for advisers. It is generally regarded as swanning by the admin-officers.'

Difficulties encountered by advisers

As the three previous comments suggest, adviser training should be a priority, but there is often a difficulty in translating into action the need for adviser in-service training, and its provision rarely ended up receiving very much priority. Part of the difficulty occurs in translating a general need into specific provision – advisers' needs change over time and tasks. The project asked advisers to list the main difficulties they encountered (a) in their first year and then (b) in their subsequent years of advising. The two distributions are presented in Table 6.3.

Table 6.3: *The difficulties advisers report encountering (a) in their first year, and (b), in their subsequent years of advising*

Nature of difficulty:	1st year		Subsequently	
	N	%*	N	%*
Balancing roles and establishing priorities – lack of guidance of what role should be	452	43.9	317	33.7
Difficulties with schools/lack of experience of the 'other' sectors	279	27.1	71	7.5
Not knowing the ways of County Hall and its staff	270	26.2	10	1.1
Getting used to advisory work, its autonomy and the personal difficulties of being an adviser	220	21.4	62	6.6
There being too much of the appropriate type of work to do/too much work	195	18.9	518	55.0
Lack of induction training	192	18.6	1	0.1
Lack of team ethos/lack of advisory service management/lack of management structure	187	18.2	149	15.8
Insufficient resources/not enough money to do the job/not enough time to do the job	150	14.6	524	55.6
Personal (time) management/learning to manage my work	127	12.3	101	10.7
Difficult and awkward communication with officers and members/red-tape/political interference	108	10.5	115	12.2
Too much administration and trivia to do	62	6.0	156	16.6
Learning new skills, committee work/negotiating skills, difficulties with providing and planning INSET	50	4.9	31	3.3
Coming to grips with changing and proliferating roles, greater LEA emphasis and involvement in initiatives	45	4.4	154	16.3
Coping with the diversity of tasks	42	4.1	88	9.3
Other difficulties	38	3.7	24	2.5
Total no. of responses	2,417		2,321	
Total no. of respondents	1,030	234.8	942	246.3

* Percentages based on number of respondents.

As might have been anticipated, the most frequently reported difficulties in the advisers' first year related directly or indirectly to a lack of induction and induction training, and of the four most frequently stated difficulties, all but the problem of balancing the role diminished drastically after the first year. As advisers stay in post longer, other issues then begin to come to the fore, and the way they change from the first to the subsequent years' column is indicative of how the job develops over time. Thus one in five advisers complained of too much work in their first year, and this then rose to more than one in two after the first year. Similarly, the lack of resources and time only really raises its head as a serious issue after the first year.

Matching INSET needs to provision

While some of the reported difficulties can be directly translated into in-service training programmes, a number are not so susceptible to improvement through the provision of in-service training alone. Furthermore, in a number of cases, what the advisers were saying really reflected upon LEA management and resource policies rather than specific training needs.

In trying to identify the advisers' in-service needs the project asked chief advisers to record what they thought were the advisers' main INSET needs. We also asked advisers to record (a) those areas they would most like to receive help with (assuming it were available), and (b) the content area of any INSET they had found to be beneficial, excluding anything in their main subject specialism. The three sets of responses are presented in Table 6.4.

The chief advisers' views are listed in order of the frequency with which they were given. Obviously there is a strong emphasis on broadening the advisers' range of knowledge and experience, increasing their management skills and generally updating their knowledge of many of the initiatives and other changes. In a way, this list reflects past appointment policies – even though they were not asked to exclude it, most chief advisers gave little or no emphasis to main subject training, just on everything else advisers are expected to do, but then many advisers were appointed on the assumption that they were already expert in the subject requirements of the job.

If, on the grounds that it is not an INSET provision *per se*, we ignore the advisers' requests for more resources, then their rank ordering more or less follows that of the chief advisers with the biggest difference being in the first two categories where the advisers put more emphasis on gaining management skills than learning about other possible aspects that their role could encompass.

Table 6.4: (A) Chief advisers' views on advisers' INSET needs, (B) advisers' self-reported INSET needs and (C) advisers' views on the most significant types of INSET received

Type of INSET:	A CA view of need %*	B Adviser view of need %*	C Adviser view of INSET %*
Acquisition of knowledge of other phases and specialisms (beyond one's own); finance, education law, IT	48.4	22.0	11.0
Management skills; leadership skills; the management of change and the management of time	46.9	37.7	22.9
General updating on curricular and other issues, central initiatives, DES reports, research, etc.	39.1	13.0	10.4
Counselling; interpersonal, group and communication skills; stress management	28.1	17.8	14.8
Appraisal techniques; school self-evaluation and review	28.1	13.6	9.7
Inspection; evaluating; observing and supporting teachers; report writing	26.6	9.2	4.7
Cross-curricular work: multicultural education; PSE; mainstream SEN; industry links; equal opportunities, etc.	18.7	9.7	14.7
Help on the role of the adviser	17.2	7.1	4.8
Courses: CAID, NAIEA, DES, higher degree, etc.	12.5	0.8	24.7
Institutional management; staffing; special procedures	4.7	7.0	14.7
Interviewing techniques; recruitment; selection	4.7	4.9	5.7
Time for research, reflection, reading	4.7	4.2	
INSET planning, funding, running and evaluating	3.1	7.8	5.8
Assessment procedures; GCSE, etc.	3.1	4.1	6.0
Discussions with colleagues, meetings, combined visiting and working, teamwork	3.1	1.2	18.8
(More advisers, more resources, more advisory teachers, more help with administration, more clerical support, more resource centres)		27.2	
Curriculum management and development	1.6	7.6	11.0
Other	4.7	0.8	1.2
Total no. of responses	189	1,770	1,395
Total no. of respondents	64	905	770

* percentages based on number of respondents.

Unfortunately, the significant INSET experienced by advisers did not seem to match their reported needs to any great extent (and, once again, this ignores the fact that experiencing 'significant' INSET does not necessarily imply 'satisfactory' INSET). Obviously more research needs to be done to explore the relationships between difficulties and needs and between needs and INSET programmes and content.

Work is also needed to explore the ways of providing INSET which are best at actually meeting these needs. In this respect, the responses to these questions, as given in Table 6.4, can only advance our thinking a certain amount, for there is a degree of confusion between content and methods of provision. Nearly a quarter of responding advisers thought that CAID (Wakefield LEA), NAIEA and DES (COSMOS) courses were beneficial, but we do not know what elements were good, nor how many advisers went on these courses and found them to be poor (although in the case of the CAID courses a body of evaluative information is being built up with the help of those attending them). Similarly, nearly a fifth of advisers rated working and communicating with colleagues to be beneficial and listed it under the INSET heading. They were suggesting that certain elements of working practice, and certain team activities, can be among the most useful ways of learning about the work they do.

Appraisal for professional development and enabling change

In recent years there have been many developments in education, and advisers' roles have had to change to meet these new challenges. But for those carrying out these very individual and at times isolated jobs, change is not easy. In the management of this change there is obviously an enhanced role for INSET, for joint working practices and for team meetings, but even together these cannot be successful without additional support. None of the three can particularly identify the individual's position in the change process (for instance, so that next year's targets can be planned in respect of last year's results), none can readily offer the feedback, response and support that are essential when change is imposed on someone carrying out an isolated, stressful and changing job, and none can really identify the *individual's* particular INSET needs. Furthermore, none of them can effectively offer the necessary continuous evaluation of the whole service that is essential if the service is to change in a coordinated and coherent fashion. What seems to be needed, and what has been tried in a number of authorities, is appraisal.

As with INSET, appraisal is a time-consuming, costly and as yet, an imprecise art with a very flexible use of language. For instance, when talking to the case-study chief advisers, it appeared under the various names of 'appraisal', 'evaluation' and even 'review'. Patently, the appraisal of advisers is a field fully worthy of its own study and it is appreciated that it has only been given a brief consideration here – furthermore, the authors can only comment on what others regard as its potential since they have only attempted to describe rather than evaluate its practice. As such little space has been afforded here to the mechanics of the appraisal process itself; however a number of chief advisers have offered us detailed and most useful thinking on this subject and some of their comments are given in Appendix Table A6.1 (p. 215). Throughout this section appraisal is only considered in the light of its being part of a wider management package – appraisal on its own is thought unlikely to achieve anything.

The developmental state of adviser appraisal

The project asked both chief advisers and advisers about the current state of their authority's appraisal systems. Of the 68 responding chief advisers, 30 described their LEAs as having no discernible appraisal system, and this included four that had had systems which were now no longer operational. Twenty-two of these 30 LEAs without systems were, however, planning some form of appraisal programme for future use. However, 38 LEAS (68 per cent) had active systems, but of these, only 25 reported operating anything more than an 'informal' programme of interviews and discussions. Most of the more formal systems employed regular interviews with some form of pre-completed materials. It appears that, for most of these LEAs, appraisal consisted of discussing last year's performance and agreeing next year's targets – perhaps, helping to implement one part of a new policy in all schools, achieving some particular aspect with a group, or setting up a new series of INSET sessions for teachers.

There were no accounts of appraisal being related to any form of contractual or pecuniary rewards, though apparently until quite recently one LEA had offered financial incentives based on the completion of agreed targets. There was scant comment on how either the goals or criteria had been determined, nor of how evidence was collected, apart from the adviser recording it him/herself. One chief adviser, however, leant heavily on reports from heads and members and backed up this with occasional observation of work-in-progress. As with the accounts of INSET, there was a considerable imprecision in the language, and this made more detailed analysis difficult.

A number of more direct questions were addressed to advisers. Just over 20 per cent of the 1,077 responding advisers reported that they had been formally appraised, with no significant differences being shown by sex, age or type of work done between appraised and non-appraised advisers. Advisers' pay, however, was found to be related to a small but significant extent, such that those on higher Soulbury scales were more likely to have been appraised. One possible reason for this would be that, in some LEAs, only some of the advisers had been appraised, and indeed this was supported by the data which showed the advisers' responses to have a high-level internal inconsistency within LEAs. Fifty-four LEAs had ten or more advisers responding to this question. Of these LEAs, 21 had all 'No' answers, one had an all 'Yes' answer, and 32 had a spread of 'Yes' and 'No'. It is, of course, possible for appraisal systems to be at different stages of development – implementation of full systems will take some years.

Advisers were therefore asked to say what they felt was the developmental state of appraisal within their service. The responses for the whole sample are given in Table 6.5 and clearly show that appraisal was at various states of development ranging from 'not yet on the agenda' to 'fully operational'. As with the previous question, within LEAs the advisers' responses showed considerable variation – typically several advisers would say appraisal was at the discussion stage, while others would say it was at the trial stage and one or two would suggest it was fully operational. There may, of course, be good reasons why this was the case in some LEAs, for instance, not all advisers may have been involved in its development. The alternative explanation is that internal communication within the service was such that few would be very sure about what was actually happening.

Table 6.5: *The state of appraisal in your authority**

No. of advisers answering each option:	N	%
1 Fully operational	108	10.2
2 Undergoing a trial phase	154	14.6
3 At the discussion stage	246	23.3
4 Considered but rejected	11	1.0
5 Discussions planned	110	10.4
6 Not yet on the agenda	231	21.9
7 Don't know	197	18.6
Total no. of respondents	1,057	100
(59 advisers failed to answer the question)		

* Advisers were asked to describe the state of appraisal in their authority as they knew it then – i.e. we were interested in what they knew rather than the details of the appraisal scheme.

If advisers had said that appraisal in their LEA was at the discussion stage or more advanced, they were then asked about their involvement in its implementation – the very principles of appraisal would surely advocate the full involvement of all those concerned during its development and implementation. Their responses, which are shown in Appendix Table A6.2 (p. 217), demonstrated that only 16 per cent of those in authorities with some form of appraisal system had had a system implemented around them without their involvement. Fifty per cent of advisers in such authorities had been involved in discussions within their own service, and a fifth involved in discussions which included other personnel from the authority. However, given that the respondents could reply to more than one of these options, it is apparent that participation was far from universal, and if we look at deeper levels of involvement, we see that although 56 per cent of chief advisers reported operating an appraisal system, only six per cent of advisers considered they had been involved in its formulation.

Advisers' views on the benefits and problems of appraisal

Apart from considering the state of the art, the project was also interested in advisers' perceptions of the benefits and problems accruing from appraisal. Table 6.6 shows advisers' thoughts on the individual and team benefits of appraisal, with 1,037 advisers offering an average of just over two 'open-ended' benefits for each. The benefits are listed in order of the frequency with which they were given in respect of the individual adviser; and quite clearly, the ideas of self-improvement, a clarification of objectives and goals and the opportunity to be more effective are all stated. Overall, the benefits seem no less emphasized for the team, although there are differing weightings. Interestingly, we see that appraisal is thought to help develop and strengthen the team concept, as well as offering an opportunity for the team to become more effective. Appraisal would appear to have had a 'good press'.

With 20 per cent of advisers having experienced appraisal, it was possible to compare the answers of those who had been appraised with those who had not. In the main, the distribution of both groups' responses followed similar patterns – the reality was not that different from the expectation. However, those who had yet to be appraised tended to give more emphasis to the potential end-products of appraisal . As a group, they gave greater emphasis to appraisal clarifying roles, aiding professional development, improving effectiveness

Table 6.6:   *The main benefits of adviser appraisal for (a) the adviser and (b) the team*

Main Benefits:	Adviser		Team	
	N	%*	N	%*
I The opportunity for self and team improvement with feedback helping to point in the right direction and highlight weaknesses	618	59.6	307	29.7
2 The clarification and ordering or re-ordering of advisers' objectives, goals and responsibilities	579	55.8	380	36.8
3 The opportunity to be more effective through reflection, discussion and feedback	474	45.7	418	40.5
4 Improved self-awareness, feelings of job satisfaction, self-worth and security	292	28.2	151	14.6
5 The opportunity to discuss one's work with senior management, to share concerns and learn more about what others in the team do and think	211	20.3	207	20.1
6 The development and strengthening the team concept and letting others know what the team does	83	8.0	587	56.9
7 Opportunity for careers advice and development	75	7.2	17	1.6
8 Provides overall picture of the service and allows for its review	23	2.2	100	9.7
Other	56	5.4	46	4.5
Total no. of responses	2,411		2,213	
Total no. of respondents to each question	1,037	232.4	1,032	214.4

* percentages based on the number of respondents.

through the provision of feedback on performance, enhancing efficiency, identifying strengths and rectifying weaknesses. In contrast, those who had experienced appraisal tended to give more emphasis to the process benefits: they gave more weight to the opportunity appraisal presented for reflection, for the time it allowed with the chief adviser and for the opportunity to express views. Thus although the differences between the two groups were slight, with members from both groups giving both process and product responses, there is a suggestion that those who had experienced appraisal were perhaps more realistic than their colleagues in that they aimed for a more achievable set of goals.

The advisers' thoughts on the problems of appraisal are shown in Table 6.7 and basically fall into four categories: (1) the difficulties of setting up a system – i.e. of finding the right appraiser, finding the right system, finding time to do it, and actually implementing the chosen system; (2) difficulties with appraisal once implemented, – i.e. not liking some of the changes it may bring about; (3) problems making sure that the process has sufficient follow-up; and (4) problems with advisers who might be reluctant to participate fully.

Table 6.7:   The main problems of adviser appraisal

Main Problems	N	%*
The appraiser: finding, selecting and training the right appraiser; someone with good experience of advisory work and with the necessary appraisal skills and sensitivity.	568	29.7
Developing an acceptable appraisal system: this includes (a) finding a consensus about aims and roles of advisory work; (b) determining the agreed appraisal criteria to meet those aims; (c) overcoming the organizational problems in the advisory service that make appraisal difficult to operate	508	26.5
Time: this includes the lack of time: (a) to prepare for it; (b) time to do it; and (c) to implement any resulting suggestions	327	17.1
Problems of living with appraisal: e.g. reduced autonomy and confidence; increased workload, anxiety and frustration	162	8.5
Problems with follow-up: a lack of real commitment to it; the inability of senior management to respond to what comes out; difficulties in affecting change	141	7.4
Problems with advisers: e.g. an unwillingness to comply, a suspicion of motives and some difficult personalities	93	4.9
Problems of implementation: difficulties implementing the system, especially when there is no one person with the remit, responsibility or authority to do it	37	1.9
Sundry	76	4.0
Total no. problems offered	1,912	100

* Percentage based on the number of respondents (data provided by 1,022 respondents, 94 missing)

Once again, it was useful to split 'appraised' and 'non-appraised' advisers and to consider their answers separately. Although they gave basically similar answers, the 'non-appraised' gave more attention to the implementation and theoretical problems of appraisal – they concentrated more on the difficulties of setting up the system, of choosing the method to be used, of how to overcome unwillingness in advisers, of finding a suitable appraiser and of determining the criteria to be used. They also appeared to be slightly more apprehensive about the outcome and gave more emphasis to some of the possible negative outcomes, for instance, a reduced autonomy, an increased workload (from having to appraise) and an increase in anxiety and frustration, the latter as a result of appraisal offering improvements to the individual which would rarely be fulfilled.

It might be anticipated that implementation problems would 'disappear' once a system was implemented, and indeed the 'appraised' gave much less attention to this aspect. In place they gave slightly more emphasis to the day-to-day organizational problems of operating and living with appraisal – that is, to the difficulties of getting people together, to the manner of carrying it out, and to the discomfort of being appraised by someone they worked closely with and/or of working closely with someone who had appraised them. However it should be recalled that in offering these difficulties, these were also the advisers who were describing the benefits in the previous question.

Appraisal would appear to offer a very powerful technique for helping this group of professionals to change and develop; but returning to the chief advisers' comments in the appendix, clearly also adviser appraisal needs a great deal of thought before it can reach its goals.

Conclusion – facing change with forgotten needs

In many ways, this chapter could be seen to draw to a rather depressing conclusion. While this research has highlighted the rate of change advisers have been subjected to, it is clear that for many of them there is little evidence of coordinated management to help them individually to cope with their own change. Equally, many services appear to have little in the way of systematic programmes of evaluation and review to help them build and maintain a coherent approach to meeting their clients' ever changing needs. However, the evidence is not at all depressing since the examples we see of these techniques being tried, and the willingness of advisers, officers and others now to consider these matters, suggests that a growing number of people are concerned to tackle the problems and seek solutions. It is possible that we are observing the beginnings of a period of remediation and development rather than the continuation of a period of stagnation.

With this in mind, advisers were asked what changes they thought would be necessary in their jobs to help them meet new demands in education over the next five years. Thus from a period of change they were being asked to hypothesize the needs of the next round of unknown changes. Their 'pre-Great Education Reform Bill' responses are given in Table 6.8. Advisers clearly stated that their roles would need to be rationalized, their workloads reduced and their work better supported. They also looked towards better management, an increase in teamwork and a move towards accepting the generalist role (less than three per cent advocated greater subject specialization). Built into their recommendations were requests for adviser appraisal and more INSET. All these aspects do, of course, cost money, either directly in the shape of more personnel and resources, or indirectly in the need to spend time off the advisory task in order to manage or be managed. Obviously a part of the greater management emphasis will need to promote these priorities, for there must be a political will as well as a management need. In this chapter we have considered how these needs have been met over the past few years, and it would seem that overall it has taken some time for LEAs to realize the extent of the changes that have occurred and the need for fresh measures to be taken. In many respects, it seems that a number of those with influence in the LEAs still regard advising as a job that can be done for many years by a competent teacher without any specialist training. In suggesting that LEAs should look at issues, such as increasing the pool of experience from which advisers can be appointed, improving and increasing induction training, providing more and better targeted in-service training and using or introducing adviser appraisal, the project is considering techniques that might not only allow advisers to catch up with the last set of changes, but also to face the next. We are also suggesting that advisory work is a separate and different professional role from teaching and headship and that to consider it as anything more than a very vague extension of these areas is to do it no justice whatsoever. Once this difference is accepted, then what is being asked for makes more sense.

But the management approaches discussed here are not at their best when used in isolation, and those who have contributed to this project have consistently advocated the necessity for their complementary use. In essence, there are a number of approaches that can be used to complement each other and to help the adviser and the service to be more effective and less overworked, but rarely did the research encounter reports of these approaches being used on a broad front. Advisory services are faced with having to respond to a great many demands at once, and this pressure would seem to be pushing coherent management planning to a lower priority.

Table 6.8: *The changes advisers felt would be necessary for the future*

Nature of change	N	%*
More advisers and advisory teachers; a reduction in the workload, more time	377	41.1
A rationalization of adviser work; a reduction in peripheral work, some internal reorganization	304	33.1
More resources, better accommodation, more clerical support and proper IT	278	30.3
Better teamwork, better management, more meetings, more adviser appraisal	174	19.0
A greater generalist role; more involvement in appointments and governing bodies; a wider spread of age coverage; more involvement with industry	143	15.6
More management and provision (but not necessarily the giving) of teacher INSET	138	15.0
More INSET for advisers, more briefing papers	136	14.8
Less school-based work, more management of advisory teachers, closer interaction with officers and members, increase in executive and policy-making function	106	11.5
More time for reading and reflection, more secondments	67	7.3
More school-based work, closer relationship with schools	62	6.8
More inspection work	52	5.7
More cross-curricular developments	52	5.7
More involvement in teacher appraisal	41	4.5
Greater streamlining of role towards subject specialization	26	2.8
Other	93	10.1
Total no. of responses	2,049	

* Percentages based on number of respondents (918).

In conclusion it is useful to consider the advisers' thoughts on the question of what were the best ways of providing the help needed for their jobs. Their replies, as shown in Table 6.9, showed that in-service training receives a very high priority – both as an external provision and as part of a team's normal working practice, for instance in joint working, team cooperation, meetings and seminars. Again, resources appear as necessary, and although little time is given to them here, their necessity is not to be underrated. Surprisingly, for all the benefits advisers offered for adviser appraisal, it appears to have a low priority on their list of ways of providing help – perhaps, it should really be viewed as just one method in the whole management basket?

Table 6.9: *The best ways of providing help for advisers, as reported by advisers*

Method of providing help	N	%*
More (adviser) INSET sessions, meetings, seminars, conferences, problem-solving sessions, workshops, etc.	299	34.8
More national or regional courses, CAID, HMI/DES, etc.	274	31.9
More opportunity to see experienced advisers at work; more joint working, cooperation, teamwork and sharing of expertise	157	18.3
More advisers, advisory teachers, less workload	122	14.2
More secondment, study visits and opportunities to work in and/or visit other LEAs	113	13.2
More time, opportunities and machinery for meetings, better contact within the advisory service	91	10.6
More resources, time, money	91	10.6
Better management of the service; better profile	86	10.0
More in-house courses and INSET sessions	81	9.4
Better premises; more office equipment; more IT; better clerical support	76	8.8
More liaison and contact with HMI, DES, MSC, university and HE lecturers, consultants and people from industry	70	8.1
More information of how advisers work elsewhere	65	7.6
More time for research, reading and reflection	31	3.6
A national centre for advisers	21	2.4
The use of (adviser) appraisal, peer appraisal, self-appraisal	16	1.9
Other	52	6.0
Total no. of responses	1,645	

(Information provided by 859 respondents – 257 omitted this question.)

* Percentage based on the number of respondents.

7 Conclusion: Change and the Future

Introduction

Some 45 years ago section 77(3) of the Education Act 1944 gave the then 154 local education authorities the right to inspect their schools and, by implication, the right to set up and fund the necessary services. A small number of inspection and advisory services already existed and this legislation paved the way for all LEAs to provide them. However, at that time there were a number of very small LEAs, and in some cases their operations were effectively divided further into smaller units: the take-up of this opportunity to develop advisory or inspectorate services was very varied. Some LEAs built on past practice and maintained inspectorates, some built up advisory services and others employed a number of 'organizers', though the latter were employed mainly in the practical subjects. Some LEAs apparently did very little at all.

In the 1960s, with growing emphasis on curriculum development across all areas of the curriculum, the limitations of the organizer's role became apparent, and they were mostly phased out to be replaced by advisers. While the new role was still designed to concentrate on the single subject and to be self-motivating and independent, there was now a greater focus on the curriculum and on its management.

With the local government reorganizations of both 1968 and 1974, the minimum size of the authorities and, for the first time, of their advisory services, became significant issues. Most of the smaller LEAs disappeared, and for the first time, many authorities gained a reasonable establishment of advisers. In building their new teams these LEAs, and their chief advisers where appointed, had their first opportunity to try to balance the expertise across subjects and between subject and 'general' (pastoral and school management) issues and, at the same time, to build a management structure into the service. Although the

104 new LEAs reached very different solutions, it is really from this time that we see the beginnings of the services as we now know them.

However, it is difficult to determine from what was reported at the time where the actual balance lay between subject and general work, and equally, just how much emphasis was ever given to managing the services. Many of the interviews conducted as part of this research suggested that during the mid-1970s there was a recognizable '1974' model for the adviser's role where the subject role predominated, with an adviser being appointed for each of the main secondary subjects. This approach had a strong secondary bias, and although LEAs typically had more children in primary than secondary school, there were proportionately far fewer advisory staff allocated to this age group.

These new services were allowed little time to settle before further changes struck. Immediately after the LEA reorganization and the raising of the school leaving age, at a time when many in education were still trying to come to terms with the implications of the growth in comprehensive schooling, a financial crisis arose which was promptly followed by falling rolls and a serious political questioning of the state education system. For advisers, there were three further issues which added uncertainty. According to Fiske (1977), following a round of pay comparability bargaining, the employers had doubts about the advisers' roles; a growing number of vacant posts were left unfilled as a result of financial constraint; and an attack from the President of the Headteachers' Association suggested that there should be drastic and permanent reductions in the number of advisers. The late 1970s was not a settled or confident time for the advisory services.

With the Auld Report in 1976, and the Green Paper and the Taylor Report, in 1977, there were overt indications that LEAs and their advisory services ought to have specific roles, but since the three reports each promoted a different role (evaluation, curriculum development and pastoral), this still left advisers with an uncertain balance and a range of demands that would be difficult to meet with only limited resources. With the 1980s came even more innovations, but the intended role of the advisory services in their implementation still seemed to vary from the marginal to the essential. One cause for this presumably arose because very little was actually known about advisers and what they could do. For instance, in the early 1980s the numbers of advisers employed by the LEAs was not known with any certainty, there were nomenclature problems of knowing who was and who was not an adviser, and when questions about subject coverage arose, little was known about how many advisers could devote how much of their time to any particular subject in each authority. Nor indeed was it known how much time they should spend on each subject and, in this respect, the new cross-curricular emphases posed even more difficulties. It was apparent that although the advisory services were being leant upon more and more to support the implementation of various innovations in schools, and also to support the schools through this period of enormous change, there was little knowledge about the whole field.

There was, however, an increasing call at this time for the advisory services to reshape themselves so as to be able to meet these new demands, but identifying the essential features of change was difficult when little information was known about how different advisory services operated – especially when it is likely that the degree of variation, in practice, was not fully recognized. In response to the need for this information, this research project was set up to study the roles, management and practices of LEA advisory services throughout England and Wales. Working in close collaboration with LEA advisers, officers, the NAIEA and HMI, and using both case-study and national survey approaches, the project's aims included:

(1) describing the various roles and responsibilities of advisers;
(2) studying the working practices of advisers and identifying the skills, knowledge and strategies used in their jobs;
(3) describing LEA policies on the role of the advisory service and on the recruitment of advisers;
(4) exploring the views of those the advisers work with; and
(5) identifying the advisers' in-service training needs.

Perhaps not surprisingly, virtually all those we talked with emphasized the changing nature of what we were looking at, and although they liked their jobs and worked extremely conscientiously over long hours, they were aware that the changes had disorganized what they did and were often unsettling. The NFER LEA Advisers Project was therefore as much a study of how change was being handled as a description of the LEAs' advisory services – and indeed, such was the pace of change, that the goalposts moved while the research was in progress. New legislation is bringing in financial delegation to schools, the National Curriculum and testing at just about the same time as new governing bodies will assume increased responsibilities. Inevitably these changes will have a fundamental impact on the role of the adviser, and to reflect this our concluding chapter has been shaped to give as much space to the issues of change as to summarizing the previous chapters. 'We start with a summary of Chapters 2–6 before turning to look at how chief advisers and advisers contemplated the mechanics of change. The chapter concludes by considering the possible impact of the new legislation – but that, of course, must be somewhat tentative.

A summary of the advisory service position

Coming to grips with change

Throughout the case studies we were constantly reminded that today's LEA advisory services are very much the product of past events; specifically, it was felt they had been influenced by a stream of recent legislative and attitudinal changes. Seven pieces of recent legislation were frequently cited as being significant: the raising of the school-leaving age (ROSLA); the Education Acts of 1976, 1979, 1980, 1981 and 1986; and, of course, the 1988 Education Reform Bill. Over and above this legislative battery, seven other major influences were identified: (1) the 1974 reorganization of local authorities; (2) the 1974 model or perception of how an advisory service should be; (3) the oil crisis and its ensuing financial recession; (4) falling rolls; (5) a perceived growing dissatisfaction with state education and the apparently consequent demand for greater accountability; (6) increasing central government intervention in the curriculum and teaching matters; and (7) the government's targeting of money to encourage LEAs to take on advisory teachers for certain initiatives.

Since each LEA was at a different starting-point when it responded in its own way to the demands of change, it is not surprising that at the time of the research their practices and philosophies varied. However, the scale of this variation was enormous and affected the advisers' involvement in the core issues of advisory work, for example, in monitoring, in pastoral support and in the LEAs' appointments procedures. The differences were such that it would appear that, at least at the time of the research, instead of there being one basic role with variations in practice, there were several models of what advisers and their services should be and should do, and that these were virtually incompatible with one another.

The project asked CEOs and chief advisers about their advisory services' policies and roles. Their responses suggested that there were four significant factors underlying most of what we saw in the advisory services: (1) the degree of centrality of the advisory service in the authority's policy-making and activities; (2) the way the service was required to face (i.e. towards the LEA or the teachers); (3) the importance of institutional monitoring and evaluation in the LEA; and (4) the local outcome of the subject specialist vs the subject generalist debate. As the research progressed two further factors emerged: (5) the degree of priority afforded the management of the advisory service, and (6) the degree of recognition that advisory work was a specialist task which required specialist training.

All these six factors can be seen as representing attitudes which will determine how the advisory service operates and is received. Of prime importance is the fact that they are all associated with how the decision-making part of the authority values, and thus promotes and identifies with the various functions of their advisers. Obviously there are exceptions to this pattern and we would not wish to suggest that it applied exactly in all cases. However, the six factors do seem to provide a most useful way of perceiving what is happening within an authority and are discernible throughout all the data collected by the project.

A national perspective on the people and the posts

Part of this project's brief was to provide a national database on LEA advisers and advisory services, and to do this two surveys were carried out: one was sent to all those in charge of advisory services, and the other to all LEA advisers and inspectors (referred to as advisers in this book). Unfortunately, it was often difficult to work out who, if anyone, was actually in charge of an LEA's advisory service, especially as quite often there was no Chief Adviser post per se. Equally, with the various terminological problems, it was often just as difficult to define who was, and was not, an adviser. Neither title nor job description was in itself sufficient for this task, and salary definitions fared no better. Around the country the research identified officers who advised, advisers who administrated, advisory teachers who had the right to inspect, advisers and inspectors who did not have the right to inspect, and advisory teachers who were paid more than advisers. As with Bolam, Smith and Canter (1978), the final decision as to who to include in the two research survey populations had to be made locally in each authority. The research clearly showed that at the national level there was a problem with advisory service titles, and although this would be reduced at the local level since all those concerned would only have to relate to the one pattern of titles, there does seem to be a case for the rationalization of the nomenclature in order to improve the effectiveness of the adviser–client relationship. This is not, however, a case for rationalizing adviser tasks and job descriptions.

The chief adviser

The 68 chief advisers who responded to the first questionnaire had been in-post on average for just over six years, but there was a wide spread with four having been in-post since 1974, in contrast to a number who had been appointed much more recently. Although the evidence is difficult to interpret, more LEAs now appear to be establishing chief adviser posts. However, having someone with the title or responsibility of 'chief adviser' does not guarantee that sufficient time was allocated to managing the service; even where there was someone indentifiably in charge, the amount of time they were left to manage the service and to carry out other chief adviser functions was often well under 50 per cent and, in one case, as low as ten per cent.

The research identified three types of chief adviser post in terms of titles and job descriptions:

(1) the 'Chief Adviser', whose main role was to be the chief adviser;

(2) the 'officer/chief adviser', whose title was likely to emphasize the officer element and for whom the chief adviser role was just one of several busy roles; and,

(3) the 'adviser/chief adviser', whose main role was to work as an adviser with the chief adviser elements having to be fitted in to an already over-full day.

The average amount of time chief advisers in each of these groups could spend on advisory service issues varied considerably. The first group, the Chief Advisers, reported that approximately 80 per cent of their time was left free, while the officer group had, on average, just less than 60 per cent left. The advising chief advisers, the third group, were left with the conflict of having to undertake a complete adviser job as well as taking on the broader advisory service management issues, and these they often had to do with few resources and little, if any, extra status. Even allowing for the very real shortages of money, it was surprising how many authorities declined to create a full-time chief adviser (or equivalent) post.

Chief advisers with 'Chief Adviser' titles were more likely to have adviser backgrounds than those with 'officer' titles, who were more likely to have officer backgrounds. There was little overlap between the backgrounds of the two groups, and few advisers had any experience, of officer work. The majority of chief advisers had secondary experience and nearly half had some experience of FHE. However, only one in seven had worked in the primary sector and only one was initially trained in this sector.

The LEA adviser

Approximately three-quarters of the respondents to the advisers survey were called 'Advisers', and one-quarter 'Inspectors': nearly 30 per cent also carried the term 'General', and one in five occupied some form of senior position. Two-thirds of those responding were still in their first appointment and, for many advisers, the first advisory post was also the last. Advisers were on average appointed to their first advisory post at approximately 40 years of age, with some variation between different LEAs which suggested that appointment age might be pay-related, that is the higher the pay offered, the higher the likely appointment age. Eighty per cent of advisers came straight from school posts, and 20 per cent came from advisory teacher, research, Schools Council and other such jobs. Two-thirds of the respondents had middle-management experience in schools and/or colleges, and about half of these (i.e. about a third of all respondents) also had senior management experience. Surprisingly, over a third of all senior positions were taken by advisers in their first advisory post, and indeed five of the 68 responding chief advisers had taken up their new roles straight from headship posts. Equal opportunities? Men outnumbered women by three to one in the advisory services, with the proportion of women being highest in the primary phase roles (40 per cent) and lowest in the youth and FE roles (15 per cent).

The number of appointments made each year has varied greatly since 1974. In that year, there were probably more than 250 new appointments in total; but from 1976 to 1979 this figure dropped to no more than about 50 per year. Since approximately 40 per cent of all new advisory appointments were made from within the appointing LEA, we can see that in some years there would have been very little inter-LEA adviser movement, and inter-LEA movement by established advisers occurs in only about one per cent of the total workforce per annum – i.e. only about 20 established advisers each year. Since about 1982 the number of appointments per annum has increased and, more recently, it has regained the 1974 value.

All our research showed that advisers and their chief worked very long hours and that many found great satisfaction in their work. They all reported being involved in an enormous range of activities. However, with the variation in practice and terminology between LEAs, it seemed that each and all of these activities could be done under any or all of the three well-known advisory 'hats', that is by advisers working in their subject-specialist, generalist or phase roles – see Table 3.11 (p. 66). Only one in six advisers described themselves as having a pure subject-specialist role – five out of six reported having generalist and/or phase roles, as well as or instead of subject roles. Since most advisers had some form of general role, the use of the term 'General' appeared anachronistic when applied to only 30 per cent of them, and there seemed little reason to support its continued and inconsistent use.

Although the research did not specifically study advisory teachers, the survey data showed that there were almost as many advisory teachers as advisers, and that while adviser numbers were increasing, those of the advisory teachers were fast outpacing them. The extremely rapid growth in advisory teacher numbers, much of which has been in response to a succession of government initiatives, was often described as having been achieved in a none-too-coherent fashion. There is considerable concern over the advisory teachers' management and about how short-term secondments will actually help their longer-term career needs.

The average LEA had just under 20 advisers, and just over 18 advisory teachers, with an area- or LEA-wide remit. In terms of adviser 'density', this represented approximately 0.35 advisers per 1,000 pupils (5–16 years), 5.9 advisers per 1,000 teachers and 97 advisers per 1,000 schools. There were substantial differences between LEAs, with the most 'generous' LEA having proportionately more than four times as many advisers per teacher as the least generous. The range in advisory-teacher 'density' between LEAs was greater still. Advisory teachers did not, however, appear to be used to compensate for low adviser numbers, indeed, quite often, the more generous the adviser density, the more generous was the advisory teacher density. Metropolitan boroughs tended to have higher adviser densities than county LEAs, though this may have arisen for a variety of reasons including demography, politics and those of their size, since smaller LEAs tended to have proportionately more advisory staff.

Curriculum and subject coverage

In looking at the advisory service's subject coverage, four main features arose. First, advisers tended to cover more than one subject area, with extra subjects being gained over time by a process akin to that of accretion – new subjects seemed to be added on top of old ones and it seemed rare for the old responsibilities to be taken away. Secondly, different subjects commanded different status. The core subjects were more often listed as the advisers' main or title subjects, while foundation and other subjects were more apparent as the advisers' second or 'other' subjects. Thirdly, where new subjects appeared as advisers' second or 'other' subjects, this was more likely to reflect their more recent introduction into the LEA's responsibilities without sufficient funding rather than their lack of status. In this respect, some of these new subject areas more often appeared as advisory teacher rather than adviser subjects.

Finally, in looking at the advisory teachers' subjects, overall there was a much smaller range of subjects and, in the main, these covered either the new initiatives or those of the more conventional subjects which were receiving enhanced attention. Advisory teachers have so far suffered less accretion, though there was some evidence of it beginning to occur with some advisory teachers seeking broader and possibly more satisfying remits at the same time as some LEAs were finding other tasks to give them.

It appeared that advisory teachers were mainly being used in those curriculum areas which were being given special emphasis and funding. They appeared to offer the funding agency a responsive, cheap and flexible workforce, though the flexibility was achieved through changing the personnel involved: as the initiatives change, one group of advisory teachers can be 'returned' to the classroom and another group brought out. It may well be that this style of management is inimical to the individual advisory teacher's best career interests and that in the light of experience, some better form of management may be brought in. There was ample evidence that the return to the classroom was not easy, especially because of changed perceptions and enormously expanded horizons. The way that advisory teachers have been brought in has enormous ramifications for advisers. These involve the issues of advisory service flexibility and subject coverage, and indeed the advisers' role vis-à-vis the time spent in classrooms. This element of their work has already been considerably reduced since 1974.

Advisory service management

The advisory service's organization and its position within the authority can also be viewed as being influenced or even determined by the same set of attitudes that determined the characteristics of its members and the work they were given to do. In this light, the research looked at the role of the chief adviser in terms of his or her lines of communication and the emphasis on managing advisers.

The project analysed the chief advisers' descriptions of their structures. By using three elements – the amount of chief adviser (time) available to the service, the use of a middle-management tier and the chief adviser's membership of the LEA's senior management team – a ten-part scale was devised. This categorized a range of structures starting with the most hierarchical systems, employing highly structured middle-management strategies, and ending with the basic 'flatarchy' or 'pancake' approach where there was no real management and little prospect of any adviser joining in the authority's decision-making process. While the majority of services offered something better than the 'flatarchy', by no means all went for the fully hierarchical systems. Size was found to be a factor in the degree of hierarchy adopted, but it was not the only factor: attitudes, philosophies and the difficulties of change still seemed to play important roles.

Advisers reported favouring the higher levels of management and it was only when they experienced them that the concept of the 'team' was described as actually working. These tighter structures were not completely without their detractors though, and a small number of advisers described them as constraining their work or voiced concerns about communication problems within them. Many of the advisers' comments were, however, conditioned by what they had become used to. In one LEA a gradual relaxation of management practice attracted criticism as the advisers felt the relaxed system frustrated their work and that decisions took too long to be made. In another LEA a recent increase in the service's organization to a position about equivalent with the one just described was this time most warmly welcomed.

Headteachers and heads of departments tended to show little concern about the advisory services' management structures, but clearly focused upon the advisers' roles and deployment as they saw and interacted with them. Both groups almost universally stressed that there was a lack of advisers and adviser time. They argued that this led to poor long-term planning and deployment within the service and that for the individual adviser it presented difficulties with access, the appropriate balancing of tasks and of completing jobs properly. Heads of department raised two further points. First, many suggested that advisers ought to spend more time with them in the school and classroom, and less time in County Hall. Their second point, however, made some allowances here as many added that they really did not know what advisers did when they were not in schools and giving INSET, so it was difficult for them to comment objectively. It generally seemed as if each of the advisers' client groups knew little of what the advisers did when not with them and thus perceived themselves to be the advisers' main *raison d'être*. Such misapprehensions can hardly lead to effective interactions between advisers and their clients. It was notable, however, that virtually all the criticisms were addressed to the lack of resources rather than the basic adviser role or the individuals concerned and that in most cases heads expressed considerable support for advisers. Heads were also asked about how they and their staff might help the advisory service in its work. A number had clearly given little thought to this question in the past, but others offered three possible roles:

(1) in the provision of curriculum and/or management expertise;

(2) by offering an enhanced facilitating, introductory and administrative role to improve adviser visits; and,

(3) by using the headteachers' 'voice' within the authority they could offer a 'political' role.

One or two heads commented that although the staff had skills to offer, it was the LEA rather than the school that had apparently not wanted or bothered to use them, and in this respect there was a feeling of resentment and of missed opportunities. Where the head and staff were involved in helping and supporting the authority's advisory work, this was liked and seemed to be regarded as being good both for individuals and for the LEA.

Adviser work patterns and team membership

The research also noted aspects of how advisers went about their work, and the evidence consistently showed the majority to have a very individualistic style of working. However, this was often described as being incompatible with meeting the current demands made upon advisory services, and it was also felt to inhibit the process of change – by its very nature, it restricts the communication, teamwork and support thought necessary to promote change.

A number of advisers have recognized these problems and have suggested alternative ways of working which give more emphasis to a rationalization of their work and an increase in teamwork and directed leadership. Similarly, there were chief advisers who talked of wanting to help advisers change their working practices and headteachers who said they would welcome greater team ethos. A few heads also argued that they wanted advisers to have broader remits and broader experience; elements that they felt would more closely reflect the schools' working practices and needs. It was generally accepted that the encouragement of teamwork and improved communication within the service would help equip advisers and their services with the skills, experiences and work practices that were argued to be appropriate to meeting today's demands.

Many chief advisers expressed a wish for greater commonality and teamwork among their advisers, but moves to create such ideals were patently not easy. For instance, over a quarter of advisers reported that they did not feel they belonged to a team. Interestingly, the advisers' working practices appeared to affect this. More 'inspectors' than 'advisers' acknowledged feelings of team membership, as did more non-subject specialists than subject specialists. Most LEAs contained a mix of responses with some but not all of their advisers feeling they belonged to teams. However, the proportion varied from LEA to LEA with some demonstrating much stronger overall team membership than others. Overall, the issue with change was not one of recognizing the way forward so much as of how to get there. It appears that although collaboration has been encouraged in many areas of adviser work, it is only just beginning to be seen as a viable practice. Many advisers still regard inspection as (one of) their only team activities: ordinary advisory work in schools and classes remained very much an individual activity.

Teamwork can also be encouraged through team meetings and the normal day-to-day interactions of the office, but the advisers' very mobile work make this difficult. Furthermore, the research showed that the communication and administrative support systems provided for the advisory services tended to be unsuited and inadequate both for their team needs and for carrying out their work in an effective fashion. Contacting advisers during the day was difficult for everybody. (Moreover, only rarely was there evidence of it being improved for schools by the provision of clear and comprehensive information about who did what and how they might be readily contacted.) Advisers also had difficulties contacting teachers at convenient times. In general, there seemed much reluctance to embrace the information technology available which could ease many of these problems, improve the quality and effectiveness of advisers' work and possibly improve within-team communication, too.

Relationships within advisory teams were reported to be more difficult with area-based services. Similarly, communication problems with the LEA's administrative and executive arm were exacerbated where advisers were based in offices away from the main education department – a facet which inevitably reduced their involvement in policy-making and the central running of the LEA. Many chief advisers were very clear about their liking for advisers to be accommodated in the middle of the education department, but then not all services have chief advisers and there are problems beyond these of geography. For instance, communication also seemed affected by the individual's role: subject specialists appeared to be more isolated (to be more likely not to know all the team) than their generalist colleagues, and the higher the adviser's salary, the more likely he/she was to know the whole team. As before, the advisers' answers to how many of the team they knew also varied by LEA, with some, but by no means all, of the differences being attributable to geographic considerations.

It would appear, then, that much of current advisory work is still based upon this single-subject lone worker 1974 model, which neither seems appropriate to meeting the new demands from schools and LEAs nor helpful in managing the transition to another style. Advisers reported being busier than ever, but if their work is to evolve to meet these new demands, and if it is to avoid the pitfalls of their being marginalized within the LEA, an occurrence that was observed where developments took place without the advisers' involvement, then time is going to need to be spent on learning new approaches and on communicating them to the clients.

There appear to be at least three elements which could help ease the advisory services' transition. The first involves the development of the team approach with improved communication both within the service, and between the service and the rest of the education department. The second encourages more joint working – the acceptance of one person saying 'I don't know', and the subsequent bringing together of several people's expertise to resolve problems, a process which should help broaden advisers' individual expertise but which will need a clear management emphasis over time. The third must lie, initially at least, with an enhancement of adviser in-service training, and in the longer term with a detailed review of adviser recruitment and induction training.

Adviser recruitment, training and appraisal

We were told by a number of those we interviewed that in terms of recruitment, under the 1974 model the adviser's role was seen as an extension of that of the head of department, and therefore the features that made excellent heads of department would apply to advisers. Times have changed and the chief advisers we interviewed were now looking for a wider range of skills to reflect the type of work they now saw being done in the service. While headteachers also followed this line, heads of department still tended to give more emphasis to teaching skills but then that is the role in which they mainly saw advisers.

Apart from looking at the selection criteria, we were also interested in knowing why people wanted to become advisers. Surprisingly, only a quarter of the advisers interviewed had positively sought advisory work with the rest, more or less, falling into it. But then in talking to current heads of department there was a certain confusion over the precise nature of adviser work, and further confusion between the roles and salaries of advisers and advisory teachers. Such difficulties cannot help in the provision of the necessary pool of applicants.

In looking to get the best people to apply for adviser posts it would seem that there is need to: (a) give those in schools and colleges a better understanding of the nature of the role; (b) reduce the gap between the schools' perceptions of what advisers should be doing and the reality of the situation, and (c) encourage the establishment of a pool of pre-advisory experience.

Once the adviser is appointed, there is a strong argument for providing both the induction information that allows him/her to get to know the people and the system, and the induction training that allows him/her to get to know the principles of the job. Over the years the amount of induction offered appears to have been very small, and while it may be improving, only 30 per cent of post-1981 appointees claimed to have received any. There would appear to be considerable scope for improvement.

The need for advisers to have adequate and appropriate in-service training was equally expressed most strongly by many of those we met during the research. Unfortunately, the provision over the past few years does not appear particularly to have met the advisers' needs, but there are several basic problems here which involve all those concerned:

(1)   INSET is perceived as taking advisers away from their work. Since they are under considerable pressure, they find difficulty finding the time, even though the INSET may be designed to help them manage their time more effectively.

(2)   INSET costs money and, along with other aspects of the advisory services, this has not always been given the (political) priority it perhaps deserves.

(3)   Effective adviser INSET requires the management to have a clear set of goals and roles for advisers, and an effective method of identifying individual and group needs with respect to their goals and roles.

(4)   Adviser INSET is a relatively new art, and as yet there is little firm consensus over what forms of INSET best meet specific needs.

Here the first three problems are, of course, management issues and like the others before them, they are tied up with attitudes. The fourth problem, however, requires the pooling of experience and perhaps a little research. British educational advisory services are sufficiently small to deny us a large adviser INSET industry, but similar INSET is being provided abroad and in other professions – perhaps, it is time for a central initiative to draw all the skills together?

Back within the local authority, there was a growing recognition of the role that appraisal could play here in targeting the appropriate INSET and, more generally, in helping with change. However, although many LEAs were actively considering it or had actually implemented it, only about one in five advisers had any real experience of it in operation. Here two very firm caveats were offered us. First, its implementation was argued to need very careful thinking to get right. Secondly, it was felt that it could only achieve anything if it was just part of, and supported by, a broader package of positive management approaches. Appraisal on its own was not regarded as a viable proposition. Appraisal with the necessary backup was, however, considered to be a most powerful management tool in the development of the service.

Looking back over this brief review of the research, it is evident that the LEA advisory services were in a state of flux. There have been enormous changes in education over the last few years and the advisory services would have had to move very fast to have been able to keep pace with them all. Unfortunately, however, many advisory services were not in a position to handle this sort of evolution – there were awkward structures, resources were short and the political climate was often far from sympathetic to such change. Some advisory services, however, have come through this period well. They have managed to keep pace with the changes and to develop their services coherently in line with the changing demands from schools, colleges and the LEA itself. Others have been slower to see what was happening or have found themselves unable to promote the necessary changes over and above adding and pruning in a reactive and *ad hoc* fashion. They often found a lack of financial and political will to support them, many had no effective leadership and on top of that, their new structures of 1974 actually denied them the ability to initiate change themselves since their advisers were appointed and encouraged to be out of the office ploughing their lone furrows for days on end. The work the services were doing might have been essential, but the lack of priority given to their management and planning simply put them in a weaker position to contemplate change.

Since the early 1980s there appears to have been a significant change of climate in these matters, though whether it is reactively or proactively initiated would be difficult to say. More authorities now seem to be attempting to provide themselves with the management equipment to cope with the demands they currently face and we see an increase in the number of chief advisers. In some authorities the management implications seem to have been embraced: we see a growth in adviser induction, INSET and appraisal, there is an increasing interest in the use of information technology to support the advisers' role and there is a greater recognition of the need for a clear management framework for advisers to work within. In other services, however, and perhaps too in the establishment, there still seems to be a residual desire for advisers to maintain the single-subject inspectorial role and for these expensive management blandishments to be regarded as unessential – after all, computers break down too frequently, the best training must be acquired on the job and who needs managers when there is work to be done! It will be interesting to consider how LEAs will now respond to the next round of initiatives, but first, it seems worthwhile to look at how they have experienced change over the last few years.

Elements of change – the advisers' responses

The case studies showed that the majority of advisers were vastly overworked and/or took on too much work, and it is in this light that the many changes they advocated should be seen. For instance, many argued for better management, for the rationalization of their tasks and for the writing of clearer job descriptions. Equally, there were similar demands for better administrative and clerical support, for the introduction of proper office systems, for more time to do jobs properly and for the provision of more and better training. Their requests can be seen to seek three goals:

(1) greater external and personal control over their work by having a more defined role and by being party to the process of rationalizing and defining it;

(2) an increase in the effectiveness of the work done by being able to use their skills more efficiently and effectively and by being able to deploy sufficient resources – time and money – to complete the work they start; and

(3) a general reduction in their workload, both to reduce the hours spent working and to enable them to undertake the necessary reading and thinking to fulfil their jobs effectively.

There were also arguments for a change in nature of what they did, and here the issue of the balance between the subject specialist and (specialist) generalist work attracted much attention. Throughout the research we were constantly given the impression that in the days immediately after 1974 there was a clear(er) idea of what advisers were supposed to do. It seemed as if the maintenance and development of the curriculum, subject or phase was the principal task for most advisers, and that generalist, cross-curriculum or pastoral duties were, (where recognized) more the domain of senior and/or area posts.

A valuable insight into what was happening in those days is available from the research of Bolam, Smith and Canter (1978); in their conclusion, when dealing with advisers' tasks, the team reported that:

> The project data indicates very clearly that the work styles of subject and general/subject advisers are different . . . . subject advisers were more likely than general advisers to spend a higher proportion of their time on giving individual advice to teachers, on in-service training activities and on the implementation of LEA or district-wide organisational and curriculum changes . . . (subject advisers) are more likely to concentrate on work related to their subject and to be less involved in matters relating to the school as a whole, including general inspections . . . On the other hand, general advisers were more likely . . . to concentrate on . . . staff appointments at all levels, staff evaluation, indirect advice to the Education Committee, advising on school-wide innovations and liaising with administrators. (p. 231).

This is neither the picture we saw nor the one we were offered by advisers and their clients. Our research showed that adviser titles no longer indicated significant differences between the general and non-general emphases (except that 'general' advisers tended to have higher salaries and be more involved in the appointment of headteachers than those without the title). Advisers' descriptions of how their tasks were distributed showed most of them to be involved in most areas of work – the demarcation described by Bolam has mostly disappeared.

The changes can be seen in a variety of ways, and three advisers' opinions are offered here. The first sees the growth in work comprising very positive elements, the second highlights difficulties, with this growth overloading the service as a whole. The third adviser expands upon this point and explains the current frustrations in the work:

> 'The job has increased in pressure and scope because it seems to have no clear-cut parameters – new initiatives, requests for help, advice, involvement, arrive from schools and individuals – and new demands or job priorities arrive regularly from 'on high'. Certainly, the general role just grows and grows in one's Pastoral 'hat' vis-à-vis secondary and primary schools. Trying to know and have credible contact with 100+ secondary teachers and 70–80 primary teachers, to be involved in the life of the school, to share its curriculum debates and pastoral concerns, and so forth, is incredibly time-consuming and demanding.'

'The key problem for all advisers is that extra demands are being loaded on us annually and the advisory team is not big enough to cope with the workload. All of us are frustrated at not being able to follow-up important initiatives, whether at school or county level, as we are constantly having to drop jobs in the middle and leave them unfinished through lack of time. Whilst it is important for specialist advisers to have general duties, it is unrealistic to expect one adviser to service more than five or six general schools with a total of about 80 staff. There is no way in which I, for example, can ever get to know the 80+ staff in my two secondary schools, let alone the further 120+ in my primary schools.'

'Advisory work has radically changed over my ten-year experience of it:
(1) The power relationship has seriously shifted towards administration, we are used much more for personnel work.
(2) The government keeps shifting the goalpost leaving the service uncertain and insecure.
(3) Advisers are under very great pressure, time for collaboration, reflection and reading is not available as it was.
(4) Teachers have become seriously disillusioned – generating enthusiasm and commitment is so much harder.
(5) The status of advisory work has steadily declined, whilst its range of responsibilities has steadily increased.
(6) There is increased political interference in professional matters – appointments, curriculum and administration.'

In all, there would seem to be an urgent need for advisers and their services to come to terms with these changes. They need to develop systems to accommodate the changes, to rationalize individual and team workloads, to correct current imbalances in the work done and to look towards appraisal and training to strengthen and consolidate what they do. But more changes are in store and there is need for advisers and their services to prepare for these, too. Changes are coming on top of a state of change, and however much some or all of these constitute improvements, the process of change, its assimilation into the system, and the resolution of the best way forward are all difficult processes.

It is in the light of this that the specialist–generalist balance remains so important. The indications are that the advisory services will continue to remain the LEAs' main way of monitoring, evaluating and developing the work of institutions. As such the services' range of duties will remain wide and will often include conflicting elements:

expertise will continue to be needed for subject, cross-curriculum, phase, assessment, school management, and monitoring and evaluation work. Similarly, the services will continue to have to work to three client groups: the schools, the LEA and the DES. There is no reason to suppose that the tensions we have seen develop over the last few years will do anything but increase unless there is effective management to help advisers cope and a considerable increase in resources. Has anyone yet really tackled the issue of the overall amount of work to be done, or are all the solutions just permutations of that same too much work between the same too few advisers?

The arguments about how the advisory service should divide up its responsibilities between the available personnel are important and subject to many issues, not the least being a consideration of just which responsibilities should fall to the advisory service to start with. On the whole the research would suggest that over the past few years there has been a move towards increasing the generalist emphasis. Some subject–specialist advisers argued that they would willingly embrace this and have offered various arguments:

> 'If we had a more general brief, we would have greater access to heads and governors. [Currently] we are ultra specialists. In terms of efficiency we are probably doing the right thing, but for ourselves we have little opportunity to come into contact with the whole school.'

> 'Being entirely a subject specialist can be restrictive – we need to know more about schools as total entities with total curriculum.'

> 'The general–subject division as practised here has effects:
> (1)   It frustrates internal promotion seeking general experience.
> (2)   It frustrates promotion outside the authority.
> (3)   It creates a "door-to-door" salesmen impression of subject advisers in schools/institution.
> (4)   It creates salary divisions – resentments within the team.
> (5)   It accords seniority to phase advisers.
> (6)   It depresses the salary for new subject advisers.
> (7)   It creates paperwork, preferential treatment and prevents scrutiny of, and team involvement in, the advice given directly by general advisers to senior administrative officers and to institutions.'

However, for others the benefits of this change are not so certain. One chief adviser commented: 'Advisers are responsible for professional advice based on their experience and should not be involved in administration and advice which is beyond their experience.' He was expressing a concern that we encountered elsewhere, particularly in LEAs where the pastoral role was not in operation. In effect, advisers worried that they would not have the expertise to take on such roles, and hence that they would lose credibility, and heads were concerned that they would be having advisers telling them what to do when they had no experience of headship.

In authorities where the pastoral role was in operation there seemed fewer doubts and most of those we spoke to endorsed the system, even though it was unusual for a subject or secondary adviser to have been the head of a secondary school. Perhaps, the main thing that had happened in these authorities was that the actual pastoral role had been worked out over the years and had been found to be neither dictatorial nor threatening? Indeed, where it was in operation it was generally well regarded. For some, however, the worry about general work was that the specialist role would be undermined. One adviser wrote that:

> I feel the trend is such that my most valuable contribution of
> subject- and school-based vision and inspiration will not be
> used, and that any competent, caring and organized person
> could do what I am now being asked to do. I feel that I can no
> longer contribute to the enrichment of the curriculum the
> children receive in a very significant way because of the
> administrative workload. I cannot give the teachers the
> self-confidence and morale boost they need to be adventurous
> and exciting teachers because the time is insufficient to build
> up that sort of relationship with individual colleagues. I can
> accept this change of role, but ask if this is not at the cost of
> impoverishing the diet of our children.'

One problem with finding any consensus in these arguments was that there was an enormous variation in what people meant by 'specialist' and 'generalist' work. Moreover, the term 'generalist' has two meanings, the familiar one with the management/pastoral connotation, as well as that of the cross-curriculum generalist. As such a curriculum generalist can argue against one type of general work while trying to protect another!

> 'I feel very strongly that my particular skills and expertise in
> equal opportunities, INSET planning and management
> development are being underused because of the hours spent
> on things like interviewing and pastoral duties, and that the lack
> of central planning in this authority means we will continually
> totter from crisis to crisis.'

The main problem has thus centred on the three institution-led demands upon the advisers' time – the 'pure' subject, cross-curriculum and pastoral support roles. And for each of these institution-led demands there is also a parallel LEA-led demand for reports, papers, supervision and work to be done for the new initiatives that will inevitably arrive in each area.

There are problems, however, in moving completely from one emphasis to another, not the least being that after integrating the team and individuals' work, and after deskilling them of their original subject expertise, it would be difficult to know if any real benefits have been brought about. Furthermore, it may well be that pressures will then reappear for the specialist emphases to be re-introduced. One adviser commented:

'Many LEAs seem to be moving towards a greater general and pastoral emphasis. This is well and good because it is a need expressed by many schools. Unfortunately there is no consequent reduction in specialist duties, nor would the schools wish there to be. They would like additional generalist help without a decrease in the effectiveness of their specialist advice. Many authorities are expanding their team and adding advisory teachers to cover gaps left by the changing adviser's role. This seems reasonable. Some authorities are simply expecting more from existing staff and this does not seem reasonable. It is interesting that some authorities who were first into the generalist approach have taken a "U" turn or are experimenting with specialists grouped in faculties.'

It is difficult to surmise whether any regrouping done at the moment would be more able than any other to meet the range of LEA, DES and school needs unless it first tackled the very basic question of the overall amount of work to be done.

In looking at change, the research also considered the advisers and their views. Advisers were asked to respond to three possible categories of change in the balance of their work – i.e. that they should move towards more subject work, more generalist work, or maintain the status quo. They were asked to give their answers in respect of (a) their job satisfaction, (b) their career prospects and (c) the needs of schools and colleges. Their responses are given in Table 7.1.

In terms of job satisfaction, the majority of advisers reported being 'happy' with the current balance. For their careers, however, there appeared to be a movement towards the general position, and in terms of the schools' and college's needs, a slight trend toward the subject position. However, when considering their answers in the different self-reported work groups, the information basically suggested that with job satisfaction proportionately more specialists wanted change than generalists, though the direction of the desired change was unclear. The position with respect to careers was less equivocal: the majority of generalists thought their balance was correct, and the

Table 7.1: *Advisers' views on the specialist/generalist balance*

How advisers would like their work to change in terms of job satisfaction:	Advisers' self-reported job classification*								
	pure spec	pure phase	pure gen	spec/ gen	phase/ gen	phase /spec	jack of all trades	all advisers	
	%	%	%	%	%	%	%	N	%
more subject	17	8	15	27	12	16	24	222	21
status quo	52	83	70	49	70	59	54	608	56
more general	31	9	15	24	18	25	22	248	23
Total (%)	100	100	100	100	100	100	100		100
Total. (N) (missing: 38)	187	66	39	252	87	61	386	1,078	

How advisers would like their work to change in terms of their career prospects.	Advisers' self-reported job classification*								
	pure spec	pure phase	pure gen	spec/ gen	phase/ gen	phase /spec	jack of all trades	all advisers	
	%	%	%	%	%	%	%	N	%
more subject	3	5	3	8	10	2	8	67	7
status quo	27	82	80	42	70	42	48	478	47
more general	70	13	17	50	20	56	44	459	46
Total (%)	100	100	100	100	100	100	100		100
Total (N) (Missing: 112)	167	62	36	240	77	59	363	1,004	

How advisers would like their work to change in terms of the needs of schools and colleges:	Advisers' self-reported job classification*								
	pure spec	pure phase	pure gen	spec/ gen	phase/ gen	phase /spec	jack of all trades	all advisers	
	%	%	%	%	%	%	%	N	%
more subject	23	13	10	40	10	28	37	319	37
status quo	50	74	69	35	65	42	37	473	37
more general	27	13	21	25	25	30	26	266	26
Total (%)	100	100	100	100	100	100	100		100
Total (N) (Missing: 58)	184	62	39	246	85	60	382	1,058	

Note: The self-reported classification is taken from Table 3.12

majority of those with a subject specialism wanted to move to a more general position. In looking at the needs of schools and colleges there was an even split across all three categories and no clear pattern emerged from the adviser groups except perhaps that phase and general advisers again appeared more satisfied with the current position than those with any subject specialism in their role. It is possible that what we are seeing here is the problem of schools needing both subject and general advice, and that the question thus comes back to how the team should best be trained and deployed to meet both demands. What perhaps should also be raised here is the issue of whether 'meeting demands' necessarily means possessing all the skills and knowledge within the individual or team, or whether it means being able to bring together those with the needs and those with the skills and then helping them to work together. Obviously, while there is no need for a complete polarization of these approaches, they do present very different training and deployment models for the advisory services.

Elements of change – the chief advisers' responses

It was apparent that chief advisers had strong views on these matters as well, and they were thus asked about their particular specialist/ generalist deployment patterns. Just over half the respondents, 32 out of 61, mentioned the benefit accruing from their advisers having both specialist and generalist roles, whereas 20 referred to the advantages of allowing the specialist to specialize. When asked about future changes, 33 out of 43 responses stressed a movement in the generalist direction.

A particular example of the polarization can be seen in the issue of appointments. With the generalized approach, involvement in the appointment process was seen as promoting a partnership with education officers, allowing the chief adviser and his or her staff to influence policy issues in the appointment of senior staff in schools, and generally enhancing the adviser's credibility. Five chief advisers rejected these arguments and argued that involvement in appointments was time-consuming and the advisers should be able to get on with the curriculum without being involved in the promotion of teachers.

The chief advisers offered four areas of difficulty with their current systems: (a) the current size of their service and the need to appoint more personnel; (b) the lack of time for advisers to carry out all the functions required of them; (c) the need to prioritize functions, especially with advisers with a dual role; and (d) the professional ability of some of their advisers to undertake the roles asked of them.

As with the advisers, the issue appears to be partly to do with balance, and partly to do with the amount of resources available and the degree of management operated. Chief advisers were thus asked to comment on their management structures – were they satisfied with how the service was organized and did they want any changes to be brought in? Twenty-eight of the responding 67 chief advisers reported being satisfied with their existing systems and offered examples of their systems' strengths. However, these were very varied and frequently at odds with one another and, as ever, demonstrated the enormous diversity in the services' character and philosophy – the 27 chief advisers gave 37 main strengths which covered 21 different areas. No individual strength was given by more than four respondents! Some chief advisers saw strengths in the way their system separated the subject and generalist roles, while others, marginally more, saw strengths in the way they combined them. In the same way, some emphasized the benefits of a small team for cooperation and communication, while others, with larger teams, saw communication and cooperation being promoted in other ways. Several commented on the advantages of the service being linked into the administration, while one with many such links saw the advantage of independence as being most significant. Much depended upon the advisory service's current position and the respondent's philosophy. Patently, the field was wide open.

The 39 chief advisers wanting change were slightly more consistent. First, as is evident in Table 4.4 (p. 103), across all LEAs, the less of a management structure a service had, the more likely the respondent was to want to change. Secondly, the less of a structure it had, the more likely he or she was to want it to increase. There was a fairly consistent desire for there to be more chief adviser time available, and for there to be a stronger middle-management system built in. Respondents argued that these measures were necessary to give unity, direction and coordination to the work of the service, as well as helping to facilitate the change to more general work where this was being implemented. In all, the most popular goal for those wanting change was for a system that would match position 2 in the hierarchical model, that is where the chief adviser was a member of the LEA's senior management team and was supported by a 'relaxed hierarchy' with a middle tier of senior/area advisers. In most of these cases, pastoral matters, which would be shared by all, would be routed through the senior/area advisers while subject–specialist work would be (still) directly routed to the chief adviser. In no instances did a chief adviser express a wish to move towards a less structured position.

There were also a number of suggestions which, while they would not affect the service's hierarchy, would certainly influence the working conditions for advisers. For instance, almost half of the 39 wanting change (16), wanted to improve their phase coverage and structure, with a good many of them emphasizing their need to 'get into' the FE sector. Eight chief advisers wanted to 'convert' some or all of their specialists to generalists (three wanted fully generalist teams), seven directly 'requested' more advisers, and three wanted more teamwork. In many ways, what we are seeing here echoes what the advisers sought.

The problems with change

Linked with the issue of wanting change is the consideration of the constraints involved in achieving it. Chief advisers were asked to describe any problems they might have encountered when proposing or implementing change in their advisory service. In all, 59 chief advisers offered 144 problems. Of the nine other respondents, seven said there were no problems and two were just blank. The problems the 59 listed fell into four main groups:
(1) difficulties within the advisory service itself   – 42 entries;
(2) a lack of money and resources   – 41 entries;
(3) difficulties with the LEA leadership (CEO and/or
     Education Committee)   – 25 entries;
(4) difficulties with the LEA's administrative arm – 23 entries.
(There were 13 other problems listed which covered ten different categories.)

Difficulties within the advisory service
The first category incorporated several basic themes. Much reference was made of advisers having a general inertia and a preference towards maintaining the status quo – one person even used the term 'entren-ched'. Some chief advisers felt change was held back because advisers feared the direction of the change – for instance, the introduction of management and team practices, the loss of individual autonomy and having to develop cross-phase and cross-curricular expertise. Some chief advisers questioned whether advisers would have enough skills to operate in the new areas: there were doubts about whether they had

either the necessary skills or confidence to operate successfully and questions were also raised about whether such skills were actually available in the market place.

A final theme was very different. It was argued that with small, stable advisory services there were few opportunities to implement change by bringing in 'fresh blood', and there were a number of chief advisers who would have liked the turnover to increase to enable change to take place. Indeed, one phrased the problem as having to wait for early retirements − a rather sad reflection both for the individual who realizes that people are waiting for him or her to go, and for the status of management which appears to have given up hope of developing the individual.

The lack of resources

The lack of resources affected change in several ways. First, it could be difficult to buy in extra staff − thus expansionist change was often ruled out. Secondly, it could be difficult to promote existing advisers within the service because of the extra salary resources that would be needed. Thirdly, with a lack of resources it could be difficult to plan, promote and engineer the change. Finally, the advisers' relatively high salaries (which caused problems with expansion), were argued to be too low to attract staff with (sufficient) senior management experience in large schools − in all, there seems here to be a catch-22 situation.

Difficulties with the LEA leadership

Some chief advisers described constraints arising from the attitudes of their CEOs, Education Committee members and other council committees. In so doing they revealed some of the tensions existing within local government. In response to the question about the problems of change we received some telling answers:

> 'Convincing the CEO that such a change would be appropriate.'

> 'CEO caution! (In process of being overcome.)'

> 'There is a resistance from the CEO for any increase in advisers.'

> 'The Education Committee approves changes and expansion but the Personnel Committee will not approve the changes.'

> 'Dogmatism on the part of the elected members.'

> 'Elected members have decided there will be no advisory teachers.'

Difficulties with the LEA's administrative arm

In this group chief advisers described conflict and sometimes even rancour, between advisers and officers − the flavour is perhaps best described in their own words. As before, the extracts were given in response to the question: 'Please describe any problems you have encountered when proposing or implementing change in your advisory service.'

> 'Difficulties with consultative negotiations where advisory service changes impinge on other branches of the LEA.'

> 'Administrators' preoccupation with administrative problems. Getting administration to move.'

> 'Lack of cooperation by senior administrative officers (sometimes because they are overworked).'

> 'Other colleagues in administration – the CEO accepts [change], but professional jealousy is met within.'

> 'Resistance from officers against the advisory service empire-building.'

> 'Opposition of some administrators who do not wish to see the advisory service strengthened.'

Before leaving this section, it is important to note that while problematic relationships between advisers and officers were reported on many occasions during the research, and these were often described as causing unnecessary difficulties, many reasons for these problems were outside the control of either side, not the least being a system which has salary conflicts built into it; some of the problems may well be regarded as 'natural' and 'healthy' in as much as a certain degree of overlap and tension between subgroups in a large organization may be argued to enhance effective working; and there were many examples of good and cooperative working relations which went unsung.

Elements of change – what the future will bring

Currently there are four important and related developments being introduced into education which, in the short term, look likely substantially to affect the nature of advisers' work and, in the long term, present the possibility of completely changing the way they are funded. These are:

(1) The continuing developments in the funding and management of teacher in-service training, especially the emphasis on a school focus.

(2) The introduction of financial delegation to schools (otherwise known as local management of schools (LMS), or local financial management (LFM)).

(3)   The enhancement of the governors' role in the management of the school and its curriculum.

(4)   The introduction of a National Curriculum with its associated attainment targets and testing at various ages.

The effects that these developments will have on advisers and their services can be grouped into three discrete but overlapping stages:

(a)   the new work which the advisers will have to take on to help implement the developments;

(b)   the ongoing work these developments will require once implemented;

(c)   the long-term effects they will have on the nature of advisory work and on advisory service organization and funding.

The effect of implementing these four developments

Over the next few years advisory services will be needed to help implement all four of these developments. For instance, as the planning and funding of teacher INSET moves over to the schools, they will need a good deal of help if they are not to become swamped in the planning, administration and organization. Some of the early experiences with school-run statutory INSET days have shown that these are difficult and time-consuming events to organize and that the advisers' experience in this area could be a most valuable asset. Since the decentralisation of INSET within the LEA comes at the same time as there is an increase in the amount of INSET provided, there is obviously scope for considerable advisory work here.

Similarly, increased levels of work will be needed with the introduction of financial delegation to schools (where advisers will need to offer help and to learn how things work under the new system), and with the enhanced role of governors. To date, much of the emphasis with governors has been to do with training them to be able to undertake the new kinds of work, and much of this training has fallen to officers. However, the combination of financial delegation and the 1986 Act will require effective management delegation within both the school and the governing body. It will also require there to be effective dialogue between the staff and the governing body. If these two developments are to work, then the governing body and the school staff will need to learn to work in unison, and this will require patience and assistance for both parties. For instance, it means that much of the decision-making that currently takes place within the department will soon have to incorporate both school and governing body policies, and it will also have to be undertaken in liaison with the governing body. This might not be too popular initially, but it seems a direct consequence of the legislation. There would appear to be an enormous role for advisers.

But having undertaken these two generalist tasks, there is the National Curriculum. Once each subject's curriculum is nationally determined, or at least a framework is laid out, the LEA will need to produce its own statement and the schools will then need to respond likewise. Where these new curricula take schools into new areas, or further down partially established avenues, for instance, as in the greatly enhanced primary science emphasis, as in encouraging the moves towards balanced science, or as in developing assessment procedures, then the advisers' subject and curriculum development expertise will be needed along with all the support available from advisory teachers.

But there is a further area of new work for the advisory services, in that three of these four developments are accompanied by a demand for greater monitoring and evaluation than generally exists at present. Although most of the evaluation will eventually take place when the developments are implemented, and in itself will become one of the most powerful influences on the nature of future advisory work, time and effort will be needed at this stage for the development of appropriate evaluative skills, criteria and systems of working. Given the variety of techniques available to monitor what is happening in schools and colleges, the enormously enhanced potential of IT to handle information, and the number of initiatives concerned with teacher appraisal and school self-evaluation, now would seem a very good time to develop the appropriate systems to use over the next few years, but time and resources must be given to this task.

The full and efficient implementation of the National Curriculum and the other three developments will require a great deal of work and support from the advisory services. But advisory services already have a large and important workload and are not necessarily in a good position easily to change what they do and how they are structured. To assist fully with the implementation of the new developments the advisory services will need further training, support and resources. They will also need a political climate that acknowledges the importance of using some of the resources to plan and manage changes within the service.

The effects of these developments once implemented

As has been suggested, these developments are accompanied by a greater emphasis on evaluation and monitoring. Unless many more advisers are appointed, it is likely that this enhanced emphasis will have the effect of reducing the advisers' involvement in school management and curriculum issues. Furthermore, financial delegation, the new roles for governors and school-focused INSET all move education decision-making nearer to where it is implemented (i.e. to the school) and all serve to reduce county hall involvement. Together, the emphasis on evaluation and the reduction in county hall involvement stand to reduce the advisers' involvement in the curriculum and management areas. The introduction of the National Curriculum is likely to continue this trend by reducing both the schools' and the advisers' influence on the main curriculum emphases, though it remains to be seen whether in the tension between the school, LEA and National Curriculum there might still be some room for innovation and useful manoeuvre – it must depend upon how prescriptive the National Curriculum will be.

All this suggests that the advisers' role is likely to change over the next ten years and that they are likely to become more involved monitoring and evaluating what others have done, and, as a consequence, lose out on many of the current developmental areas of their work. There is little doubt that the evaluative role will grow, especially since it is written into the Reform Bill and it is being suggested as a key element in the successful running of Local Management of Schools (LMS) (Coopers and Lybrand, 1988), but can education authorities afford to allow it to push out the supporting and developmental role and is there still some room for manoeuvre? Once again, the best time to establish the desired (local) pattern for the next few years would appear to be before all the systems are fully implemented.

A number of LEAs have already moved towards creating two-tier advisory services, with one part more or less solely concerned with the evaluative and monitoring roles while the other is concerned with curriculum development and helping schools and teachers respond to the evaluation. In essence, this is the same issue that was raised earlier about how an advisory service's tasks should be divided up. Then it was the specialist/ generalist debate: now it is the developmental and support roles vs the monitoring and evaluation task – should each adviser carry a part of each role, or should some do all of one while some do all of the other? In many respects, as far as the end-products are concerned, in the short term there will be little difference as both approaches will serve both roles. The long-term arguments are perhaps more interesting, though, and they raise four important issues: the advisers' professional development, careers and job satisfaction; the relationship between the evaluator and the evaluated (is it healthy for education to support such roles within the LEA); can evaluation be valid or effective if divorced from the developmental process; and can the developmental process be effective if divorced from the evaluative role? One might further question whether it is cost-effective to have the evaluated staff playing a passive role when they patently know more about the local (classroom and school) situation than any external evaluator can do without expending a great deal of time and effort.

Of course, it may be that the multiple roles of the service are too many and varied for any one adviser to cover successfully and other solutions are beginning to appear. In one case the pastoral/monitoring (but non-inspectorial) role has been split from that of curriculum development, and in others, advisers for evaluation and for assessment have been sought to enhance the overall expertise available within the undivided advisory service.

One of the strongest themes that has appeared in this research, however, is that there is no one solution that is right for all LEAs. Whatever solution is sought, it must meet both national and local goals, be more or less compatible with existing philosophies and work within existing strengths – whatever extra resources the government provides, the majority of the new teams will still inevitably comprise existing staff. New solutions must acknowledge this.

The long term effects on advisory work and the advisory service.

Even in such a speculative and cursory analysis as this, it is important to recall that these four developments form part of a larger package which is concerned to reduce the role of local government. In this light, the LEA adviser is a local government officer standing on a platform which is being purposefully eroded. At the same time, however, all these developments need the help of the adviser if they are to be fully and efficiently implemented. Historically it would be fair to say that the role of the adviser has not always been particularly well appreciated by central government, but now this point seems to be more or less accepted though without any reduction in the tension between the evaluative role (necessary for political reasons though too expensive to be maintained by the government) and the supportive/developmental role (politically too soft and too near the LEA role, but essential for the implementation of the government's developments). Thus while we see support, resources and recognition being offered, the exact nature of the adviser's future role, both in terms of its balance and organizational structure, still seems undecided, and perhaps this is the appropriate way to allow the local solution to be found. However, we should also consider the long-term effects of financial delegation.

At the moment, it seems accepted that advisory services should continue to be funded by the LEA, that is schools are not yet being expected to pay for the advisers' services. There are good reasons for this, not the least being that schools might not see the need to pay for the evaluative part of the advisers' role and indeed, if it were fully analysed, they might not choose to pay for the advisers' role in implementing government initiatives. But having said this, Coopers and Lybrand's (1988) report looks to the future and wonders whether parts of the advisers' work might eventually be paid for directly by schools. With this scenario, there exists the eventual possibility of the monitoring and evaluation part of split services being maintained by money held back by the LEA, while the curriculum development and support unit would only survive by selling its services. This presents both attractive and most worrying prospects, and whatever the eventual outcome, which again may vary from one LEA to the next, the potential for this to happen should most certainly be on the current agenda when discussing how advisory services should distribute their work.

Perhaps, finally, we should return to the issue and mechanics of change. The four developments all assume that the LEA advisory services are in a position to handle considerable change in a coherent and planned way, but are they? Looking back over the research, we can see that there were many difficulties with previous initiatives and that some of them are still with us today. To successfully achieve the aims of these four developments will require the acknowledgement that change is difficult, even for the change agents. This acknowledgement will also be needed if we are to allow the advisory services to move into the twenty-first century as an effective force in the promotion of our children's education. But we should also ask whether it is yet recognized that advisory work is a highly specialized role within education, a role which is more than just an extension of the conventional teaching role? Allied to this question must be that of providing advisers with effective resources and management, and this is perhaps the biggest step. As the four developments start to define the nature of education over the next few years, have we yet accepted that the small group who will be most influential in their implementation and evaluation will themselves need effective support and management both to help them undertake this role, and to help them handle the changes that will come about as a result of these innovations?

Appendix 1

Table A2.1: *Post titles of the respondents to the Chief Advisers questionnaire*

Post title	Total	%
Chief Adviser	22	32.4
Chief Inspector	16	23.5
Chief Adviser/Inspector	1	1.5
Assistant CEO/Director – Chief Adviser	4	5.9
Principal Adviser	7	10.3
Principal Inspector	1	1.5
Chairman of Advisory Team	1	1.5
Senior Adviser	2	2.9
Senior Inspector	1	1.5
Senior Phase Adviser (secondary)	2	2.9
Senior Phase Adviser (primary)	2	2.9
Deputy CEO/ Deputy Director	7	10.3
Assist CEO / Assist Director	1	1.5
Principal or Senior Education Officer	1	1.5
Total	68	100.1

Table A2.2:   *Extracts from the Soulbury Committee's 'Joint Education Services Circular:
JESC: I, Decisions of the Soulbury Committee on 22nd September 1987:
Education Advisers'*

2.c

Assistant Advisers:	from points	1–5
Advisers:	from points	5–19
Senior Advisers:	from points	12–22
Principal Advisers:	from points	19–28

(Note: Salary scales for appointments made under this salary structure should be of not more than four consecutive points in length.)

Annexe III

1. Education advisers are drawn from senior members of the teaching profession in order to advise local authorities and education institutions on a wide range of professional, organisational and curriculum issues, with the overall aim of enhancing the quality of education.
2. The organisational structure of advisory services within LEAs varies widely according to local factors such as geography, the local organisation of schools and colleges and the historical development of the LEA's advisory services. Whereas in the past a distinction could often be drawn between subject and general advisers, recent developments in curriculum and organisation matters have been such as to make that distinction too inflexible.
3. Consequently the national framework for the grading of advisers needs to accommodate a very wide range of circumstances, set against the reality that, for reasons of recruitment and retention, salary scales need amongst other factors to pay regard to those of senior members of the teaching profession.
4. In most LEAs three categories of adviser are likely to be found: adviser, senior adviser and principal adviser. But within and between LEAs there need to be several grading options for different levels within the categories to allow for differentiation according to the local distribution of responsibilities and the size of the LEA concerned.

Table A2.3: *Regional variation in adviser 'density': pupils, teachers and schools*

		Advisory staff per 1,000 pupils*			Advisory staff per 1,000 teachers†			Advisory staff per 1,000 schools‡		
		Advisers	Advisory teachers	All team	Advisers	Advisory teachers	All team	Advisers	Advisory teachers	All team
ALL LEAs	mean	0.35	0.34	0.69	6.1	6.1	12.2	101	97	198
	SD	0.12	0.35	0.39	1.9	6.1	6.7	44	96	116
No. of LEAs		64	64	64	64	64	64	64	64	64
REGION:§										
North	mean	0.38	0.30	0.69	6.5	5.0	11.4	111	85	196
	SD	0.12	0.26	0.37	1.5	4.2	5.5	42	78	114
	No. of LEAs	9	9	9	9	9	9	9	9	9
York and	mean	0.37	0.29	0.66	6.4	5.1	11.5	106	87	193
Humberside	SD	0.11	0.21	0.25	1.6	3.3	3.8	31	62	79
	No. of LEAs	6	6	6	6	6	6	6	6	6
North	mean	0.33	0.38	0.70	5.9	6.8	12.8	100	116	216
West	SD	0.14	0.42	0.46	2.4	7.8	8.5	43	124	139
	No. of LEAS	12	12	12	12	12	12	12	12	12
East	mean	0.27	0.25	0.52	5.0	4.5	9.5	64	62	126
Midlands	SD	0.04	0.13	0.10	0.95	2.2	1.3	2	36	35
	No. of LEAs	3	3	3	3	3	3	3	3	3
West	mean	0.32	0.29	0.61	5.7	5.2	10.9	99	87	186
Midlands	SD	0.09	0.18	0.21	1.6	3.3	4.0	39	54	74
	No. of LEAs	7	7	7	7	7	7	7	7	7
East	mean	0.26	0.34	0.60	5.0	6.3	11.3	66	81	147
Anglia	SD	0.08	0.32	0.36	1.5	5.8	6.3	26	78	86
	No. of LEAs	3	3	3	3	3	3	3	3	3
Greater	mean	0.48	0.33	0.81	7.8	5.5	13.3	165	116	281
London	SD	0.13	0.28	0.33	1.8	4.7	5.2	48	102	123
	No. of LEAs	8	8	8	8	8	8	8	8	8
South	mean	0.31	0.18	0.50	5.9	3.5	9.4	83	50	133
East	SD	0.11	0.14	0.16	2.1	2.2	3.1	26	39	42
	No. of LEAs	8	8	8	8	8	8	8	8	8
South	mean	0.27	0.38	0.65	5.3	7.4	12.7	64	86	150
West	SD	0.07	0.34	0.34	1.5	6.5	6.5	13	77	70
	No. of LEAs	4	4	4	4	4	4	4	4	4
Wales	mean	0.34	0.91	1.25	5.8	15.5	21.4	78	208	286
	SD	0.08	0.81	0.88	1.3	13.8	15.0	23	210	231
	No. of LEAs	4	4	4	4	4	4	4	4	4

* These are registered pupils aged 5–16 years inclusive.
† Teachers in schools with pupils 5–16.
‡ Schools for pupils 5–16 – i.e. excluding sixth-form colleges and nursery schools.
§ Regions as defined in DES usage.
(The correlation between the adviser–teacher and adviser–pupil ratios = 0.96. Both the adviser–teacher and adviser–pupil ratios have correlations of 0.9 with the adviser–school ratio: all correlations significant at the 0.001 level or better.)

Table A3.1: *Distribution of advisers' pay and pay scales*

| Officer scales | | | Burnham and Soulbury scales | | | | | |
| Officer scale point | No. of advisers | | Burnham and Soulbury scale point | Burnham HT No. of advisers | | Soulbury No. of advisers | | |
	N	%		N	%	N	%
1	3	0.3					
2	1	0.1					
3	7	0.6	3			3	0.3
4	12	1.1	4	2	0.2		
5			5	2	0.2		
6	18	1.7	6	3	0.3	1	0.1
7			7	12	1.1	49	4.5
8	2	0.2	8	41	3.8	291	26.9
9	5	0.5	9	38	3.5	233	21.6
			10	40	3.7	251	23.2
			11	8	0.7	51	4.1
			12	2	0.2	6	0.6

| Total no. of advisers: | 48 | | | 148 | | 885 | |
| Percentage of total no. of advisers: | 4.4 | | | 13.7 | | 81.9 | |

Mean scale point: officer = 5.06; Burnham HT = 8.80, and Soulbury = 8.96

Note: There is no implied relationship between the Officer and the Burnham and Soulbury Scales. (Information missing from 35 of the 1,116 responding advisers.)

Table A3.2: *Advisers' current work, grouped by their last job*

Current Post	Assistant teacher	Middle manager	Senior manager	Headship	FHE lecturer	Advisory work	Near advisory	Officer	Total
Main subject specialist	15	156	50	14	78	145	87	12	557
Cross-curriculum/ Curricular initiative	–	17	8	22	14	31	13	8	113
Primary	2	1	1	89	5	51	12	2	163
Secondary	–	3	7	7	1	24	2	1	45
FHE	–	4	1	3	5	7	6	4	30
Adult/youth	–	1	3	–	6	4	1	1	16
Other	1	16	7	25	12	67	11	7	46
Total	18	198	77	160	121	329	132	35	1,070

Note: Other previous jobs = 45. No. of respondents = 1,115.

Table A3.3:   *The post: functions and tasks*

10) We are interested in knowing your involvement across a range of key activities which are listed below. Please note this is not an exhaustive list of advisory tasks and does not set out to include all activities in which advisers are engaged. We would be grateful if you would respond to all three categories A, B and C	A — Under each heading please tick, where appropriate, all those activities in which you have been actively involved over the last 12 months			B — Using only those activities ticked in A, please tick those you find to be			C
	When acting in a subject or curriculum area specialist capacity	When acting in a phase, i.e. age–range, specialist capacity	When acting in a generalist capacity	The three most time-consuming	The three most professionally demanding	The three which have most increased in emphasis in the last 5 years	From all the activities listed please tick the three you consider most important for the institutions with which you work
Subject advice primary							
Subject advice secondary							
Subject advice FE/tertiary							
Appointing primary staff							
Appointing secondary staff							
Appointing FE/tertiary staff							
Appointing special school staff							
Advice on institutional management							
Attendance at governors' meetings							
Careers advice for school/college staff							
Involvement in redeployment							
Reorganization (closures, etc.)							
Building design/accommodation							
Planning of new INSET arrangements							
Formally inspecting or reviewing institutions, departments or aspects							
Cross-curricular initiatives, including multicultural, equal opportunities, SEN.							
Curriclum development initiatives, e.g. TVEI							
Assessment initiatives e.g. GCSE CPVE, profiling							
Management of advisers and advisory teaching staff							

Table A3.4: *The distribution of inspection across inspecting and non-inspecting LEAs*

	Advisers in inspecting LEAs	Advisers in non-inspecting LEAs	Total
Inspecting adv, %	63.5	12.6	77.9
(N =	513	99	612)
Non-inspecting adv, %	8.5	13.6	22.1
(N =	67	107	174)
Total, %	73.8	26.2	100
N	580	206	786

Note: (Because this table takes its information from two totally separate sources, full information is only available for 786 advisers which represents 100%.)

Table A5.1: *The nature of the advisers' subgroups*

Nature of Subgroup	No. of references	Percentage of respondents
1 Area or divisional group or team	109	26.3
2 Primary phase advisers	97	23.4
3 Various single academic subject groups	90	21.7
4 Task-oriented groups that exist only to carry out the task in question – i.e. inspection, resource planning, libraries, etc.	58	14.0
5 Secondary phase advisers	34	8.2
6 Various specific cross-curriculum groups, including SEN, multicultural, equal opportunities, etc.	28	6.8
7 Phase advisers (as opposed to non-phase advisers)	26	6.3
8 Self-selected, mutual interest or support group	24	5.8
9 FE, FHE and post-16 phase advisers	22	5.3
10 Specific working parties	21	5.1
Other *(in toto)*	26	6.3
Total from 414 respondents	535	129.2

Table A6.1:   *Chief advisers' comments on adviser appraisal and service evaluation*

It seems to me that the question should be concerned with three processes: (1) appraisal of individual advisers; (2) appraisal of individual teachers; (3) the evaluation of the whole service. In this authority we are not yet at an advanced enough stage to answer these questions with any certainty. Advisers, psychologists and education officers have spent a residential period with visiting consultants and have identified the issues to be addressed. A steering-group has been formed of the above with the addition of teachers and representatives from the professional associations. It is intended to establish a number of pilot schemes in the authority using the following variables: purposes; self, peer or hierarchical systems; internal or external assessors; the relation to student-centred reviewing and profiling; differential finance; issues of confidentiality; the relation to career advancement; and INSET. We believe that unless the CEO, assistant directors, schools officers and advisers are appraised and have experienced the process at first hand, we shall not be in any position to set up a system for the education service in general.

I would like to set up a form of self-evaluation link to appraisal of individual advisers. Each adviser would formulate his/her own evaluation of performance during the preceding school term. This would be talked through with the appropriate senior adviser in a one to one situation with self-evaluation as the focal point, but also with the freedom for both parties to introduce discussion points to and about each other. It must be realized that the performance of the senior adviser over a period and the decisions he takes will have an effect on the performance of those within his responsibility. This same procedure will involve the self-evaluation of senior advisers with the director as appraiser. The evaluation of the whole service would be included to some extent in the adviser/senior adviser situation, and to a larger extent in the senior adviser/director dialogue. Following on from these appraisal situations the senior advisers would produce a written document outlining possible improvement in the service. This would be made available to all advisers and the director, and all of them invited to add riders, comments and suggestions as each felt desirable. This whole process would be done annually.

Since the advisory service is not inexpensive it seemed proper to pose questions about its evaluation and the quality of what it provides. Open University Course E364 suggests six criteria:
(1) It should be fair and perceived as fair by all the parties involved.
(2) It should be capable of suggesting capable remedies.
(3) It should be methodologically sound.
(4) It should yield an account that is intelligible to its intended audience.
(5) It should be economic in its use of resources.
(6) It should be an acceptable blend of centralised and delegated control.
     Point 1 raises the question of who is concerned. Apart from the advisers, there would appear to be the Education Committee, the chief education officer, some of his staff and the client groups such as schools and colleges. The latter would include governors, teaching staff, and possibly pupils if they directly encounter advisers in music, outdoor education, and so on. One aspect of fairness would be for the other parties to be similarly subject to evaluation. I do not see why advisers should be a separate group for the process.

The issue of fairness also arises since the various parties all have a stake in the outcome. Headteachers are a major consumer group, but would they be impartial since they may see the advisers as eroding their autonomy, as rivals for the loyalty of their staff and as a drain on education resources which might otherwise have come to them. Equally, education officers are not entirely impartial, if only on the issue of salary, and the Education Committee experience of advisers may be very circumscribed. Nevertheless, any evaluation will involve people who are not strictly speaking disinterested, and the advisory service will simply have to cope with that.

Associated with the general problem of fairness is the question of the criteria against which the service should be judged. Presumably, it should be against its objectives, but what are they? If all the above groups were involved then there could be a conflict of interests in the evaluation's suggestions and it might be incapable of suggesting viable remedies. For example, the headteachers might want to see the advisers more frequently in school at the same time as the Chief Officer might want to see them giving more time to supporting the administrative thrust of the authority.

Point 3, that procedures should be methodologically sound, raises many difficulties, especially in the initial stages. It would be difficult for an LEA to judge how well its advisory service was doing simply by reference to itself − evaluation implies comparison. However, it is conceivable that an evaluation of one advisory service could be undertaken by a team from another, or that HMI might provide such a service. Independent management consultants might be another possible group, although it may take them some time to understand the nuances of advisory work and there would be a real financial cost involved.

Point 5 refers to the economic use of resources, and it is hard to judge at this distance whether an evaluation would be economic. It is scarcely likely to be cheap, however.

Point 6 suggests there should be a suitable blend of centralised and delegated control. Depending upon the process determined, it is conceivable that this could be reached − e.g. through blending the interests of the Education Committee, the chief officer and the advisory service.

I see very considerable difficulties inherent in evaluating advisory services, given the present state of the art. In that sense, I think any effort, time and resources invested in it might more usefully proceed from the assumption that the advisory service is useful. From that point one can imagine a forum of interested and representative parties covering all levels of the LEA, meeting, debating and agreeing the objectives for that education service for a given year. They could then suggest a reasonable contribution for the advisory service to make to that objective. If the objectives could be agreed, then it would be proper for the advisory service to have the autonomy to decide how to organise itself to achieve them. This then could provide the baseline for an annual review in which the success of the advisory service's contribution to the achievement of the objectives could be commented upon and the objectives for the coming year determined. Within this framework the chief adviser could undertake a review or appraisal of individual adviser's work and performance.

Table A6.2:   *Adviser involvement in setting up adviser appraisal schemes*

No. of advisers answering each option:	N	%*
1 Discussions within the advisory service	317	50.4
2 Discussions including others from within the authority, i.e. officers, etc.	114	18.1
3 Discussions with advisers from other authorities	62	9.9
4 Actually formulating authority's scheme	36	5.7
5 Participating in trial runs as the appraisee	96	15.3
6 Participating in trial runs as the appraiser	49	7.8
7 No involvement, system running before appointment	47	7.5
8 No involvement, system implemented since appointment	100	15.9
Total no. of responses	821	

Note: There were 629 respondents in total – i.e. all those who answered categories 1–5.
* Percentage based on the number of respondents
Where advisers had reported that their authority's appraisal scheme was at least at the discussion stages, they were asked to describe their involvement in its implementation at that time.

Appendix 2 Members of the Steering Committee

W.H. Cubitt (Chairman)   Director of Education, Gateshead
C. Banks   HMI
D. Felsenstein   ILEA Inspector (retired)
A.P. Matthews   Principal Adviser, Northumberland
                           (President of NAIEA, 1985–6)
C. Noble   Headteacher
J.J. Pearce   Senior Inspector, Cambridge
M. Sansome   Controller of Education Services, Harrow
B. Wilcox   Chief Adviser, Sheffield
G. Wilson   Chief Inspector, Hillingdon, latterly HMI

References

ANDERSON, N.V. (1975). 'New Advisers' Course at Dyffryn,' *NAIEA Journal*, 1, 3, 14–15.

AULD REPORT (1976). *Report of the Public Inquiry conducted by Robin Auld, QC, into the Teaching, Organization and Management of the William Tyndale Junior and Infants Schools, Islington, London N1.* London: ILEA.

BIRCHENOUGH, M. (1976). 'The Authority's Inspectorate: the present positions and future developments'. Appendix to the Education Committee Agenda: Tuesday, 18th May. London: ILEA.

BLACKIE, J. (1970). *Inspecting and the Inspectorate.* London: Routledge and Kegan Paul.

BOLAM, R., SMITH, G. and CANTER, H. (1978). *LEA Advisers and the Mechanisms of Innovation.* Windsor: NFER-NELSON.

CLARK, L. (1976). *The Inspector Remembers.* London: Dobson.

COOPERS and LYBRAND (1988). *Local Management of Schools.* London: DES.

COX, B. and BOYSON, R. (1975). *Black Paper 1975: The Fight for Education.* London: Dent.

EDMUNDS, E.L. (1966). *School Inspection of the Future.* London: Schoolmaster Publishing.

EDUCATION (1972). 'The change of a decade for justice on salaries'. *Education*, 6 October.

EDUCATION (1976). 'The advisory service'. *Education,* 20 February.

FISKE, D.A. (1969). 'The Local Inspectorate in Redcliffe–Maud's England'. Address to NAIEO.

FISKE, D.A. (1977). 'Week by Week', *Education,* 25 November.

GENTLE, K. (1976). The significance of advisory work', *NAIEA Journal*, 1, 4, 15–16.

GREAT BRITAIN (1944). *The Education Act 1944.* London: HMSO.

GREAT BRITAIN. (1979). *The Education Act 1979.* London: HMSO.

GREAT BRITAIN. (1980). *The Education Act 1980.* London: HMSO.

GREAT BRITAIN. (1981). *The Education Act 1981.* London: HMSO.

GREAT BRITAIN. (1986). *The Education Act 1986.* London: HMSO.

GREAT BRITAIN. DEPARTMENT OF EDUCATION AND SCIENCE (1977). *Educating our Children: Four Subjects for Debate.* London: DES

GREAT BRITAIN. DEPARTMENT OF EDUCATION AND SCIENCE (1985a). *Report by Her Majesty's Inspectors on the Effects of Local Authority Expenditure Policies on the Education Provision in England – 1984.* London: DES.

GREAT BRITAIN. DEPARTMENT OF EDUCATION AND SCIENCE (1985b). *A Draft Statement on the role of the Local Education Authority Advisory Services.* London: DES.

GREAT BRITAIN. DEPARTMENT OF EDUCATION AND SCIENCE (1986). *Report by Her Majesty's Inspectors on the Effects of Local Authority Expenditure Policies on the Education Provision in England – 1985.* London: DES.

GREAT BRITAIN. DEPARTMENT OF EDUCATION AND SCIENCE (1988). *Draft Consultative Document Education Reform Act: Financial Delegation to Schools.* London: DES.

GREAT BRITAIN. DEPARTMENT OF THE ENVIRONMENT (1972). *Local Government Reorganisation in England: Areas of New Counties.* Circular No. 107/72. London: HMSO.

HOUSE OF COMMONS. EDUCATION, SCIENCE AND ARTS COMMITTEE (1986). *Achievement in Primary Schools.* London: HMSO.

HOUSE OF COMMONS. SELECT COMMITTEE ON EDUCATION AND SCIENCE (1968). *Report: Part 1, Her Majesty's Inspectorate (England and Wales).* London: HMSO.

HOWARTH, T. (1974). 'Advice on advisers', *Times Educational Supplement,* 22 November.

HUGILL, B. (1988). 'Councils put a price on Reform Bill', *Times Educational Supplement,* 10 June.

KOGAN, M. (1974). 'Advisers in conflict', *Times Educational Supplement* 5 April.

MALLABY, G. (1967). 'Size of an authority and effect on recruitment of professional staff'. In: *Committee on the Staff of Local Government.* London: HMSO.

NATIONAL ASSOCIATION OF INSPECTORS AND EDUCATIONAL ORGANIZERS (NAIEO) (1968). *Evidence to the Royal Commission on Local Government.* London: NAIEO; as referred to in Bolam *et al.*, 1968.

PEARCE, J.J. (1986). *Standards and the LEA – the Accountability of Schools.* Windsor: NFER-NELSON.

REDCLIFFE-MAUD, R. (1969). *Royal Commission on Local Government in England.* Cmnd 4040. London HMSO.

ROBINSON, J.A. (1972). 'The role of the local education authority adviser'. In: *'L'Information Universitaire et Culturelle'.*

SHEPPARD, R. (1975a). 'Talepiece: The Soulbury saga,' *NAIEA Journal* 1,2, 20–23.

SHEPPARD, R. (1975b). 'How long is long? The Soulbury saga Part 2', *NAIEA Journal* 1,3, 19–22.

TAYLOR REPORT. GREAT BRITAIN. DEPARTMENT OF EDUCATION AND SCIENCE. WELSH OFFICE (1977). *A New Partnership for our Schools.* London: HMSO.

THE NFER RESEARCH LIBRARY

Titles available in the NFER Research Library

TITLE	HARDBACK ISBN	SOFTBACK ISBN
Joining Forces: a study of links between special and ordinary schools (Jowett, Hegarty, Moses)	0 7005 1179 2	0 7005 1162 8
Supporting Ordinary Schools: LEA initiatives (Moses, Hegarty, Jowett)	0 7005 1177 6	0 7005 1163 6
Developing Expertise: INSET for special educational needs (Moses and Hegarty (Eds))	0 7005 1178 4	0 7005 1164 4
Graduated Tests in Mathematics: a study of lower attaining pupils in secondary schools (Foxman, Ruddock, Thorpe)	0 7005 0867 8	0 7005 0868 6
Mathematics Coordination: a study of practice in primary and middle schools (Stow with Foxman)	0 7005 0873 2	0 7005 0874 0
A Sound Start: the schools' instrumental music service (Cleave and Dust)	0 7005 0871 6	0 7005 0872 4
Course Teams–the Way Forward in FE? (Tansley)	0 7005 0869 4	0 7005 0870 8
The LEA Adviser – a Changing Role (Stillman, Grant)	0 7005 0875 9	0 7005 0876 7

For further information contact the Customer Support Department, NFER-NELSON, Darville House, 2 Oxford Road East, Windsor, Berks SL4 1DF, England. Tel: (0753) 858961   Telex 937400 ONECOM G Ref. 24966001

R

The LEA Adviser – a Changing Role

Andrew Stillman
and
Mary Grant

NFER-NELSON

Published by The NFER-NELSON Publishing Company Ltd.,
Darville House, 2 Oxford Road East,
Windsor, Berkshire SL4 1DF, England

First Published 1989
© 1989, National Foundation for Educational Research

British Library Cataloguing in Publication Data

Stillman, A

The LEA adviser: a changing role
1. England. Local education
authorities. Advisory services
I. Title II. Grant, Mary
379.1'53' 0942

ISBN 0-7005-0875-9
ISBN 0-7005-0876-7 Pbk

Typeset by First Page Ltd., Watford.
Printed by Billing & Sons Ltd, Worcester

ISBN 0 7005 0875 9 (Hardback)
Code 8309 02 1

ISBN 0 7005 0876 7 (Paperback)
Code 8310 02 1